Internationalization at Home in Iceland

Stories of Faculty Engagement

Casey J. Dinger

STARSCHOLARS NETWORK
Baltimore, Maryland

STAR SCHOLARS NETWORK

First Published 2023

by
STAR Scholars
Baltimore, Maryland (USA)

In collaboration with
Open Journals in Education and
Journal of International Students

Category
Education/Higher Education

Series
Comparative and International Education

Series Editor
Krishna Bista

Typeset in Garamond
by HBK Digital

Cover Design
Mary Watts

Author
Casey J. Dinger

ISBN: 978-1-957480-12-1

Library of Congress Control Number: 2021943756

Faculty Engagement and Internationalization at Home in Iceland

Subject: Education/Higher Education – United States | International Education | Student Mobility | Comparative Education

Krishna Bista (series editor)

Library of Congress

US Programs, Law, and Literature Division
Cataloging in Publication Program
101 Independence Avenue, S.E.
Washington, DC 20540-4283

Printed in the United States of America

Praises for this book

Internationalization at Home in Iceland

Faculty and administrators throughout the university will find Dinger's work on *Internationalization at Home in Iceland* to be timely reading. The discussions on theoretical frameworks in this work and the insights gained from faculty leading these efforts will support our colleagues engaged in global learning, education abroad, and transnational education efforts on our campuses. An important contribution to the literature.

Jon W. Stauff, Assistant Vice President for International Affairs
South Dakota State University, USA

Dinger offers insights into faculty's perceptions of internationalization in Iceland. The book provides an in-depth examination of faculty's motivation and understanding of the concept by sharing several teachers' profiles. Dinger highlights how teachers change their curricula and research interests to better connect with their students. The book is timely and offers a glimpse of a geographical area rarely included in the literature.

Amany Saleh, Professor of Curriculum and Instruction and Comparative Education
Arkansas State University, USA

In *Internationalization at Home in Iceland,* Dr. Dinger makes a compelling and well-documented case for institutions to move beyond an emphasis on curriculum and academics in Internationalization at Home (IaH) programs. Instead, institutions should adopt a holistic approach where IaH is a prioritized (and supported) "cornerstone of student-centered internationalization efforts"; efforts where intentional faculty engagement – and their own resulting enhanced learning – is central and can lead to genuinely transformative campus internationalization. Highly recommended for educators seeking to address the limitations and inequities of mobility in international education.

James E. Callaghan, Assistant Vice-President for International Education
Georgia College & State University (Georgia College), USA

Internationalization at Home in Iceland is a meaningful book about faculty members' perspectives on internationalization, particularly IaH in Icelandic society. Dr. Casey Dinger has shown how diverse perspectives on this research impact the internationalization process through personal and professional accounts and how exposure and daily engagement strengthen and transform the connection between learning and executing internationalization-related teaching, research, and practice through change. A fascinating read and an authentic contribution to international higher education.

Ruth Lu, International Higher Education Researcher
The Ohio State University, USA

Internationalization at Home in Iceland

Stories of Faculty Engagement

Cross-border physical mobility has dominated the discourse and practice internationalization of higher education. Yet, global crises of climate change, sustainability, pandemics, social equity among others are challenging traditional mobility paradigms. Internationalization at Home (IaH) has been promoted as a way to increase international and intercultural education, and faculty members are central to achieving any success with this program. This collective case study at the University of Iceland examines faculty members' engagement and practices of IaH. What emerges from this portrait of adult learning is professional and personal growth from these practices, a growth that cultivates a more transformative orientation toward internationalization. Findings can inform both faculty and program development around institutional IaH.

CASEY J. DINGER is the Executive Director for Internationalization at the University of Denver in the United States.

STAR Scholars Network Titles

We seek to explore new ideas and best practices related to international and comparative education from the US and around the world, and from a wide range of academic fields, including leadership studies, technology, general education, and area and cultural studies. STAR Scholars publishes some titles in collaboration with Routledge, Springer, Palgrave Macmillan, Open Journals in Education, *Journal of International Students*, and other university presses. At STAR Scholars Network, we aim to amplify the voices of underrepresented scholars, epistemologies, and perspectives. We are committed to an inclusion of a diversity of racial, ethnic, and cultural backgrounds and are particularly interested in proposals from scholars who identify with countries in the Global South. More information at https://starscholars.org/open-access/

Recently Published Books

1. *Chinese Students and the Experience of International Doctoral Study in STEM*
2. *Developing Intercultural Competence in Higher Education*
3. *International Student Mobility to and from the Middle East*
4. *Inequalities in Study Abroad and Student Mobility*
5. *The Experiences of International Faculty in Institutions of Higher Education*
6. *International Students at US Community Colleges*
7. *Critical Perspectives on Equity and Social Mobility in Study Abroad*
8. *Online Teaching, Learning and Virtual Experiences in Global Higher Education*
9. *International Student Support and Engagement in Higher Education*
10. *Impact of COVID-19 on Global Student Mobility and Higher Education*
11. *Global Higher Education During COVID-19: Policy, Society, and Technology*
12. *COVID-19 and Higher Education in the Global Context*
13. *Reimagining Mobility in Higher Education*
14. *Cross-Cultural Narratives: Stories and Experiences of International Students*
15. *Reimagining Internationalization and International Initiatives at HBCUs*
16. *Delinking, Relinking, and Linking Writing and Rhetorics*
17. *Global Footprints in Higher Education*

Table of Contents

List of Tables

Acknowledgements

I am humbled to be in a space and position where I have had the latitude to guide this monograph to fruition. In the spirit of collaborative learning, there are numerous individuals to recognize for their support and co-construction. I am chiefly indebted to the participants named and unnamed in the following chapters. Their willingness to engage in this project was unfettered and authentic. The stories they shared underscore the need for more faculty voices in furthering international education. The University of Iceland leadership and staff also played an important role in developing this project. While there is a list that could fill pages, I would like to thank specifically Tryggvi Thayer for important historical and contextual insight and Guðrún Eysteinsdóttir for tangible and intangible support during data collection.

From the University of Minnesota, I am eternally grateful for Ilene Alexander and sustained insight into faculty development and learning theory. Her depth of knowledge, probing questions, and thoughtful reflections were foundational to this work. I also thank Darwin Hendel, Christopher Johnstone, Deanne Magnuson, and Gerald Fry for their support and feedback. Although I was only able to connect with him once, I owe a deep intellectual debt to the unparalleled Joe Mestenhauser whose life work continues to shape and challenge my thinking.

Colleagues at the University of Denver were also instrumental in realizing this work. Liz Collier and Aubrey Schiavone provided manuscript feedback, Mike Furno provided insight on reframing methods, questions and data and Luc Beaudoin offered avenues for my own continued learning and a platform to apply this work. This platform allowed me to try new ways of advancing international and intercultural education. Thank you all.

As this project was starting, I received great deal of inspiration and encouragement from some of important international educator colleagues Emily Gorlewski, Melissa kirk, Chris Sippel and Christian Wilwohl, and Bonnie Bissonette. During these the final stages, Christina Paguyo offered verbal confetti, communal silence, creative input and insightful feedback. She was instrumental in helping this project over the finish line.

Finally, Diana Davila who was and is my companion, logical sounding board, first-reader and constant encourager. You are a gifted teacher and mentor. I continue to revel at your intercultural skills and capacity for empathy. I'm forever grateful to you, Isela and Diego.

Preface

In the pages to follow, I capture a snapshot in time, place, and space of certain key aspects of a society, institution, and individuals. I leverage this snapshot to provide an intimate portrait of how five faculty members came to be engaged in Internationalization at Home, what practices they use and how they support intercultural learning. This is only part of the story; there's always a dialectic tension between the static (what continues to be true) and dynamic (what changes).

During an interview for this research, Terry Gunnell, asserted that as faculty members, "we're always changing, we're always adapting, we're always learning." This indelible quote has stayed with me – always in the back of my mind. It captures the essence of the study in ways I couldn't have penned myself. It reflects that through a lens of adult learning, faculty members grow and develop in their understanding of their craft and relationship to others and the world itself. This quote also captures a more fundamental reality that we all change as time moves on – whether it is recognized, reflected on, credited or not.

As we change, the world around us changes as well. Contexts and environments have shifted since I collected data for this project starting in 2015 and ending in 2018. The city of Reykjavik Iceland, for example, has made significant advancements in increased commitment to being a more inclusive international place (Intercultural Cities, 2020). For the institution, the University of Iceland has developed a new equality action plan that increases support for students from immigrant backgrounds, establishes new credit-bearing coursework on diversity and equality issues, and advances support for intercultural pedagogies in the classroom (University of Iceland, 2020). And the faculty member participants – their roles and positions, understandings, and practices, have grown and developed.

I, too, have changed as an outcome of this project. Terry's quote underscores a crucial point: to learn is to change – sometimes radically. Learning about faculty members' processes of engagement has transformed my perspectives on higher education, Internationalization at Home, and questions of equity, sustainability and interculturality. These developed throughout the years I spent on this endeavor and are reflected in this monograph. More significantly, my ideas and understandings continue to shift beyond what is in this text in ways that cannot be captured in a static document, in ways that are yet unknown. I invite you to reflect on your own personal or professional growth in whatever areas in this work are relevant to you, and it is my sincere hope that your perspective changes as you reflect on the topics in this work.

Chapter I: Introduction

There is growing uneasiness among educators about the direction of projects of internationalization in higher education. Global crises around climate change and sustainability, health, social injustice, and equity among others are challenging traditional mobility paradigms. Not only are such specific activities being questioned, but there are emerging critical questions of who gets to drive and shape what counts as internationalization. Despite these challenges and questions, many of us who international educators are still deeply value developing multiple perspectives and intercultural learning. Internationalization at Home (IaH) through intercultural pedagogies and practices has emerged as an important advancement toward these outcomes for students and all campus members without relying on the significant issues that come with mobility.

IaH shifts focus to the curriculum and co-curriculum on a home campus, meaning faculty members must be the key to achieving any success. What do we know about their practices, their engagement? Unfortunately, not enough, which is hampering efforts in this area. When discussing the work of faculty members, this word engagement often refers to being part of a specific initiative or involved in an institutional project. The term is frequently used without much attention to the nuance of the concept or its component parts.

Organizational psychology and related fields position employee engagement as more than solely participating, satisfaction with work, or involvement in projects or tasks. Kahn (1990) conceptualizes engagement in the context of organizational psychology and defines employee engagement as "…the harnessing of organizational members' selves to their work roles; in engagement, people employ and express themselves physically, cognitively, and emotionally during role performance" (p. 694). This is a state of psychological presence in professional contexts requiring authenticity by bringing in the self, which then "allows growth, learning, change and productivity to occur" (Kahn, 1992, p. 324). Other researchers have demonstrated the connection between engagement and a growth mindset (Caniëls, Semeijn, & Renders, 2018). This more holistic engagement concerns the "relational contexts that shape how, when, and to what effect people disclose and express themselves in the course of role performances" (Kahn, 2014, p.83).

Thinking how this translates for faculty members, Livingston (2011) proposes that their engagement is unique, defined as "perpetual focused attention, enjoyment, and enthusiasm for the activities associated with faculty work through which the individual finds purpose, senses congruence with personal values and talents, is challenged to use knowledge and skills, and experiences productivity even during difficult times" (p.11). This definition aligns with Kahn's ideas of personal engagement in self-expression and acknowledges engagement as a psychological state that allows for learning and change. While still nascent, scholars are starting to take up faculty member engagement in the internationalization of higher education more intently. Leask, Whitsed, de Wit, & Beelen's (2020) for example looks at faculty member engagement in study abroad contexts. However, we still need to hear more faculty voices in these efforts. There have long been calls for increased research which presents faculty member perspectives, that focus on the teaching and learning processes within local intercultural dimensions. Yet, work centering faculty member perspectives on internationalization – especially Internationalization at Home – is still surprisingly limited.

My primary goal in this book is to start filling in this gap – to offer one window into faculty members' experiences and practices, centering their own voices to deeply understand their investment. This approach affords a more authentic view of their activities, behaviors, and mindsets around IaH. I investigate how those who are at the heart of carrying out what could be a transformative process, construct meaning, enact and grow from practices of internationalization broadly. The second goal is to illuminate, through a constellation of learning and adult learning theories, the personal and professional development faculty undergo when they engage in these practices. Applying these theories results in a portrait of faculty members' learning as an ongoing process of individual internationalization, which is scarce in a sea of literature focused on internationalization as institutional-level process and strategy. While the focus is primarily on these faculty members own experiences, I will also briefly explore contexts that texturize their stories. These include institutional supports and challenges that they navigate as academics as well as the national and societal backdrop at a time of increased global migration and intercultural contact.

Toward a More Ethical Engagement

A dominant development in higher education has been the shift toward a more global and relational focus as the world becomes increasingly interconnected through migration and technology, leading to significantly higher contact between peoples from various cultures, identities, and backgrounds. While international educators have been arguing this for years, there is mounting recognition among higher education that internationalizing is not simply an admirable goal, but rather a fundamental dimension of post-secondary learning to engage with a globalizing world. As a testament to its central position within higher education, internationalization has become more institutionalized in policy and practice (de Wit, 2019) with growing interest from all segments of the field.

Internationalization will always "mean different things to different people" (Knight, 2011b, p. 1) because regional, national, institutional, departmental, and personal contexts and cultures influence how this complex idea of internationalization is conceptualized and carried out. Yet there are trends that impact its development. The economic and social benefits of internationalization on individual and often national levels are far and away the leading narrative, yet there are serious negative repercussions about how it's implemented and who it privileges. Recent work (see Buckner & Stein, 2020) has criticized the very positioning of this imperative, questioning the parameters of what qualifies as internationalization in Western contexts and contesting the depoliticized, decontextualized nature of how it's currently conceptualized and practiced.

The ramifications of internationalization practices have led to frequent rethinking of what internationalization of higher education is and should be (Buckner & Stein, 2020; Deardorff, 2012; Teferra, 2020; Whitsed & Green, 2013). This tension is often driven by a desire to reposition internationalization as value-based (Knight, 2011; Merrill, 2012) —even if those values are themselves diverse. While international educators must continue shaping what internationalization is and means, there is also a clear need to interrogate and address the global impacts and human relations involved in internationalization through multiple and even conflicting perspectives. Institutions of higher education are agents in globalization and arguably have a responsibility to develop humanist-driven values and accompanying skills sets toward solving global issues. Despite these seemingly laudable goals, Teferra (2020) reminds us that "even 'good' intentions are subjective and are presumed worthy by a certain sector of society (scholarly or otherwise) for a certain period of time and to a certain extent" (p.157). Yet if internationalization is to be transformative rather than only symbolic, then definitions, approaches and frameworks need to consider the experiences and views from those who carry out internationalization day-to-day (Jones & de Wit, 2012). This means that efforts should not be on the theoretical question of what internationalization is, but rather on gaining insight about how internationalization is understood and enacted by those who it impacts the most, including faculty members (Robson, Almeida, & Schartner, 2017). Hearing faculty voices address how they conceptualize and realize internationalization is a crucial initial step in understanding faculty members' impact on fostering internationalized institutions. Such institutions then create transformative experiences for the faculty, the campus community and greater society. Faculty perspectives on internationalization are pivotal to better understanding how student learning outcomes can be designed to promote a more ethical, equitable, sustainable, and interculturally sensitive approach to our world.

Internationalization at Home: Beyond Mobility

While broad conceptualizations of the scope of internationalization abound, student mobility has long been the primary strategy associated with internationalization of higher education in Europe. Yet, a consistently low number of European students have studied in another country (Gvetadze, 2014) despite extensive efforts to increase participation primarily through the supra-national Erasmus student mobility program. De Wit (2011a) concludes that even if as many students were able to study abroad as institutions or governments hoped, there is no guarantee that assumed outcomes of this mobility such as "personal development, employability, diversity, intercultural communication, multilingualism, cooperation and competition" (p. 12) would be achieved solely through the mechanism of mobility itself. While certain institutions, organizations and program providers have made advances in deepening such experiences, these outcomes are still illusive.

At the turn of the 21st century then, IaH developed as a response to this problem of a stagnant 10% of European students gaining international experience abroad (Nilsson, 2003). Bengt Nilsson developed an initiative at Malmö University with the aim to start internationalizing the 90% of students who did not go abroad, but rather stayed at their home university. The idea was that Malmö itself could provide the context for an international experience by engaging with the ethnic and cultural diversity on campus and in the surrounding community. This concept received quick support from other international educators and was later moved forward by a special interest group in the European Association for International Education consisting of over 100 international academics and administrators (Wächter, 2003). Although Nilsson initially proposed that IaH was defined as "the provision by universities of international and intercultural learning opportunities for those students who for various reasons do not go abroad" (Paige, 2003. p. 52), the definition was later expanded to include "any internationally related activity with the exception of outbound student mobility" (Nilsson, 2003, p. 31) to which Wächter also added the exception of staff mobility. IaH became part of an attempt to broaden the understanding of internationalization from the physical crossing of borders to embedding international education and intercultural learning throughout institutions themselves. Moreover, the concept includes advancing a structure to the internationalization of the "home" so that the process is embedded across the campus, rather than solely by individual efforts (Wächter, 2000).

It is vital to briefly describe some of the context, rationale and goals established by early architects of IaH. When Bengt Nilsson first proposed IaH in Malmö Sweden, the university was a new institution, situated in an ethnically diverse region with 35% of the surrounding area's population being immigrants or the children of immigrants (Nilsson, 2003). Nilsson made it a goal of the university to integrate with this local diversity. One of the core components of IaH then is to connect the university communities to local diverse communities through face-to-face communication with the goal of fostering both cooperation and external spaces for intercultural exchange. A related goal is to increase the diversity on campus, drawn from both international and domestic populations and this in turn would create internal spaces and opportunities for intercultural interaction (Leask, 2009) through "sustained interaction between students and faculty of diverse cultural backgrounds" (Crawford & Bethell, 2012, p. 192). The presence of such students and faculty then is a key resource in the development of intercultural competencies and is used to assist in the internationalization of domestic students and faculty, leading to a more diverse campus (Mertova & Green, 2010). Additionally, such internationalized campuses can act as a bridge between concepts traditionally associated with multicultural education such as exploring issues of privilege, power (J. Bennett, 2008), and equity within a framework of international education which then has ramifications for the larger society in which the university operates.

Several scholars have introduced additional perspectives on IaH elaborating and extending the original concept. Despite the original parameters set by early architects, Crawford and Bethell (2012) argue that outward mobility has a place in IaH as well. If "the knowledge, experiences, perspectives, and skills gained by students and teachers while abroad" (p. 192) are integrated throughout the institution in a systematic manner, they too can act as a resource to assist in internationalization of those who don't engage in mobility. Hoffman (2003) posits that IaH "necessarily involves the study of transformation within countries, cultures, and institutions" (p. 78). In other words, approaching IaH from the inside with considerations of local demographic and cultural shifts, rather than focusing on traditional lenses of interactions between institutions, universities can act as "international sites" as well as regional and structural harmonization sites (Hoffman, 2003), which are so dominant in Europe (de Wit & Hunter, 2015). Moving beyond intercultural aspects, Mestenhauser (2006) discusses IaH in terms of the international perspectives and creating institutional structure for the process. More specifically, he advocates taking a systems approach, where IaH is understood as a sub-system of larger systems including international education, higher education, and international relations. Focusing on aspects of IaH that intersect with transforming how we approach knowledge will deeply impact higher education, not the least faculty domains of scholarship, teaching, and learning.

As part of a systems approach, IaH must have implications beyond curriculum and academics. While Jones (2013) draws many of the key elements from more traditional understandings of IaH such as "internationalization of the formal curriculum for all students"; "international campus culture and informal curriculum"; student diversity; and development including both academic and non-academic staff (p. 166) she also includes other aspects. She lists points to governance, leadership, strategic planning, assessment of internationalization efforts and deployment of resources. Jones also adds "guidance and support for students outside of the classroom" (p. 166), which aims to internationalize student services and related staff specifically in areas such as advising, libraries and career services. This notion extends idea to include co-curricular programs and non-academic staff as ways of including less visible in the IaH discussion.

The emphasis of IaH is squarely on integrating dimensions of international perspectives and intercultural competence through both formal and non-formal teaching and learning processes (Beelen & Jones, 2015; Crawford & Bethell, 2012). Quoting Teekens, Anderson et al. (2008) argue that IaH is more inclusive than the broad label of internationalization because "it focuses our attention on 'academic learning that blends the concepts of self, strange, foreign and otherness'" (p. 4) and by actively seeking connections with diversity internally and in the greater community. The concept of IaH is intended to be malleable and evolutionary; however, approaches to IaH must include a foundational balance of infusing international perspectives and intercultural competence. Early conceptualizations include the importance of developing international perspectives and intercultural competence in both students and staff alike (Nilsson, 2000; Otten, 2000) and recent (re)conceptualizations still consider the need for academic staff development – even if such wording does not appear in formal definitions (e.g. Beelen & Jones, 2015). While the focus is ultimately on students, developing and leveraging of internationalized academic staff are prerequisites for preparing and delivering the international perspectives and intercultural competence in the formal and informal curriculum (Agnew & Kahn, 2014). The root of any conceptualization of IaH must include a continued focus on the activities and development of academic and non-academic staff. Unfortunately, while there are certainly exceptions, much of the current scholarship misses the holistic approach of IaH when discussing the intersections of faculty and internationalization because it doesn't attend nearly enough to the intercultural aspects.

Despite the promising outlook, there is debate over the effectiveness of IaH at developing intercultural competence in students (Crawford & Bethell, 2012; Prieto-Flores, Feu, & Casademont, 2016). However, evidence suggests that well-planned implementation of IaH activities can be effective (Bhat & McMahon, 2016; Custer & Tuominen, 2017) and may be even more effective in increasing global, intercultural, and international competencies in students than study abroad (Soria & Troisi, 2014). The reality is that IaH is often understood the presence of more international students' on campus, which is frequently expected to enrich the classroom and university by their very presence. Just as mobility in and of itself does not guarantee positive outcomes often associated with being abroad, so it is with the increasing quantity of international students on campus and the positive outcomes associated with IaH. Regardless of the more specific parameters, the process of developing international and intercultural competencies through IaH must be directed (Jones, 2013), facilitated and supported (Crawford & Bethell, 2012) to be effective throughout the institution. Despite convincing rhetoric and increasing scholarly attention, there is little evidence that many institutions have implemented IaH systematically. There are, however, institutions and, importantly, individuals working toward advancing the cause starting from positionsgrowth and learning.

Internationalizing as a learning process

Five streams of research on learning inform this present project on IaH: the growth mindset (the internal condition for learning), adult cognition (capacities that are developed), authenticity in teaching (merging core essence with profession), the academic Self (continual stretching, adapting and (re)creating professional identity) and collaborative learning (coming into communities of practice) provide a foundational basis for exploring faculty learning in the context of internationalization. I expound more on each these theories below, but two particularly relevant themes emerge from this portrait of learning. First, the sort of learning described here is very much rooted in the idea of identity, which can be at the same time, a core essence and "an ongoing construction" (Kreber et al., 2007, p. 40). Second, these concepts are part of a process of lifelong learning, which is at the center of what Stier (2006) called an ideology of educationalism. Institutions can learn through the process of internationalization and such learning starts with the individuals who experience the grassroots and tangible aspects of that process daily. Although they are key components in the process, theories that intersect with the self are underutilized in investigating successful learning (Yorke & Knight, 2004) and much could be gleaned from their use.

Aspects of this study stem from a deconstruction of Sanderson's (2008) ideas on internationalizing the Academic Self. Sanderson contends that within this framework, it is central to extend the concept of understanding through self-reflection that allows for exploration and understanding of others' value-systems, identity, and social culture;(p. 288) this self-reflection is subsequently realized as "notions of openness, interconnectivity, interdependence, reciprocity, and plurality" (p. 294). This conceptual framework allows for paths of faculty member development specifically through extending the self-reflection exercises related to authenticity in teaching into a context of internationalization. The chapters that follow provide evidence of efforts to develop and grow from practices of IaH through a lens of engagement as a process of learning.

Chapter Organization

This book is organized in sections covering the broad concept of faculty development, context for the study, and analysis of data from the participants. Chapter 2 frames the centrality of faculty members to the process of internationalization in higher education in addition to their understandings, motivations, and barriers to engagement. I shift to describing the spaces and places of Iceland that the participants operate in, providing brief context of with attention to immigration and changing demographics in chapter 3. I go on to discuss the University of Iceland where the participants all work and certain key elements related to IaH.

Chapter 4 then pivots to exploring the central figures heart of this study, the faculty members participants. Here I offer profiles including their early international experiences and background on how they came to be interested in international-related teaching and scholarship. I move from their backgrounds to explore the specific practices of IaH that the participants engage in as part of their work. While many of these practices are related to the classroom, others are co-curricular, part of their research or engaging with Icelandic society. In chapter 5, I discuss the participants' understanding of internationalization as a concept, their role in it and what meaning they derive from engaging before discussing the daily practices of IaH in chapters 6 and 7 with attention to areas of teaching, networking, and research. In chapter 8, I analyze the faculty participants' engagement using a constellation of theories to discuss their development. These theories serve as a lens used to understand the participants' experiences in the continuum of symbolic and transformative internationalization. This analysis shows that faculty who engage in practices of IaH continually grow professionally and impact their own spheres of influence within their departments and beyond, shaping and advancing IaH. Finally, in chapter 9 I consider the paths forward supporting for faculty development, internationalized teaching and learning as well as implications for the University of Iceland. The hope is that this concluding chapter sparks thoughts for the reader on how these ideas may translate to other higher education institutions.

Chapter II: Centering Faculty in Internationalization

Just as there are a variety of approaches among researchers to internationalization, there are also significant differences among faculty as well. The literature provides a basis for further exploration of faculty in the context of Iceland despite such differences. It isn't new that faculty members serve a vital function in the internationalization process (Brewer, 2010; Romani-Dias et al., 2019; Stohl, 2007) and arguably and even greater role in the more focused IaH (Bedenlier & Zawacki-Richter, 2015). Allen (2004) bluntly asserts that faculty are the "most critical factor in achieving a more internationalized campus" (p. 1) and it is clear why this is the case. Faculty members are intimately connected with many central elements of the internationalization process as they are the generators of new knowledge through research, the architects of the curriculum, and then the teachers of that material. Their efforts result in significant influence on students who then impact the greater society. Additionally, they act "as catalysts and initiators of international programs and collaborations and as the day-to-day implementers of new developments" (Finkelstein et al., 2013, p. 326). Without their engagement, effective and successful internationalization efforts will always be on the peripheries. Unfortunately, the argument about faculty members' centrality has been washed out by the avalanche of narratives fixated on institutional strategies and easily quantifiable data points. Even in the current scholarship available, the relative lack of research accounting for faculty perspectives and voices regarding internationalization bears witness to the persistent challenge that exists in this arena. (Re)centering faculty members in the conversation is a necessary pre-cursor to implementing IaH beyond the superficial.

Faculty understanding of internationalization

Many studies on internationalization in higher education go directly to rationales for participating without considering meaning. There's a much small number focused on how faculty members understand the concept. What we do know is that that faculty members' understanding is often influenced by their scholarship and experience in international spheres and varies significantly across discipline, unit, or school (Childress, 2010; Jiang & Carpenter, 2013; K. Thomas, 2012). The advancement of state-level strategies for internationalization means that national policies and frameworks are impacting their understanding as well (Clarke & Hui Yang, 2019; Li, Khattak, and Jiang, 2021). Much of the literature addresses faculty members' view of internationalization as understood as an institutional process or strategy. In one of the few empirical studies investigating UK academics understanding of internationalization, the researchers report that "the group universally accepted that internationalization was a fact of their working lives, nonetheless people felt uncertain about precise definitions of what internationalization meant" (Turner & Robson, 2007, p. 9). This finding mirrors what many see in their institutions: a disconnect between buzzwords or concepts that senior leadership and support offices use and how faculty translate that to their own understanding and practice. Other studies show that faculty members more solidified vision of what internationalization means, but see it more as global corporatization. Friesen (2012) finds that certain faculty see institutional internationalization as an effort to increase reputation and rankings, while others report a belief that their institutions pursue internationalization primarily as an economic-driven enterprise (Clarke & Hui Yang 2019; Hanson & McNeil, 2012). The faculty members' responses in these studies are informed by internationalization as messaged and framed by senior administration. This paints a discouraging picture of how faculty perceive the entire project because there is often a mismatch and tension in rationales and values between the organizational economic factors and missions rooted in liberal arts traditions.

When internationalization is framed as an academic project related to how faculty conceptualize core principles of pedagogy and how faculty view the relationship to their research, however, faculty members show significantly greater interest and understanding. More importantly for our purposes here, connecting internationalization with the key aspects of IaH including internationalizing the campus and curriculum by focusing on developing global, international, or intercultural learning and development engages more faculty. We can infer their investment from the copious amount of conference presentations, scholarship and activities centered on these outcomes from faculty across various fields. As Godwin (2019) asserts, outcomes (learning-driven) rather than outputs (economic-driven) must be central to internationalization as a concept. While this tension demonstrates the disconnect between many institutions' messaging and how scholars and leaders in the international education field position the concept, we must hear more from individual faculty themselves as to how they have come to understand and then navigate the various narratives of internationalization in their daily work.

Faculty member motivation and participation in internationalization

Understanding of internationalization is inextricably linked to faculty members' motivations to participate. In his essay, "The role of faculty in international education," Allen (2004) argues that universities that desire to have a more internationalized institution must encourage faculty members to engage in internationally oriented activities in the three traditional areas of faculty members' activity: research, teaching and service. The term "faculty engagement" is widely used throughout literature concerned with faculty members' involvement in internationally orientated activities without exploration of the full meaning or definition. "Engagement" is frequently used interchangeably with "participation", which can point to a variety of domains that may or may not relate to the psychological investment and presence. At a minimum, it means faculty member involvement in internationally oriented activities such as transnational collaborations; internationalizing curriculum, and learning; international conferences; internationally-oriented research and service; leading study away courses; and campus events or committees related to internationalization. This book is concerned with the construct of engagement specifically, but it is necessary to consider related work even if they lack precise definitions.

Many institutions provide some extrinsic motivation and incentives for participating in internationalization-related endeavors, though these are often less related to developing IaH. Institutional-driven supports can have an impact especially in ramping up new initiatives or programs, but they only go so far. Unless faculty members internalize extrinsic motivations to join internationalization efforts with their own goals, participation frequently falls off when the resources are no longer offered. Certainly, much of the evidence suggests intrinsic incentives generally outweigh extrinsic incentives in motivating faculty toward individual internationalization (Li & Tu, 2016). In many ways faculty life is driven chiefly by these intrinsic drivers and personal interests whether in research, teaching, or service. Emmanuel (2010) suggests that self-development in an important intrinsic factor as there is a recognition of growth that comes from engaging in internationalization. Researchers found that "self-knowledge" that is to say, "the professional values, orientations and self-concept over a career within particular institutional contexts" (Finkelstein et al., 2013, p. 338) was the most powerful predictor in individual faculty internationalization of research content and networks. Other motivations are more explicitly social and civic-minded. Klyberg (2012) shows that a commitment to developing empathy in students, sense of responsibility and doing something that "matters" were dominant among participants. These social and civic-minded rationales are rooted in prioritizing learning and self-development which is a theme of across much of the literature on faculty member motivation. This personal and learning-centered approach to internationalization informs core aspects of IaH and why it has emerged as an important alternative to the mobility focused models.

There are differing levels of involvement with internationalization and specific models such as IaH. We can look at many institutions and see faculty members who serve on internationalization committees, lead study away programs and actively integrate intercultural or global learning in the curriculum. These faculty members are often highly visible at the institution and have strong international connections or experience. Others are entirely disconnected. In her review of related literature, Childress (2010) categorizes different degrees of faculty engagement in internationalization from the most outspoken advocates who are "champions", to those who resist to internationalization, called "the uninterested skeptics" and outright "opponents." Green and Olson (2003) parse out the category of champions into those who will take the reins and lead campus-wide efforts, those who home in on developing specific aspects of internationalization and those who are focused on internationalizing their own teaching and daily work. Results from Childress' (2010) case studies reveal that faculty champions of internationalization are drivers of the process who can be particularly key figures in realizing organizational internationalization goals. Similarly, the presence of internationally oriented and persuasive champions among faculty contributes to a greater degree of internationalization within their unit (Ellingboe, 1998) and can shift a department's culture and collective mindset toward more comprehensive internationalization (Bogotch & Maslin-Ostrowski, 2010) which is a more holistic approach. It is clear champions can have a significant and lasting impact in supporting the development of internationalization at various levels, particularly among their colleagues.

Aligning institutional motivations and rationales with faculty member's own personal drivers (Nyangau, 2020) are more likely to engage them and advance efforts related to IaH specifically. Institutions deeply interested in developing IaH must find ways to dedicate more time and resources cultivating champions given their power to affect change. Particularly because targeted investment in even a small number of these highly engaged faculty members can influence and impact their colleagues, institutions, students, and society. To be successful, developing these champions of IaH must be coupled with empowering them to drive initiatives and be recognized and rewarded for their efforts. Unfortunately, this is not the reality for many institutions or faculty member where the activities and components of IaH is considered just another area of interest rather than central to the function of education in a more global world.

Barriers to involvement in internationalization

There are always barriers to engaging faculty members in higher education initiatives and internationalization is no different. This is particularly true when there is not consensus or a well-laid out idea of what the term even encompasses. Beelen (2011) suggests there is a lack of faculty engagement and expertise in the internationalization process. This is expected as much of the messaging which is often on rankings and student mobility is not directed at faculty or their daily work in the classroom and in research.

Barriers for faculty members participating in internationalization are governmental, institutional, and personal. Governmental or geopolitical barriers are mostly beyond the individual and institution's direct influence. Calikoglu, Lee & Arslan, (2020) for example find issues with restrictive visas and travel regulations as well as differences in national systems and accreditation. While there are often ongoing attempts to improve harmonization through initiatives such as the Bologna Process in Europe, challenges remain, and it only impacts a single region. Many more barriers are institutional, however. The lack of funding is the most frequently cited institutional obstacle in faculty participating in internationalization (e.g. Criswell & Zhu, 2015; Nyangau, 2020), but it is not the only barrier. Despite significant funds devoted to internationalized initiatives from the institutions in the study, Klyberg (2012) for example, concludes that faculty questioned the institution's long-term commitment and attributed their minimal participation to lack of institutional and administrative support. Faculty report frequently feeling unsupported in their internationalization efforts (Clarke & Hui Yang, 2021; Calikoglu, Lee & Arslan, 2020) or found that there is only rhetorical support (Criswell & Zhu, 2015) which may suggest a more symbolic approach to internationalization by many higher education administrators.

In addition to feeling unsupported in their efforts, there is evidence that faculty balk at institutional rationales for pursuing internationalization that are rooted in marketization. As Turner and Robson (2007) note, "linking commercial revenue-generating approach with internationalist rhetoric may frustrate the development of an international orientation in an institution; and increasing academic disengagement with the commercial agenda possesses the potential to obstruct management intention." Other researchers report a gap in communication, as faculty do not recognize a link between the goals of internationalization strategies and their day-to-day work at all (Dewey & Duff, 2009). Instead, many faculty members report seeing their activities as raising department and individual profile, ultimately unintentionally reinforcing an entrepreneurial and competitive rationale for internationalization itself (Mitchell & Nielsen, 2012). A core challenge is that often institutional internationalization in practice works around the central purpose of education, rather than being grounded in outcomes of teaching, learning and development of IaH and resonates with many faculty members.

Institutional barriers are only part of the challenge. Personal barriers exist as well. The combination of a lack of expertise and interest among academic staff is an equally significant barrier to involvement in the internationalization process (Beelen, 2011). This lack of expertise supports claims made by Mestenhauser (2011) about faculty member knowledge regarding the internationalization process and their specific disciplines. This is particularly clear when considering internationalizing the curriculum (K. Thomas, 2012). In terms of a lack of interest, Hustvedt and Dickson (2011) determine that the lack of personal engagement in international topics and research is "most related to a decrease in international activity" (p. 22). However, for some faculty interest is not the obstacle, instead faculty are hesitant to continue pursuing internationalization activities because of the excess stress on their professional and personal lives (Klyberg, 2012). This is partly the result of global or international aspects not being integrated into most review and promotion processes, but also the overall lack of internationalized campuses where incorporating global perspectives and intercultural learning is additive and not foundational.

Mestenhauser (2011) contends there are more fundamental obstacles that are both conceptual and perceptual. Green and Shoenberg (2006) agree, saying that faculty must overcome mindsets with deeply held implicit assumptions about their discipline which are part of their academic culture and broaden their perspective beyond traditional conventions. Ellingboe (1998) calls this barrier a lack of cognitive shift toward internationalization. Even disciplines which are more internationally oriented require deliberate efforts to successfully internationalize, accounting for multiple international perspectives as well as intercultural dimensions. In addition to a spectrum of barriers associated with academic culture, organizational and department culture can also be barriers to faculty internationalization (Bartell, 2003), particularly as such environments are recursive and often reinforce normative values (Otten, 2009). Rethinking courses and curriculum to integrate global perspectives often challenges the canon of knowledge and understanding central to the identity of an academic field. While transforming the curriculum is a necessary and crucial undertaking for building a more accurate and inclusive education system, it is likely one of the most challenging aspects to internationalization. It requires that faculty members across the institution reflect on their own thinking and then translate it into making time in re-evaluating courses and learning outcomes. This is an intense and ongoing process which requires time and resources and even frowned upon by the institution or colleagues. While there are important roles and functions played by non-academic staff, administrators, and students in implementing IaH, it depends on faculty. They are simultaneously the primary component and central barrier.

A Continuum of Internationalization Orientation

Internationalization in higher education is conceptually and practically complex. Understandings, rationales, policies, and activities differ across institutions. There is a continuum of institutional orientations toward internationalization, from the symbolic to the transformative (Bartell, 2003). The symbolic end of the continuum is characterized with a commercialized market-oriented approach (Gu & Schweisfurth, 2011) with a few token international-related activities scattered across campus, but no central structure or integration. Institutions taking this orientation focus on compliance with external demands as there is little desire to make radical changes to traditional systems (Turner & Robson, 2007). Institutions on the transformational end of the continuum, implement a synergistic, campus-wide internationalization through curriculum and research that impacts all stakeholders drawing on an orientation toward cooperation, collaboration springing from internal drivers (Turner & Robson, 2008).

Despite the academic, cultural, and even economic benefits that come from transformational internationalization (Gu & Schweisfurth, 2011), few institutions embrace this approach. Senior leadership tend to focus primarily on funds for institutional agendas, the transfer of knowledge and competitive rationales (Calikoglu, Lee & Arslan, 2020); and issues of compliance (Anderson et al., 2008) rather than an agenda of comprehensive engagement. Certainly, much of the current literature and practice is concerned with faculty willingness to participate in the internationalization vision, goals and strategies as determined by central administration. Not that internationalization should somehow be decentralized, but there must be a move away from the fixation on meeting quotas and toward mechanics of the process and affects those in the field.

An orientation toward more transformational internationalization is personal and qualitative, rather than institutional and quantitative in nature, springing from the grassroots which in turn shapes and stimulates institutional direction and change (Turner & Robson, 2007). In this way, IaH is more aligned with transformative internationalization as it is concerned chiefly with the personal and individual perspectives on internationalization (Anderson et al., 2008). Like Bartell, Appadurai (2001) also wrote about orientations of internationalization, but in language that is more readily applied and meant for focus on the personal. Sanderson (2004) summarizes Appadurai's concept stating that weak internationalization is characterized as "a superficial engagement with the issues" while strong internationalization is "a laborious, even contentious, deeper, more sophisticated and genuine desire to explore what it means to become internationalized" (p. 16).

In one of the most important conceptual pieces, Sanderson (2008) provides conceptual space for this personal approach to include a department level and more fundamentally, the individual level where the daily work of internationalization occurs (Turner & Robson, 2007). In this way, the focus of inquiry can be on how transformational change can occur on the individual level through a personal journey of internationalization. In their study on five universities in the UK, Anderson et al., (2008) find that academic staff speak about making individual and personal change in teaching and learning rather than departmental or institutional change. Personal attitudes, beliefs and worldview of the individual academic are central to transformational internationalization. If academics daily work pivots toward a more transformational internationalization, then so will the institution. The transformational aspects of internationalization can then come from individual faculty members as champions pushing change. While successful attempts to incorporate a transformative orientation to internationalization include employing specific methods and strategies, it ultimately is more about understanding faculty member worldviews and how they are developed and changed (Niehaus & Williams, 2012). A focus faculty member development is the necessary precursor to working toward IaH which embodies a transformative, personal, and collaborative internationalization.

Faculty Development for a Transformative Orientation

While a transformational internationalization is centered on the individual rather than the institution, faculty still deeply benefit from organizational support. A few comprehensive models been proposed to carry out this development in internationalization systematically for faculty members. Childress (2010) constructs a model for developing faculty engagement in internationalization based on data from case studies of two US universities with significant dedication to internationalization throughout the institution. This model consists of five components that an institution should provide for faculty: intentionality, investments, infrastructure, institutional networks, and individual support. While institutional environments and supports are key, the model stops short of addressing developing the individual faculty members' mindset or valuing.

In a more individual-level Turner and Robson (2008) focus more on the person than the institutional. They present a matrix for internationalizing faculty by combining competence in terms of skills and knowledge surrounding internationalization, with the commitment to the process by creating institutional partnerships that cross conventional professional cultural boundaries in order to "develop a dialog about similarities and differences of values and practices" (p. 139). This model takes a more personal and relational approach asking faculty members to (continually) work toward challenging and transcending normative structures in academia and their institutions. Values and practices are often so profoundly embedded, it takes a significant amount of ongoing work and intentional conversation for change to occur. Additionally, while institutions can provide support and opportunity, this model places faculty members growth and mindset at the center which also has implications for their own responsibility in the process.

This process includes the development of intercultural capabilities as foundational components of transformational internationalization. There is a significant body of research that solidifies importance of promoting intercultural or international-related learning outcomes for students in higher education, but little work has been done on the intercultural development of faculty members. The few studies available highlight the need for structured and purposeful growth in this area. Bennett (2010) argues that faculty members who are in ethnorelative stages of intercultural development are "more likely to recognize or design programming that really contributes to the development of intercultural sensitivity and competence" (p. 9). Moving into an ethnorelative state for faculty members requires knowing about the "self" as a cultural being, the elements of culture, culture-specific and culture-general skills, and the process of learning itself (Paige & Goode, 2009).

In one of the most persuasive studies on faculty members and intercultural competence, Crichton and Paige (2004) find two overarching themes from their study. The first is that a strong disconnect exists among the academic staff between what is international and intercultural in education. They argue that these two fields ought to be better integrated and even that intercultural education is more inclusive as a concept than international education. The second theme deals with the operationalization of the "intercultural" in teaching and learning. The researchers discover that graduates were expected to attain three dimensions of expertise that of "international", "culture" and "communication" (p. 11). The challenge then for faculty to "integrate these aspects of the curriculum, drawing on, and raising awareness of the fact that both students' and lecturers' identities are themselves 'reflexively engaged' with others in their own lives, and, together, in relation to internationalisation" (p. 12). There is a need for more practical scholarship that integrates components of internationalization theory and research with an application to policy and practice in a specific institutional context.

Even while intercultural development can be considered a core outcome of internationalization, it is only part of the picture. There is also a need for more holistic models of what it means to be a globally-minded or internationalized faculty member in the context of IaH. Faculty members must work toward an international mindset which consists of integrative, intercultural, interdisciplinary, comparative, transfer of knowledge-technology, contextual and global dimensions (Paige & Mestenhauser, 1999, pp. 504-505). Sanderson (2011) provides detailed profile of what the ideal internationalized faculty member would look like in relation to the teacher role specifically. He identifies seven dimensions for university teachers, arguing that they should,

> 1) have some basic knowledge of educational theory, 2) incorporate internationalised content into subject material, 3) have a critical appreciation of one's own culture and its assumptions, 4) have some knowledge of other countries and cultures, but a preference for being open to and appreciating other worldviews, 5) use universal teaching strategies to enhance the learning experiences of all students, 6) understand the way one's academic discipline and its related profession (e.g. physiotherapy) are structured in a range of countries, 7) understand the international labour market in relation to one's academic discipline" (pp. 665-666).

In addition to the profile, Sanderson presents practical actions that faculty members can take that could help move them toward this ideal. He also argues that they must engage in "international existentialism," whereby the understanding "cultural otherness" serves as a catalyst for an increased internationalized "self". This work should serve as an important template for administrators and individual faculty in for advancing engagement in IaH.

Faculty members are the pivotal actors in embedding IaH and because of this, it is vital to focus on how to develop their global perspectives and attitudes. And yet, there is an implicit assumption either that faculty already possess these capabilities or that these attitudes and skills are less critical than other aspects of faculty work. This reflects a significant challenge to elevating intercultural learning broadly. Although there is increasing acknowledgement of the importance, it still is often marginalized in higher education where cognitive and fact-based learning are prioritized while learning outcomes that center affective learning and critical feeling are less valued or altogether dismissed.

Senior administrators, international officers, deans, department chairs, and other campus leaders must be more explicit about the criticality of intercultural and international capabilities as part of faculty members' daily work. This also means that these leaders must offer the supports and incentives that are contextualized within the faculty members' own experiences and disciplines. We can't expect intercultural learning outcomes in students if faculty members don't embody these capabilities and mindset themselves. The next section explores the development of these capabilities and mindsets and what that means for their personal and professional growth.

Perspectives on Faculty Members and Adult Learning

Transformational or "strong" internationalization is an ongoing process realized as a kind of growth and can, broadly speaking, be understood as a process of learning (Paige & Mestenhauser, 1999) by developing new mindsets, behaviors, and capacities (J. Bennett, 2008). Stohl (2007) supports this proposition saying that scholars should examine faculty members' teaching, research, and service components in light of internationalization within the context of learning and discovery. He states, "if we think of internationalization as how faculty and students (as well as administrators) learn about, learn from, and learn with others, we suggest that internationalization has value in and of itself" (p. 369). This is because the context of internationalization presents new and emerging realities which challenge traditionally local cultural structures, identities, pedagogies, and approaches to knowledge and requires that faculty change, adapt and grow – that is learn. Consequently, faculty members are stepping into educational spaces in which they will have to experience learning about themselves as teachers, as academics, as members of their campus, society, and the world in order to be relevant and effective. Moreover, they must learn about the shifting contexts in which they operate (Mestenhauser, 2011), both within and outside of the confines of the campus and teach new material and familiar material in new ways. While this learning is often subsumed under the banner of faculty member development as outlined in the previous section, such development rarely focuses on how academic staff actually go about and experience learning, but rather frequently focuses on the acquisition of technical skills (Cranton & Carusetta, 2004).

A small number of empirical studies have explored faculty learning experiences (e.g. Niehaus & Williams, 2016), particularly experiences in internationalizing curriculum and teaching. Schuerholz-Lehr, Caws, Van Gyn, and Preece (2007) adapt an education intervention which utilizes a workshop format to assist participating faculty in internationalizing their course curriculum. Faculty report significant learning through the workshop and a deeper level of engagement with the concept of internationalization. Beuckelaer, Lievens, & Bucker (2012) reach a similar conclusion that faculty can undergo a process of transformative learning by taking part in workshops where facilitators with expertise in internationalizing of curriculum work with participants to internationalize specific courses. Odgers and Giroux (2006) move beyond investigating faculty experiences in workshops and show that over a period of a year, faculty and their teaching practices became more internationalized through a development initiative designed to internationalize curriculum.

Niehuas and Williams (2016) provide one of the most intriguing studies. As a result of a structured faculty development program, participants shifted their perspectives on course content, pedagogy, and internationalization. Importantly, the researchers also found that participants experienced "personal growth" (Niehaus & Williams, 2016, p. 70), changing their perspectives beyond their job role. While such studies are crucial to approaching an understanding of faculty members' personal involvement in internationalization, a gap still exists in understanding the experience and learning processes on a broader scale.

It is important to find a approach aligned with a transformative orientation of internationalization and a benchmark for what constitutes learning for faculty. Coffield (2008) provides a robust and accessible definition for learning saying that it:

> refers only to significant changes in capability, understanding, knowledge, practices, attitudes or values by individuals, groups, organizations or society. Two qualifications. It excludes the acquisition of factual information when it does not contribute to such changes; it also excludes immoral learning as when prisoners learn from other inmates in custody how to extend their repertoire of criminal activities (p. 7)

While the exceptions add bulk, they help to focus on palpable growth and development as well as highlighting the aspect of morality in learning. This definition is a starting block, and the concepts below are not intended to present a unified theory, but rather they are interrelated (and in ways overlapping) dimensions which help construct a portrait of faculty learning aligned with an orientation toward transformative internationalization.

Mindset for learning

Successful learning springs from internal conditions and orientations for learners that give space for embracing such development. Dweck (2006) argues learning requires what she terms a growth mindset. People with this mindset believe that they can continually stretch themselves to learn something new. They feel invigorated and smart when they take on a difficult challenge and see effort as fundamental to improving. Moreover, they look at failure as an opportunity to learn and take more risks in attempting new learning activities. Educational spaces are fertile grounds for investigation and developing new skills for those with a growth mindset. Indeed, Dweck's (2006) research shows that those with this mindset learn more naturally, perform better and attain higher levels of achievement (p. 245) which is supported by additional evidence in a study from the field of neuroscience using fMRI (Mangels, Butterfield, Lamb, Good, & Dweck, 2006). She contrasts this with those who have a fixed mindset believing that traits are set in stone, focus on constant perfection and proving themselves in every task. Failure to those in this mindset is tantamount to not being intelligent or talented enough and because of this, educational spaces are understood primarily as places for sorting learners into categories of talent and intelligence. Dweck (2006) also contends that mindset itself is not inborn and permanent; rather it is plastic and more akin to a perceptual lens that can be shifted. It is a fundamental component of how individuals engage in their own learning.

Adult cognition and capacities of thinking

When adults learn, they harness and grow into specific capacities that establish a distinct dimension of adult learning. Brookfield (2000) draws on four streams of research on learning and contends that there are four primary capacities which can be employed more frequently and developed to a greater degree by adult learners. While these capacities are not unique to adults, they make up a particular dimension of learning which takes place during adulthood. These capacities include thinking dialectically, employing practical logic, knowing how we know what we know and finally, critical reflection. Collectively termed "adult cognition," these capacities are connected by the thread of an increased awareness of context and self.

The capacity to think dialectically refers to the continual back and forth movement, or interplay, of reasoning between recognizing set universal rules or patterns of understanding of how the world works and the specific context of any given situation (Brookfield, 2000). This mode of thinking, which has implications for decision making, allows for the co-existence of what is ideal and what is actual and contradictory rationales, ideas or values are held simultaneously without dissonance for the learner. In the context of moral decision-making and reasoning, "adults become aware of how context alters the neat application of general codes, of how the rules of moral reasoning learned at earlier stages of life are reinterpreted and contextualized because of the moral complexities of adult life" (para. 9).

Another capacity that Brookfield points to in adult learners is what he calls practical logic, which is also concerned with contextually understanding. By practical logic he does not mean common sense or deductive reasoning, but an inferential logic with ability to employ a sort of close reading of a situation which results in a deep understanding. This is accomplished through "being aware of, and attending seriously to, very subtle cues whose importance only becomes apparent to those who have the benefit of a lengthy and mindful immersion in experience" (para. 12). Those who have the capacity for and employ this type of self-referential logic can reflect on their own experiences and make rapid decisions or adjustments as necessary (Brookfield, 2000).

The third capacity of adult learners that Brookfield presents is knowing how to know what we know; that is understanding about how we have come by what it means to know. In less abstract terms, this capacity is essentially learning how to learn. This is defined as "the capacity adults possess to become self-consciously aware of their learning styles and to adjust their preferred ways of learning according to the situations in which they find themselves" (para. 15). In addition to comprehending, summarizing and critically analyzing the content of information in a given situation, this capacity adds a meta-cognitive layer to the process of learning, where learners can draw on strengths and compensate for weaknesses.

The final relevant capacity that adult learners develop is critical reflection. Brookfield defines this capacity as "the process by which adults become critically reflective regarding the assumptions, beliefs and values which they have assimilated during childhood and adolescence" (para. 19). In this way, he argues adults test the validity of their long-established frame of reference to determine whether the hard and fast rules, biases and they internalized when they were young, hold up to the complexities and realities of adulthood. Mezirow (1997) provides reasoning that this is not a painless process because we as adults "have a strong tendency to reject ideas that fail to fit our preconceptions, labeling those ideas as unworthy of consideration—aberrations, nonsense, irrelevant, weird, or mistaken" (p. 5). Brookfield (1995, 2000) and Meizrow (1997, 2000) both note that in adult learning, such critical reflection can only be developed through the lived experience of contractions and ambiguity presented by interactions and decisions confronting adults. Brookfield demonstrates that there is evidence behind what that theorists posit: that some kind of disorienting or traumatic event often precipitates a period of critical reflection which leads to increased awareness the cycle of "reflection on action, further action, reflection on the further action and so on" (para. 21) that can occur in a short period of time. In addition to the connections with the broad concept of adult learning, critical reflection and the awareness that comes with that process are also central components of theories concerned with teachers and learning specifically which are addressed in the next section.

Authenticity in teaching

Like Brookfield and Mezirow, Cranton (2001) and Cranton and Carusetta (2004) also take up the idea of critical reflection, but specifically regarding developing authenticity through integrating the "self" into their teaching practice. Although authenticity in teaching has diverse meaning both among theorists as well as practitioners, Cranton (2001) and Cranton and Carusetta's (2004) approach is particularly useful because it adds an ethical component that authenticity is a moral ideal (Kreber, 2007). Through their 3-year study using methods of grounded theory, these researchers posit that there are five dimensions to authenticity: awareness of self as teachers and individuals, awareness of others' characteristics and their learning needs, developing relationships with learners promoting the mutual ability to be genuine, awareness of context and constraints of learning, and a critically reflective approach to practice (Cranton & Carusetta, 2004, p. 6-7). Rather than instrumental knowledge which is technical or scientific and more valued in today's market-driven world, knowledge gained in these dimensions is communicative (understanding of ourselves and social constructs), and emancipatory (freeing of learned oppressive norms and assumptions) (Cranton & King, 2003).

The researchers define the self as an individual's basic values, personality, and traits - that is to say, one's core identity which remains fairly stable across contexts for the individual and how the others perceive that individual (Gee, 2000). In this way, Cranton and Carusetta (2004) see the self in Jungian terms of individuation: the ongoing process of gaining self-awareness through reflecting on oneself and one's own experience. They argue that it is through the process of becoming authentic that teachers integrate personal principles, beliefs, personality and learning styles into their practice in a genuine way, which creates congruence and consistency in values and action.

Authenticity in teaching is ultimately rooted in critical theory (Brookfield, 1995) and more specifically, in transformational learning theory (Mezirow, 1997, 2000). Mezirow says that critical reflection on our assumptions can happen in daily activities when we encounter alternate viewpoints through objective reframing (task-oriented problem solving) or subjective reframing (self-reflectively assessing one's own perceptions and beliefs). Cranton (2006) shows that the learning that can come out of self-reflection manifests in different ways, it "may be rational, affective, extrarational, or experiential depending on the person engaged in the learning and the context in which it takes place" (p. 6) and "can lead to significant personal transformations" (Mezirow, 1997, p. 7). Through this experience teachers:

> transform their habits of mind about teaching. For this kind of learning about teaching to take place, faculty must be critical of the academic community collective. They need to be able to challenge the way things are done and have always been done. They need to differentiate their own thoughts and values from those of the community within which they work, which is a part of developing authenticity (Cranton & Carusetta, 2004, p. 7).

The academic Self

Hall (2002) investigates the topic of the self in relation to educators as well, extending beyond the scope of teaching and to the broader position where academics are seen as investigating and reflecting on their professional identity as it relates to their practiced professional life of teaching, research and service. In his seminal book on the notion of the academic self, Hall says that "self-reflexivity entails the seeing of one's life as a project always in the making, one that is not controlled by tradition or other external forces that may have played determining roles in the past" (p. 3). The author makes two points particularly related to faculty and learning: First, that an academic's professional identity and career, can undergo significant change which may lead them in new and productive directions in research and growth. Indeed, this is because adults can develop the capacity to undertake self-directed projects of learning (Coffield, 2008) and faculty by the nature of their profession, can be considered what Zimmerman (2002) calls self-regulated learners in forging these novel paths as new information comes to light or cultural contexts shift (Hall, 2002). Second, that despite the over-use of the idiom, academics should continually integrate theory and practice in an authentic way (Hall 2002). Here it should be noted that Hall is referring to professional identity as one of multiple identities "being recognized as a certain 'kind of person,' in a given context" rather than Cranton's (2001) concept of a core essence which is constant across such contexts.

Collaborative learning

Like theorists in adult education and authenticity in teaching, Coffield (2008) also focuses on the issue of identity, though looking less at "Self" and more identity within a larger community. Indeed, Cranton laments that what most new faculty know and enact in regard to their teaching derives from their own experience as students and what they learn from watching their community of colleagues. Coffield (2008) inverts the paradigm, turning negative association with this communal acquisition of knowledge into a positive process through which adults learn. To situate his concept of collaborative learning into a broader context, Coffield (2008) summarizes two theories using the metaphors of acquisition and participation both of which appear on the surface to deal with learning. In the acquisition metaphor, the focus is on the individual student's acquisition of knowledge, the straightforward process of transmission of information from teacher to student and finally, knowledge is understood to be form of capital that can be converted into profit (Coffield, 2008; Coffield & Williamson, 2011). This theory of learning is reflected in government policies stressing accountability and the qualification and credential-driven market model in education systems (Coffield & Williamson, 2011) which counts the stringing of facts together as learning. Coffield (2008) cites the shortcoming of this theory as constraining the benefits of learning to the individual who understands their acquired knowledge to be a possession used for economic gain. Additionally, these conceptions of the linear transfer of knowledge from teacher to student maintain the power distance and hierarchy in educational settings, leading to a less democratic classroom (Coffield, 2008). There isn't much significant change in such a theory of learning. Instead, learning aligned with a transformative orientation is multi-dimensional, reciprocal, and democratic in a process, which places learning within a social dimension. Learning is ultimately about change, which is reflected in the participation metaphor. In this more cultural theory of learning Coffield (2008) contends:

> the participation metaphor locates learning not in the heads of individuals, but in the simultaneous social processes of: learning to belong to different 'communities of practice'…; learning to recognise changes in our identity because learning changes who we are; learning to create meaning out of our experiences; and learning what it means to know in practice (p. 8).

This change then is a constant (re)negotiation of meaning and identity (Brookfield, 2000; Mezirow, 1997) through participating in new communities of practice by which Coffield (2008) means "groups of people informally bound together by shared expertise and passion for a joint enterprise" (Wenger & Snyder, 2000, p. 139). Communities of practice are connected to Gee's (2002) idea that an affinity group creates identity for its members. As the focus is on shared experience and changing identities, learning must be understood as a whole-person endeavor which recognizes the interaction of formal and informal learning spaces as well as cognition and emotion without creating artificial divisions between them (Coffield, 2008). This perspective locates collaboration and cooperation at the center of learning in which faculty are not only facilitators of students' learning but learners as well, learning about their own craft and own identities. Teaching and learning are "not two distinct activities, but intertwined elements of a single, reciprocal process, or, if you like, the two sides of one coin; perhaps they could be described as a double-sided, interactive process which transforms both tutor and learner" (p. 8) and thus, teachers and students are co-learners who constantly renew each other. The last two sections of this portrait of learning are concerned with teaching specifically, though these concepts need not be confined to teaching in the formal sense. Rather, for the purposes of this study teaching is understood in the broadest sense of the word, to include a variety of activities both inside and outside of the classroom, that faculty undertake.

Internationalizing as a learning process

These five streams of research on learning: the growth mindset (the internal condition for learning), adult cognition (capacities that are developed), authenticity in teaching (merging core essence with profession), the academic Self (continual stretching, adapting and (re) creating professional identity) and collaborative learning (coming into communities of practice) provide a foundational basis for exploring faculty learning in the context of internationalization. Two particularly relevant themes emerge from these concepts. First, the sort of learning described here is very much rooted in the idea of identity, which can be at the same time, both an essence and an ongoing construction (Kreber et al., 2007, p. 40). Second, these concepts are part of a process of lifelong learning, which is at the center of what Stier (2006) called an ideology of educationalism. As Knight (2004) and Ellingboe (1998) remind us, internationalization itself is an ongoing process. Institutions can learn through internationalization and such learning starts with the individuals who experience the grassroots and tangible aspects of that process daily. Although they are key components in the process, theories that intersect with the self are underutilized in investigating successful learning (Yorke & Knight, 2004) and much could be gleaned from their use.

Sanderson (2008) previously linked some concepts from the portrait above with internationalization and some approach in this study stems from a deconstruction of his ideas. In his framework, "internationalizing the academic self" he contends that within a framework of internationalizing the academic self, it is central to extend the concept of understanding through self-reflection that allows for exploration and understanding of others' value-systems, identity, and social culture as well through a similar process of reflection (p. 288) which is realized as "notions of openness, interconnectivity, interdependence, reciprocity, and plurality" (p. 294). This conceptual framework allows for paths of faculty member development specifically through extending self-reflection exercises developed by others into a context of internationalization, but it provides minimal assistance in understanding the faculty member engagement.

Conceptual Framework

Institutionally oriented frameworks, such as Knight's (1994) 6-cycle model, broadly conceptualize how internationalization in higher education occurs. This framework starts from the perspective that internationalization is an administratively driven phenomenon focused on policy and strategy. Even though Knight (2004) notes that internationalization must occur on the institutional and individual level, few frameworks allow for meaningful exploration using the individual as the unit of analysis (Anderson, Dickens, Hyland, & Trahar, 2008) or the specific ways in which grassroots efforts (Novelli, 2006) serve a foundational role in

Figure 1 Continuum of international orientation, Reprinted from "Competitive and cooperative impulses to internationalization: Reflecting on the interplay between management intentions and the experience of academics in a British university." Y. Turner & S. Robson. Education, Knowledge & Economy, 1(1), 65-82. Copyright 2007 S. Robson. Reprinted with permission

	←	→
International Orientation:	Symbolic	Transformative
Stimulus:	External	Internal
Management Style:	Designed	Emergent
Financial Focus:	Cost- and Revenue-focused	Investment-focused
International Impetus:	Business-led	Internationalist
External Engagement:	Competitive	Cooperative
Institutional Characterization of Internationalization:	Prescriptive	Descriptive
Style of Participation:	Compliance	Commitment
International Values:	Institutional	Personal

the internationalization process. For this project, I employ a conceptual framework focused on individual level internationalization, informed by a portrait of faculty member learning. The framework has foundations in the concepts of symbolic and transformative internationalization developed by Bartell (2003) and weak and strong internationalization developed by Appadurai (2001). Bartell (2003) posits that a continuum exists among higher education institutions where only peripheral efforts (symbolic internationalization) occupy one extreme and synergistic and deep processes (transformative internationalization) occupy the other, such that they affect all stakeholders on campus. Turner and Robson (2007) expand on Bartell's continuum to include international characteristics that align with the two orientations, each representing an end of the spectrum (figure 1). Their work provides the conceptual framework for the study as it sets out the categories and ends of the continuum.

Similarly, in Appadurai's concept of weak versus strong internationalization, the notion of weak internationalization is characterized as "a superficial engagement with the issues" while strong internationalization is "a laborious, even contentious, deeper, more sophisticated and genuine desire to explore what it means to become internationalized" (Sanderson, 2004, p. 16). Although this notion of strong and weak internationalization was developed regarding research specifically, the application to internationalization of the self has been successfully adopted elsewhere (Anderson et al., 2008; W. Green & Mertova, 2016). Internationalization, to be both transformative and strong, must prioritize and invest in individual agents if it is to truly be embedded throughout an institution. Appadurai (2001) wrote of the personal journey of internationalization; a relevant approach that only a few other scholars are incorporating into their research. This combined framework of symbolic and transformative, weak versus strong internationalization allows for inquiry regarding that journey for faculty members.

A second component of this conceptual framework bounds the focus and activities investigated in the study. The specific imagining of internationalization termed "Internationalization at Home" (IaH), focuses on internationalized activities, chiefly formal and informal curriculum, that occur on an institution's home campus as well as the dynamics between the institution and ethnic and cultural diversity in the local surrounding area (Beelen & Jones, 2015; Nilsson, 2003). The broad goal of IaH is to infuse and develop intercultural competence and multiple perspective-taking among members of the campus community. Given this commitment to the intercultural, IaH is more closely aligned with a transformative or strong orientations than many other manifestations of internationalization.

Figure 2 Conceptual model of faculty member learning through engagement in IaH

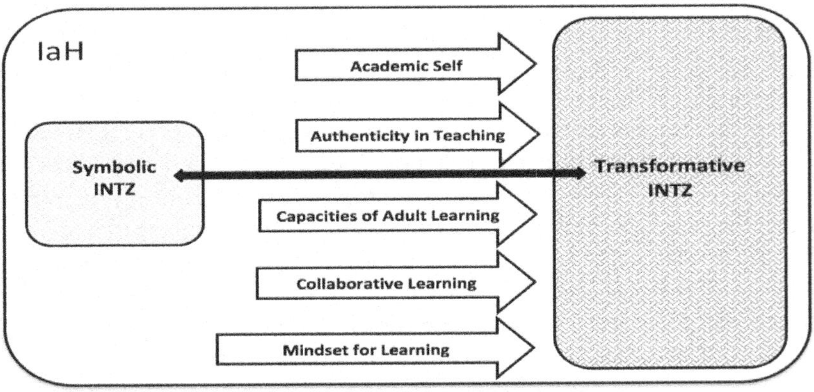

Theoretical Framework

An orientation toward transformational internationalization for faculty members may be advanced by developing such capacities and attendant practices as are described throughout this chapter and the theories of learning outlined therein.

The model below provides a visual for understanding how the components of this constructed portrait of adult learning aid academic staff in advancing along the continuum from symbolic internationalization toward more transformative internationalization. This advancement is on an individual level of internal growth, rather than focused on increased participation in activities or understanding of institutional internationalization plans. The field is the scope of the project, focusing on practices and the context of IaH. The "Symbolic INTZ" square represents a narrowly defined view of internationalization, primarily driven by reporting & external rankings, whereas the "Transformative INTZ" rectangle represents the broader, in-depth, holistic orientation, driven by personal engagement and institutional commitment (Appadurai, 2001; Bartell, 2003; Turner & Robson, 2007). The long narrow bi-directional line then represents the continuum between the two poles of symbolic and transformative orientations. An institution's position on the continuum is dynamic and not static (Appadurai, 2001; Bartell, 2003) and this is also the case for the participants who comprise important individual parts of the institution.

Finally, the arrows pointing to the right represent key aspects of adult learning developed in the context of IaH which promote a transformative orientation in faculty members and thus in the institution. The length of the arrows represents gradation, starting with the components of fundamental capacities for learning and moving toward the more professionalized, nuanced, or focused components. The longer lines are then those more generalized approaches applicable to all adult learners, and the shorter lines are those applicable primarily to faculty members as learners.

I am chiefly concerned with processes of engagement; that is, how faculty members construct meaning and enact practices aligned with IaH at a single, unique institution. The present study employs a collective, exploratory case study methodology informed by qualitative methods of inquiry conducted both through computer-mediated communication and in the participants' natural environment. Such an approach emphasizes gaining a deep understanding of the complexities of the individual cases from the participants' own voices and through direct interpretation of their experience. Findings offer a rich and descriptive narrative of the phenomenon of theories of learning at work in faculty participation in IaH.

Data collection and methods

I designed this project as a collective case study that considers several cases jointly to inquire into a phenomenon of faculty engagement. Data collection for this case study occurred in three stages: pre-site visit, site visit, and post-site visit. The research design included multiple data streams for both case participants and the institution. Interviews provided the bulk of data as they are essential in giving authentic voice to participants' meaning and understanding. The faculty member participants real first names were used, with permission, to highlight and credit the work they are doig. Some passages in the report have been edited for clarity. The process of engagement, perceptions, and constructed meaning takes place primarily within the participants' minds. Following Seidman's (2013) three-part interview structure of past (or life history), present experiences and practices, and reflection on constructed meaning and future orientation. Additional data streams included observations of participants' classrooms and office spaces leveraged to stimulate new directions for conversation, in-depth understanding, and reflection with participants. I assumed the role of "participant as observer" (Creswell & Creswell, 2018) to the degree possible. Photographs captured aspects of a physical space not found in documents or interviews. They provide contextual observations for the research itself as well as illustrating specific themes or point drawn from other data streams.

The final data stream came from document analysis. There were numerous sources of institutional documents to analyze including the institution's strategic vision, policies, public messaging, and communications. Other documents include public and government records for the context of the case. Some participant-generated work related to practices of IaH such as blogs, archival records and evaluations provided additional points for analysis. Collectively, these various methods triangulated data and provided a rich source of information for analysis.

Chapter III: A Shifting Landscape – Perspectives in Iceland

It is important to briefly sketch out certain relevant national and institutional contexts in which this study was conducted to better understand the experiences and attitudes of faculty participants. In this chapter, I describe certain key developments in Icelandic culture and at the University of Iceland. This chapter also provides the reader initial findings from the study around the context and space in which the faculty member participants operate. Iceland has experienced a significant increase in people entering the country over the past few decades. Tourism in the country has seen an "almost exponential growth" in recent years (Gil-Alana & Huijbens, 2018). In the decade prior to the COVID-19 pandemic in 2020, the number of foreign visitor arrivals to Iceland grew from approximately only around 494 thousand in 2009 to over 2 million in 2019 (Icelandic Tourist Board, 2021). While there has been an increase in how many people pass through Iceland, there has also been a significant rise in those staying in Iceland. The number of immigrants has risen dramatically in the past 25 years. So much so that Statistics Iceland, the official government-sanctioned center that collects and organizes national statistics, started reporting on immigrants in Iceland for the first time in 2009. With a total population of just over 368,000, the number of immigrants born abroad now living in this small island-nation increased from 5,357 or 2.1% of the total population in 1998 to 55,354 or 13.5% in 2020 (Statistics Iceland, 2020a). The number of those considered second generation immigrants has increased from only 345 in 1996 to 5,684 in 2020 (Statistics Iceland, 2020a).

In addition to increasing in sheer numbers, the composition of the immigrant population is changing. For most of the country's history, Iceland has been a highly homogenous population. Up to 1996, 30% of the immigrant population was still from the Nordic countries (Statistics Iceland, 2009). As illustrated in Table 1, this trend is changing as immigrants from other Nordic countries made up only 3.2% of the total immigrant population as of 2020. Most immigrants are now coming from Eastern European countries, especially from Poland where emigrants to Iceland have grown from 820 or 6.5% of the total immigrant population in 1998 to 20,515 or 37.1% in 2020 (Statistics Iceland, 2020). Data show that as of 2020, there were also larger populations from Lithuania (3,299) and the Philippines (2,223), which have increased significantly since the late 90s (Statistics Iceland, 2020).

Table 1 Number of Immigrants in Iceland 1996 and 2020

Region of origin	*Total 1996*	*Ratio (%)*	*Total 2020*	*Ratio (%)*
Nordic countries	1617	30.1%	1762	3.2%
European countries	2130	39.8%	40,928	73.9%
North America	437	8.2%	1241	2.2%
South & central America	119	2.2%	1384	2.5%
Africa	181	3.4%	1491	2.7%
Asia	816	15.2%	6820	12.3%
Oceania	57	1.1%	165	0.3%
Unknown	0	0%	1563	2.8%
Total	5357	100%	55,354	100%

Note. Data for the number of immigrants in Iceland from Statistics Iceland (2020a).

Diversity of race, ethnicity, and culture is becoming more visible in the social landscape of Iceland, and as a result, more research is now being done on immigration and the immigrant experience in Iceland (Bjarnason, Stevenson, Shuttleworth, & Meckl, 2020; Murdock, 2020). The data on inclusion of these diverse populations are mixed. Studies on immigrant experience from scholars in Iceland itself attest to the challenges of multiculturalism. One study offered a detailed review of recent immigration in Iceland by Loftsdóttir (2017), and identifies "emerging racism" in Iceland, particularly toward Eastern Europeans. The researcher also notes that as more migrants are refugees or those seeking asylum, bias against those from Muslim countries is increasing. The rise in immigrant populations and attitudes toward these groups have impacted higher education as well. Researchers note that there is an increasing amount of diversity in Icelandic universities due to immigration, and institutions are lacking in tools, measures, and capacity to support them (Ragnarsdóttir, Tran, & Jónsdóttir, 2020). In a more recent study, Murdock (2020) found that the majority of Icelanders demonstrated openness and acceptance of immigrants. Hopefully this positive trend in attitude translates into increased resources and attention to inclusion at Icelandic education institutions to rectify these gaps.

An Overview of the Institution

Beyond all being members of Icelandic society, the individual participants in this study are bound by their positions as faculty members at UI. Since its establishment in 1911, UI has played a significant, highly visible, and enduring role in many social, cultural, and political aspects of life in the island-nation; this is a role that is still increasing and evolving today. While there are several post-secondary institutions in Iceland, including the well-regarded private research institution Reykjavík University, UI is a cultural icon in Icelandic society, and it has an equal amount of influence. During interviews, one administrator stated that UI was positioned as the very cradle of Icelandic society. This position is in part due to its legal status as the national university, but also as the only university in the country offering the entire spectrum of disciplines related to culture and the social sciences. Much of the research on the country's cultural history, language, educational practices, politics, and literature flows from this single institution, which strengthens UI's influence on the country. As another administrator stated, UI "has a voice that nobody else in the education system has because it's respected and it's – huge." This reputation is enhanced by the well-regarded geological science academics who inform events such as volcanic eruptions and frequent (though often insignificant) earthquakes on the island. In addition, it houses the Árni Magnússon Institute for Icelandic studies, which is charged with investigating and preserving the country's celebrated medieval literature. The institution's messaging and their annual fact book are both strongly influenced by this unique position. The importance of UI to Icelandic society cannot be overstated.

The main campus of the university is situated in the western half of the capital city Reykjavík. The university has other facilities both inside and outside of the city too. What is conspicuously missing from the main campus of the university is the School of Education which is at another location across town. The School of Education was formerly a separate institution developed as a teacher's college and was then elevated to a full-fledged university of education. This new university merged with UI in the summer of 2008 to become the school it is today. Since this merger, UI now has five schools: Education, Engineering and Natural Sciences, Health Sciences, Humanities, and Social Sciences, each with multiple faculties totaling 25 across the entire institution. As of 2019, there were 552 tenure or tenure track academic staff and another 484 teaching and research staff. Administrative, technical and support staff number at 474. The number of students attending UI has increased by 3,000 in the last decade and a half (University of Iceland, 2020).

UI as an institution, as well as its component members, serve as advisors, consultants, and knowledge brokers for Icelandic society. Media frequently turn to faculty at UI for interviews and statements about various phenomena that span the various facets of the human experience. Several participants in the present study noted during data collection that they had just recently been interviewed for significant news stories. Seeking out experts from academia is typical media, but the limited number of experts in many fields makes the faculty at UI first-line sources for opinions and views.

A Decade of Change

For much of UI's history, the institution has been relatively domestic, focused on educational frameworks, structures, and issues that were primarily internal or those of their one-time Danish colonial power. Being the national university of Iceland, such a focus was both encouraged and aligned with governmental agendas. As a precursor to these institutional advances, one informant recounted that the Faculty of Philosophy was one of the first units to pursue internationalization in earnest, through bringing in international experts and scholars from the discipline and establishing an external-facing outlook which valued and increased a multiplicity of perspectives beyond traditional approaches. In the last decade, however, UI has undergone significant changes, not the least of which are efforts surrounding internationalization of the university. The overview and case context presented below focuses primarily on key aspects and practices of the university community which relate to IaH, rather than an exhaustive overview of every aspect of internationalization.

Global positioning

As a strategic priority is to increase its global profile, UI established a goal of being one of the top 100 research universities in the world in 2006. The impact of that priority so far is reflected in world rankings. UI reached a ranking within the 201-250 band in the Times Higher Education World University Rankings (THE) in 2016, while ranking 13th among the Nordic universities (University of Iceland, 2016b). While rankings fluctuate and in more recent years they dropped, this shows a significant investment in global endeavors. THE is a major international ranking system and includes internationalization as an explicit part of its measures, which has provided some important impetus for the university to internationalize in the ways that "count." With an aim of being in a top global institution came significant resources and efforts to improve international research, collaboration, and funding. The university focused on establishing a graduate school in 2009, which took the lead in developing new research potential. Additionally, UI has developed collaborations with close to 500 universities, which includes research, teaching, and various staff and student exchanges. Because of this goal, significant restructuring has occurred in the International Office to help improve world rankings. Beyond agreements for student mobility, the university also rapidly established and expanded both doctorate and master's academic programs. Prior to the 1990s, the university was primarily an undergraduate institution and most of the faculty members received their doctorate training abroad. While the expansion of graduate programs has allowed Icelanders to complete graduate programs at home in many fields, it also attracts foreign researchers and graduate students. Moreover, it has strengthened research collaborations and the attainment of prestigious international grants.

The international office

Through the reorienting toward a more global profile some important internal restructuring occurred which shifted the reporting line of the director of the International Office to the rector rather than the Office of Academic Affairs which strengthened the position of the International Office within the university. Cooperation agreements with international universities, which were previously housed in individual units or with individual faculty members, are now organized and centralized in this office. Agreements are also now more selectively established to align with the university's strategic plan and improve world rankings. These agreements include all external mobility, exchange programs, and logistical functions related to inbound international students.

International access and alignment

International students comprise about 8.8% of the student population (approximately 1550 students) from eighty-seven different countries (University of Iceland, 2020b). International students are not cast as revenue-generators for the university as tuition is free for everyone with only a minimal annual registration fee of 75,000 Icelandic Krona. This tuition policy is set by the national government rather than UI, so there is potential for this to shift in the future. This however rests on the Icelandic constitution which states that everyone should have equal access to education and the current interpretation is that tuition is a barrier to that access.

Iceland was one of the original signatories on the Bologna Accord in 1999, which was designed to create a common European educational area. This included establishing common degree and credit structures, improved mobility, and increased collaboration between universities. Much of the degree structure established by the Bologna process, the so-called 3+2+3 system that required separating the BA (3 years) and the master's degrees (2 years), was already standard practice at UI, so certain aspects called for little change. Curriculum and degree pathways in some fields such as engineering and medical sciences required some revamping, but most disciplines did not need overhauls.

In other areas, the Bologna process has created some significant changes; some are more challenging to implement than others. Diploma supplements were introduced, and these are handled through administrative personnel. Additionally, the change to the ECTS credit system was also primarily a bureaucratic process. Both were relatively straightforward process, despite some necessary adjustments.

The number of courses and programs offered in English has increased, especially at the master's level, and thus are more linguistically accessible for international students. There are 70 graduate-level programs offered at UI and over a dozen are always taught in English – while many tracks have specific cohorts taught in English. The master's program in Medieval Icelandic studies, for example, has been particularly successful and internally praised as a model for scaling up curriculum designed for and delivered to primarily international students.

Only one undergraduate study program exists taught completely in English despite a robust number of individual courses offered. This program is a B.A. in international education offered through the School of Education and has been written about in detail by two of the participants who we will meet later in this study (see Books, Ragnarsdóttir, Jónsson, & Macdonald, 2010; Halldorsdottir and Gollifer, 2018). One of the purposes of this program is to give students from recent immigrant backgrounds, who often do not speak Icelandic, a path to a college degree and more specifically, to work in the field of education – despite the degree not leading to a specific vocational credential. As IaH develops further at the university, this program will undoubtedly demonstrate that internationalization can and must occur within domestic contexts which will highlight the importance of this sort of work that the school is currently engaged in.

Central support for international and diverse students

The International Office purposefully and thoughtfully integrates international students into a student housing system that aims for a balanced mix of domestic and international students. While most students, both domestic and international, live off-campus, those who are living on campus have access to increased intercultural contact through these housing arrangements.

In addition to integrating students in on-campus housing, the International Office has also developed a mentoring or buddy program, where domestic students volunteer to be partnered with an international student, which is run in conjunction with the Student Council. This is designed to help international students become acquainted with the university and to give them the opportunity to connect with Icelanders. The program has resulted in some positive effects (Icelandic Quality Board for Higher Education, 2015). Another recent improvement in the support of international students has been the construction of a social and services hub in the center of the main campus (University of Iceland, 2013).

The building Háskólatorg represented a major step toward a more student-centered university. Most student services are centralized in this building including the International Office, Student Housing, Student Council, Student Registration, Career Services, IT Help Desk, and the bookstore. While this centralization has impacted all students, international students have particularly benefited with increased ease of access to coordinated services. Space for international students to socialize and meet on campus has improved because of these common areas. The more purposeful integration of international students through housing, mentoring, and more accessible common spaces has also increased domestic student exposure to diversity and cultural difference at the university, though the effects and extent of this increased exposure are unknown.

For domestic students from diverse and immigrant backgrounds, there is less formalized support dedicated to their success. UI has an Equality Officer who supports diversity broadly, including international students and domestic students from diverse backgrounds who may seek out support on issues related to equity. The Equality Officer is charged with advocating for immigrant and international students' rights at UI when such issues are brought to the attention of the office – but this is only one of many groups that require support. Moreover, this position is primarily one of advising and consultancy in addition to sitting on committees regarding equality rather than being a decision maker. Other support for such students comes only generally from traditional student service offices on campus. While there are certainly those academic and support staff on campus who provide services to such students, there are not dedicated offices to help address and champion their unique needs. UI has annual events which can be considered part of IaH activities and often highlight issues of social justice and inclusion. The number of events and programming in this area has increased in recent years, including the Equality Days event. The annual International Week at UI takes place in November and is aimed at celebrating both international culture and opportunities for students and employees.

University Goals and IaH

Like so many institutions, no specific written policy or plan for systematic IaH exists at UI, however the university leadership has more recently taken concrete efforts in areas of promoting equality for diverse peoples and culture on campus which can be considered a part of promoting an intercultural campus. An Equal Rights Committee was established as an advisory body to questions of equality at UI and is comprised of the chairpersons from each of the individual schools' in-house Equal Rights committee. This central committee then provides recommendations directly to the University Council and the rector and works on their behalf. One of the resolutions of the 2011-2016 Strategic Plan was to lead in areas of equality of gender specifically:

> The University of Iceland emphasizes democratic working methods and gender equality in all areas of endeavor. The University always wants to be at the forefront in gender equality. Diversity of students and employees is the University of Iceland's strength (University of Iceland, 2011, p. 7).

Emerging from this goal was the development of an Equality Policy, which documented the university's leadership role in being progressive on issues surrounding equal rights. While the 2011-2016 Strategic Plan called only for gender equality specifically, the English version of the 2013-2017 Equality Policy (University of Iceland, 2014) developed from that plan addressed a much broader vision of equality. The aim of that policy was:

> to ensure that all individuals are afforded their rights within the University without facing discrimination that marginalises or offends any individual or group on the basis of sex, gender, gender identity, sexual orientation, age, disability, health, nationality, race, skin colour, origins, religion, views, culture or position in any other sense (para. 8).

This vision of equality covers a host of social and physical identity differences, which extends to domestic students from immigrant or diverse backgrounds as well as international students. International students are referenced again elsewhere in this most recent Equality Policy, though they are not addressed directly. What the text of the policy does not reference is developing concepts related to intercultural or global learning for students (or any other campus community member) in order to improve the campus climate around equality. Even so, the document establishes a measure in the form of a campus-wide survey about the "wellbeing of students and staff" in attempt to understand

and improve the campus climate regarding the various identities listed above, including origins, nationality, and culture.

The 2016-2021 strategic document includes language meant to increase efforts to specifically support diverse and immigrant populations on campus and in society. The language focuses on increased support for underrepresented students in the university, university-educated immigrants, and diverse upper secondary students attempting to matriculate. In the "Human Resources" area of this strategic document, one of the stated goals is that "equality and diversity within the University community [is] promoted," This goal signaled a pivot toward addressing the need to increase the diversity on campus and reach out to students from immigrant backgrounds who are potentially the most underrepresented population in Iceland. Work done in this area was previously carried out on an ad hoc or individual school basis. The 2016-2021 strategic plan also addresses immigrants who already have attained a university education elsewhere, but often are unable to use those skills in their new country. The most recent strategic plan covers 2021-2026 and expands many of the goals in the previous iteration strengthening language around supporting society and internationalization broadly.

Teaching and curriculum

There is currently no office, tracking or position on campus that directly addresses internationalizing the curriculum. Incorporating this material and related outcomes is largely an instructor-by-instructor endeavor gauging the amount internationalized or interculturalized courses is challenging. UI offers a wide range graduate programs including food science, geology and anthropology taught in English which are designed for and marketed to both international and domestic students.

Despite the incomplete picture of internationalized curriculum, improving teaching is becoming a more deliberate and centralized effort at UI, and this has significant implications for IaH and internationalizing the curriculum including more inclusive classrooms for diverse students and exposure to new perspectives through diverse teaching methods and content. This emerging focus on teaching is primarily in response to the Quality Enhancement Framework report issued in April of 2015 (Icelandic Quality Board for Higher Education, 2015) on the institutional-level review of UI. One informant from the Center for Teaching and Learning (CTL) noted that this recent messaging about improving teaching is having an impact:

> [...] the more our services are sought after, the more I see it as an indication that people are getting engaged

> and more interested in their teaching. And you can really see quite a lot of difference in that […] the teaching is being pushed a little bit on the top of the agenda. Maybe as a counter-act to a very heavy research orientation we have had for the last six years or so, ten years maybe.

These efforts are being implemented in large part through the university's Center for Teaching and Learning with support from the administration and central committees such as the Teaching Committee and the Quality Enhancement committee. Part of this new emphasis is a shift in orientation toward more student-centered learning. While it is certainly not the case for all coursework and classes, the dominant model at UI has historically been teacher-centered lectures stemming from traditional European modes of instruction. That move to focusing on student needs and identity in learning, the CTL informant believes, represents a significant change to the approach in teaching as well as content and curriculum design.

Out of this increasing emphasis on student-centered learning has emerged conversations and subsequent efforts to employ multiple and diverse methods of instruction to meet students where they are academically while delivering content in more effective ways. CTL has created a variety of development courses for faculty, which include considering new ways of teaching courses and connecting with students to see their perspectives. One of these development programs is a ECTS credit diploma organizationally housed in the School of Education but run out of the CTL. The diploma program is a series of three courses intended to help academic staff develop their teaching practice through theory and experience. The informant from the CTL reflected on the impact of one of these experiences the faculty member participants go through:

> One of the assignments that we have in our course is that academics that participate […] there's a discussion with the students. We ask them to go and interview a group of students […] within their program. Just say […] "what are your expectations? […] and it's always our experience that they come totally like thrilled about that task. They're going like "I've never talked to students", they were so [gestures excitedly]. So, […] we try to increase a dialogue with students and respect for diversity within the student groups.

Interest in the craft of teaching is increasing and these courses and workshops offered through CTL play a significant role in both messaging about and the development of multiple teaching methods. These workshops for academic staff embody not only a push for student-centered learning, but also an attempt to help participants recognize difference in the classroom.

The informant explains further that viewing students "as a multicultural group" is the basis for all their workshops and courses. Multiculturalism here understood as difference, in circumstances or life, not necessarily regarding race or ethnicity. They went on to reflect on the efforts to help faculty members see all groups of students as diverse:

> [I]n our reading texts, in our courses, we have maybe one text that has to do with you know, multicultural in the sense of ethnicity. And that's usually not a big issue here. I mean, it just, kind of all white people here. But […] it's like the baseline of all our things that you have students that are very different from each other, in regard to how they study, what […] their background is, how their understanding of the discipline is and how their situation is like financially, and family wise and so on. And that is something we promote in all of courses, and actually trying hard to […] fight against academics' notion that everybody is the same or that "they are all like me when I was here 30 years ago."

The key is that difference is starting to be recognized for what it is: that students are not monolithic, rather a diverse group. This view is strengthened by the increased messaging and calls that faculty, especially new hires, participate in such development courses. The informant also noted that this effort targets part-time instructors as well, so that the entire body of instructors at UI can be reached. Alignment of messaging and practice is still evolving; however, the CTL is seeing an increased interest from instructors in these development courses even while they are establishing what diversity is in the classroom and why it is important. This acknowledgement of diversity in any form, is an important step toward recognizing and valuing cultural difference in the classroom and is and of itself a practice of IaH. Employing multiple teaching methods also allows for new perspectives because students are exposed to the various cultural aspects of different teaching activities and builds student experiences which add to multiple and diverse perspectives. The development and implementation of multiple teaching methods lays the foundation for increasing integration of students from different cultural backgrounds, for new types of instruction, and for strengthening equity in the classroom.

Beyond these broad approaches to teaching and learning, there are some curricular approaches and advances related to IaH that are particularly noteworthy. An increasing number of faculty at UI have more comparative perspectives in both teaching and research as opposed to more parochial views which have historically dominated teaching and research. This is evidenced not only in comments from a number of informants, but also in the increasing number of programs and courses in the course catalog which state a comparative basis in the course material. The Faculty of Social Work is engaged in efforts to support the national social work system by reportedly developing a new diploma in multicultural social work in cooperation with other departments in the social sciences. Other related projects at UI include Icelandic Online, a language course for new speakers of Icelandic, which is available to the public. There is also a master's degree program that has been established for those who want to teach Icelandic language to adult learners

Situational Factors at UI

Like many top research institutions, internationalization at UI is understood and promoted in terms of international reputation, research collaborations, and flows of people in and out of the university across Iceland's borders. This understanding is, in part, due to the historically domestic focus of the institution and the more recent increased attention to international contexts that has occurred in recent years. With the rapidity of changes at UI in the still emerging international-facing focus, the university must focus attention on a wide-range of complex issues and competing pressures.

Internationalized curriculum

As with many such institutions, barriers to one of the key activities in IaH, internationalized curriculum, are both structural and individual. The increased focus on teaching has not reached a large enough audience according to some informants and despite the efforts toward incorporating explicit learning outcomes as part of that messaging, there are no common learning outcomes for undergraduate or graduate students, which focus on global learning or intercultural competence, for curricula to map onto. Such learning outcomes – like the curriculum itself, are often in the hands of individual instructors. With no centralized office or formal systems working directly on IaH, one administrator readily acknowledged that work is needed on internationalizing the curriculum:

> So, the faculty members can play a significant role in developing their courses to become international, especially at the master's level. But like I mentioned, we, we

> need to do more there, it's our weakest point, we need more courses, and it's understandable because we are a relatively small university compared to [larger institutions] and we cannot have everything.

With institutional attention spread across a wide array of recently developing areas and significant external pressures, there is limited organizational headspace or capacity to develop more formalized efforts related to IaH. The bulk of the international curricular efforts are directed toward expanding programs taught in English, which increases the potential number of international students but retains primarily Icelandic or at best Western viewpoints. Another informant asserted that in terms of IaH broadly "we probably don't have [a] very strong attitude towards this." For the limited amount of curricula that moves beyond this mold, development has to balance continuance of important national perspectives, many of which emanate from UI as the single national university, against comparative international perspectives, which can help students make sense of multiple knowledge paradigms. However, there are pockets around the university where global learning is being infused, and there is increasing opportunity to develop this further.

Beyond some of these larger structural and organizational questions, there are individual challenges for instructors as well. A significant concern is that historically, many instructors are only familiar with teaching a student body that is considered homogenous and "just like them." They are also working within a system that has been built and maintained around such perceived homogeneity. These instructors face the task of shifting their own perceptions and approaches to increasingly recognize diversity that already exists among traditional domestic students in their classroom. The shift to incorporating multiple methods in the classroom in active recognition of such diversity is slowly developing. With discipline-based and culturally historic rationales for keeping lecture-based teaching methods in the classroom, there is a struggle to provide external motivation for moving into multiple methods across the university, which has ramifications for cultural diversity and inclusion. This theme is explored more later sections of the book where participants discuss how they bring multiple methods into their classrooms.

While moving toward more student-centered learning itself is no simple feat, the increasing cultural diversity from international students and eventually more domestic students from immigrant backgrounds, presents another layer of consideration for inclusion. Challenges then exist for individual instructors in both adjusting their own methods and understanding of teaching in a multicultural classroom, while also communicating the institutional cultural norms to international students who come from a variety of backgrounds with educational experiences that may be quite different. While the institution can adapt to incorporate a variety of learning backgrounds and develop systems that are more culturally fluid, there is a clear need for international students to be actively supported in learning the culture of institutional academic practices. The barriers to internationalized curriculum then are located both in the organization and in the individual instructors, which are often difficult to tease apart for isolated improvement when one is constantly informing the other; any advancement for IaH must address both.

Integrating international and domestic students

IaH does not necessitate international students, yet integrating them into the campus is an opportunity for domestic student contact as well as the diversity and inclusion aspects of IaH. The challenges of integrating international and domestic student populations at universities is well documented (Harrison, 2015). The university has made substantial advances in this area as described previously, and yet, there are still opportunities for increased integration of international students with domestic students. Icelandic undergraduate students tend to be older than their international counterparts and are often partnered with relatively more commitments. Many domestic and international students, both undergraduate and graduate, live off-campus as well. So even with new spaces and efforts to increase interaction, in dormitories and common areas, interactions between domestic and international students on campus can be limited.

The challenge of forming relationships between domestic students and international students is also informed by cultural differences. One participant noted that Icelanders at UI often have the same group of friends and acquaintances that they knew from their previous schooling and childhood. This provides less intrinsic motivation for them to introduce themselves to new people and make new friends, unless there is a specific need for it.

Challenges in integration between student groups extend to the classroom where a significant piece of cultural capital at UI is the Icelandic language. The limited number of classes offered in English, especially at the undergraduate level, means that many of the university classes are only offered in Icelandic. This makes it effectively inaccessible to international students who rarely have a strong enough command of Icelandic language to participate. Certain programs and courses do have a mix of international and domestic students, but others that are intentionally designed for international students or those marketed to them are majority or solely international students. The BA in Icelandic for Foreigners is one of the most popular courses of study at UI (Halldórsson, 2017); while a positive for those trying to establish a living in Iceland, there are few if any domestic students in this program. As such, there are systemic barriers to overcome to increase contact and significant cultural exchange between the two groups.

Language

As is indicated in several examples already shared here, a final key challenge in advancing practices and goals related to IaH is the language of instruction at UI. As the national university, UI is situated as being simultaneously a staunch preserver of the past and Icelandic identity as well as a progressive international university, collaborating and connecting globally. While these two positions are not necessarily at odds with each other, choices in language usage provide difficult decisions and complex pathways for moving forward. The Quality Assurance report issued by the Ministry of Education, Science and Culture highlights this tension:

> UI's stated ambition to evolve towards a high-ranking international research institution has led to an increased international presence among both academic staff and students, together with pressures to publish in high-ranking journals published in English. At the same time, the University is very aware of its national role in preserving Icelandic language and culture, and there is an undisputed need to be able to communicate professionally in Icelandic within professions such as, for example, nursing and school teaching. This inevitably leads to some competing pressures and difficult decisions concerning language of instruction at the different levels of study (Icelandic Quality Board for Higher Education, 2015, p. 46).

The report was published in April 2015 and provides a realistic assessment of the challenge language presents for the institution. Not only does the university have a general charge of preserving Icelandic language, but also they are required to do so by law. The Icelandic government dictates that courses at UI will be taught in Icelandic, yet there are numerous courses taught in English because there is an increasing number of international students without sufficient knowledge of Icelandic.

The question of what internationalization means, both for the participants as well as administrators, resulted in a many of those interviewed commenting about which courses should be taught in

Icelandic and which should be taught in English, how often, by whom and to whom. As mentioned previously, UI is the national university and it is understood to be the university for the "nation." This plays out frequently in public discourse and is used as leverage to support a variety of causes, including those on both ends of the spectrum. Language is undoubtedly the most visible site for this tension. There are those who argue that because UI is the national university, the language of the university (and therefore, instruction) should be primarily (if not solely) Icelandic, the official national language. The relatively low number of total Icelandic speakers in the world adds urgency to this argument.

Ever since the early settlement of Iceland, language has played a particularly prominent role in Icelandic identity. However, in the face of new Icelanders from immigrant backgrounds along with new immigrants arriving who are now part of the nation, an important question has become what does it mean to be "Icelandic?" Those on the opposite end of this spectrum then argue that more courses and programs ought to be offered in English as the University is for everyone, including those students from an immigrant background who may not speak Icelandic well or at all. They should be able to learn in other languages. It is argued that this means more open and supported access to immigrants or children of immigrants.

The focus on increased opportunities for all students moves the question of language at UI closer to the heart of IaH. Courses taught in English could be an important space for cultural exchange and exposure to differing worldviews for many domestic students who do not study abroad. While creating these spaces yet, the serious question of Iceland's need to educate and develop its own people in Icelandic as well as the more long-term threat of complete loss of the language remains, especially in the modern digital and globalized world where Icelandic is increasingly shut out (Andrews, 2017).

Moving forward with language of instruction and related policy is also a question of capacity and ability. The increase of international academic staff means that there are more instructors who have little Icelandic language preparation, if any. This means that there can be dual isolation for international faculty and students who don't speak Icelandic. The university provides support for these instructors through making key information available outside of Icelandic. The Equal Rights Policy covering 2013-2017 states that one of the goals for "[f]ostering diversity amongst employees at the University of Iceland" is to, "[e]nsure that essential information on studies and work at UI is available in languages other than Icelandic." Many of these non-Icelandic speaking instructors won't have time to learn well enough to lecture or conduct research in Icelandic, as this is not necessarily part of their job function when the university provides documentation in other languages. Moreover, they may not be at the university long enough to invest deeply in developing those skills. This means that more courses are also being taught in English and pushes this global language further into the daily work at the university. For the domestic instructors with Icelandic as their first language, there are other challenges as well such as:

> [...] most of the Icelandic people do speak English; to lecture in English is different than [...] just speaking it and some professors are obviously not comfortable with that.

Many instructors are trained in English speaking areas such as United Kingdom or the United States; others are trained in countries such as Germany or Denmark. While some faculty members who have Icelandic as a first language may be challenged by teaching in English, those coming from non-English doctoral training programs may be more challenged leading to resistance in teaching in English.

Much of the opposition to the concept of internationalization lies more with questions of what language of instruction to use than it does with incorporating multiple perspectives or intercultural learning. Internationalization is conflated with how many courses are offered in English and its use in daily operations. These deliberations around language choice and policy are a codified part of the university's 2016-2021 Strategic Plan. The plan reads that:

> The University official language strategy reviewed with the aim of supporting both the Icelandic language (the official language of the University) and the international work of the University (University of Iceland, 2016d, section 2, para. 5).

While the formal review of the language policy is in and of itself an important step, the wording is situated in the document as a measure under the goal of "Equality and diversity within the University community promoted", which is aimed at all campus community members. This signals that the questions about language usage and policy are matters of inclusion as much as they are a logistical necessity for university. While this is important in terms of diversity, some fundamental IaH activities require further discussion, particularly those surrounding internationalization of the curriculum. More courses use English as the medium for instruction without necessarily presenting perspectives that are more internationally or culturally diverse. The debate over language usage is a dominant question as the university intensifies its international gaze, but there is room for the university to turn more efforts toward preparing students, academic and support staff with intercultural skills and developing more global and inclusive mindsets.

Readiness to Embrace IaH

UI is progressing in recognizing and integrating diversity and pursing activities related to IaH. One piece of support for this came from an informant who commented that they have noted an increase in openness to differing cultural perspectives at the university, while another informant stated that the university is becoming more inclusive. If such initial signs develop into more collective action across the university, it will be an important step for establishing a foundation for additional IaH. Beyond this perceived increase in openness, important markers of this shift have come from recent messaging from the administration. Observations and interviews revealed a significant optimism from various informants about the increased attention and inclusion of those from immigrant backgrounds. This is in part because the rector, Jón Atli Benediktsson and other administrators have repeated support for improved integration of all Icelanders into the university, including those from immigrant backgrounds as well as broad improvements in diversity and equality.

Beyond just increasing awareness of the issues, several informants framed the issues around inclusivity and diversity as a responsibility for the university to take up with concrete actions. An informant in the International Office stressed that the university "should have a more active role in working with [...] immigrants" and another informant asserted that the university should engage with these populations because it was the "biggest" and had the broadest base of knowledge regarding multiculturalism "in terms of research to understand what's what and what are the issues, what are the problems, what do we need to do, what could be helpful; all of that." One administrator posited that the university as a collective has a responsibility in undertaking such aspects of IaH which extends to the faculty members as well:

> they should [...] develop their courses in such a way that they are attractive for students with different backgrounds. And [...] we're talking about [...] Internationalization at Home, but you know, like I mentioned previously, Iceland is so small, that we also have to think about this in a wider context.

This administrator's assertion that faculty members need to be involved in IaH was echoed by another when talking about international students and the formal curriculum, which is, first and foremost, the purview of faculty members:

> it's not only about the language of instruction, but it's also about the content of the curriculum. So that the university not only focuses on Icelandic problems and Icelandic issues, so that you take into consideration the world [...] – International context I would say.

Both administrators stressed the importance of UI engaging in instruction and practices that consider a broader context – one outside of an Icelandic-centric view in the curriculum and strategies. These statements about the responsibility of the university to engage provides evidence that core concepts in IaH are starting to migrate to the forefront of the minds of those who have the power and position to develop related efforts and activities.

Summary

The changes at UI in the last few decades have been both rapid and radical. While the changes are still developing, the university has transformed from a domestic institution focused primarily on internal issues and research, to an international powerhouse with a wide range of collaborations and connections with universities and peoples across the globe. The changing demographics, increased international student population, and ramifications of the 2008 economic challenges presented the university with a number of significant challenges in a short period of time. There is evidence that key administrators, university leadership, and faculty members are starting to consider the importance of such aspects of IaH more deeply for the betterment of the student body and Icelandic society.

Chapter IV: Faculty Profiles and Spaces for Internationalization

Five faculty members participated in this study, each as an individual in-depth case. These participants were all selected because they are champions of IaH. While they represent a variety of backgrounds and positioning, several participants converge in areas of research and expertise. Three of the faculty members were from the School of Education, one was from the School of Business, and one was from the Department of Folkloristics in the School of Social Sciences. Four participants were female, and one was male. Additionally, at data collection, four were tenured or tenure-track while one worked as an adjunct. The following section offers a sketch of each of the participant's background focusing on each of their formative experiences with difference as well as their motivations to engage in practices of IaH.

Brynja

Brynja completed her doctorate at the University of Minnesota in 2012. From 2012-2013, she was a post-doctoral researcher in the School of Education before being hired as tenure-track faculty in 2013. She brings to the unit extensive research, teaching and course development expertise and even more experience working in intercultural education. Brynja coordinates the International Studies in Education program for the School of Education. Her involvement means a significant amount of face time with the students in that program as well as being in a position to facilitate better communication between diverse students and others in the campus community. As mentioned above, this is the only full course of study entirely in English at UI, which makes it the only option for students who speak English, but are not proficient in Icelandic.

Brynja has spent a significant part of her life living outside of Iceland and points to experiences while abroad as pivotal intercultural interactions in her life, many of which center around her family and have led her to her current work. She points to one important experience when she was 8 years old visiting her uncle who worked for the Danish aid agency in Kenya. Driving through the market, one family member was visibly upset because an elderly woman with leprosy was asking for a ride and to get out of the heat. Brynja felt sympathy for the woman and didn't understand why her family member was so opposed to helping this woman. At that young age, she couldn't grasp the health and cultural values at play in that situation, but she noted that it ignited her interest in learning more. Such international experiences were not isolated. Her immediate family was connected to academics and an international community, which was already engaged in issues around intercultural learning:

> I grew up at the University, [...] in that community. There are still people working at the University that I have known since I was a little girl. So - I understand that community, but my parents were very forward thinking in that perspective. My dad taught at a University in Swaziland, my mom was a diplomat, you know and lived all over the world. So, all of this, I have a pretty unique foundation in that. I think I've always kind of been this way? And so, for me, it just seems logical for me to bring it in to this space that I'm in now, that I inhabit now.

In addition to being raised around the academy and spending time in international locations, her parents hail from two distinct cultures. Having one parent from Iceland and another from the United States, she arguably has a unique perspective among Icelanders. As she states, "I am raised bi-cultural, so that sort of has always been part of my life as a sort of a consciousness of straddling multiple cultures." This upbringing is then both a strength and a challenge. On the one hand, growing up in multiple countries and having parents from different cultural backgrounds makes her keenly aware of cultural issues, struggles, and barriers that international or diverse students may face. On the other hand, finding space and place to move freely and being regarded as an insider can be difficult. At her graduate institution in the United States, she was frequently referred to as an Icelander, a designation that she herself used during interviews. However, some at UI contend that she is "really" an American. This all-too-frequent dilemma for bi-cultural people highlights the challenging position of being accepted as "Icelandic" without being raised in-country with two Icelandic parents. She recognizes that it makes her a cultural minority.

Beyond the exposure to difference that she had growing up, Brynja also has a son who is "mixed race: African-American or Haitian African-American and Icelandic-Irish-American." This personal connection with racial diversity has widened her perspectives and has strongly contributed to her academic path:

> I guess it's like thinking about how my life would be different if I didn't have my son. Cause I mean that's

> essentially what it would mean; because I wouldn't have had a large portion of this focus if I didn't have that aspect of my life. If I had just been a white middle class European woman that had had a white middle-class family [...] I wouldn't have run into having to question any of that stuff.

While she was around cultural difference from a young age, this didn't translate to the intersections of questions about difference with race, power, and privilege. The centrality of these questions to her worldview gained traction as she witnessed prejudice toward both herself because of her personal life and her son because of his appearance.

Two other experiences were particularly salient in her early professional development in relation to intercultural and international education. The first experience was during her undergraduate career. Brynja noted that a role-playing activity was a significant moment of learning. One of her courses on Russian history included an experiential role-playing activity where students were to study a given historical character and then through the activity, establish and form alliances until the end when someone is elected the leader. Brynja ended up being elected, which she was surprised about and not specifically aiming for. However, the project taught her about effective strategies and leadership in the face of difference. Another important experience was her time spent teaching mathematics to young girls in Saudi Arabia. While the interactions with the students themselves were eye-opening, the alternative perspective she gained on how education is understood differently and how systems are created to support this understanding, gave her the impetus to pursue her doctorate in international education.

What motivates Brynja to engage in practices of IaH as part of her work at the university is intrinsic. While acknowledging the challenges of international and multicultural education, she sees the rationale for her being hired as her unique training and background in these areas:

> [Y]ou know I think about why I do this a lot because the internationalization, the multicultural education, all this stuff. It's not easy work - I watch other people who have their nice little niches, "I teach about this, and I do this" and I just thought that I can't even envision a different way to be. Well, I think, I mean I think I was expressly hired for this kind of stuff. I mean they've hired people for multicultural and diversity aspects before but, you know I'm the only person on the faculty that has a comparative international development

> experience background. So, I think that I was really, and I emphasized that and they hired me for that aspect.

This motivation lives at the core of her identity and is channeled into her daily work at the School of Education. The institution hired her for this background and this is evidence of the growing importance placed on intercultural and comparative education, which is a pivot away from the parochial framework the school has worked from in the past. This motivation not only informs the work she does in multiculturalism and the international education program, but it also is the driving factor behind her work on broad internationalization efforts across the university.

Erla

While several academic staff research and teach on issues related to immigration, culture and related fields, Erla focuses on intercultural communication. After receiving her doctorate from Arizona State University, she held several faculty positions at institutions including the State University of New York and Reykjavik University, before being appointed an Assistant Professor in the School of Business at UI in 2013. In addition to intercultural communication, she teaches research methods and leadership to business students, both Icelandic and non-Icelandic.

Like most of the other participants, some of Erla's early intercultural experiences came from traveling abroad when she was young. Her parents are from Denmark and Norway, which gave her not only a multicultural upbringing between three Nordic countries, but also frequent opportunities to interact with others from her parents' native lands. In early adulthood, she moved with her own family to the United States in 1995 and lived in three very culturally distinct states, Florida, Arizona, and New York. These three states in which she lived gave her a broader perspective of cultural diversity. It allowed her to recognize the uniqueness and distinctions in each of these areas – particularly because she was living with people from different races and ethnicities which was a new experience for her:

> Yeah, I think maybe just being White, I never thought about that identity until I moved to the U.S. especially when we were living in Pensacola, Florida and the high schools there. I have 4 daughters and they all went with me and my husband and they for example, my oldest daughter she attended Washington High School with predominantly Black students so that was sort of really, something that stands with me. Wow, I never considered being White was anything in particular. I didn't even consider that, what it meant, you know?

This was the time she was first exposed to the concept that "being White" came with certain meanings and positions: that she had privileges of space, status, and acceptance without the prejudice directed toward people of color. Recognizing that her majority white identity was invisible to her before had a significant emotional impact on her. For Erla growing up in Nordic countries, prior to the largest waves of the 20th century immigration, there were limited possibilities for personal contact with people of color without travel elsewhere.

In addition to this new experience living in a community with people of color, two critical incidents in the United States deeply informed her personal learning and transformed her perspectives on difference. The first instance was her daughter's introduction of a new boyfriend while they were living in New York. Prior to leaving for the United States, a family member who also happened to be living in the New Orleans asked Erla how she would react if one of her daughters had a relationship with a Black man. She hadn't considered this potential before, with such little contact with people of color. Erla noted that when her daughter brought him home the first time "[...]she was really afraid to introduce him because she wasn't sure how I was to act." Erla recalled that she wasn't opposed to the relationship, but she said it "just didn't fit into my picture." The second event that had a strong impact on Erla's outlook and development toward difference was her time spent interviewing prisoners for research at a facility in Upstate New York in the United States.

> So, I want[ed] to interview African-American prisoners in upstate New York. I really want[ed] to learn about it because I was pretty judgmental. So, I knew I was wrong, I started to see that of course my original beliefs were not correct. [...] I went there every weekend for several months and I was shocked because I realized that many of these young men, gentlemen, they were really smart, really kind, warm, and they were just stuck where they were.

While Erla had already interacted with more diverse populations from her time in Florida, she was still confronting her own persistent and complex stereotypes of Black males, people in prison, and the intersection between them. Her determination to change her perceptions through increased interactions and by listening to their experiences led her to understand not only cultural differences, but also cycles of poverty and oppression.

Erla's family has played, and continues to play, an important role in developing her academic and personal interests in intercultural and global learning. This is in part because of her grandchildren being of mixed race, but also that she has other family members from different cultures as well. Her home life and family bring people together from a variety of cultures and countries and she talks passionately about their importance:

> my family is intercultural, international if you will, because my closest family is diverse [...]. I have grand-kids [whose] father is from Africa, Algeria; another is from Brooklyn, New York and then my brother has a wife from the Philippines. So, it's very international in the home there because of that. Also, I emphasize during family gatherings or when we have some dinners together, birthdays, we emphasize the importance of learning about the backgrounds of the kids.

Beyond her formal education, intercultural communication and the experiences mentioned above, which were certainly strong factors in her current work, Erla pointed to her upbringing as one of her initial motivations for engaging in IaH—she felt that her interest was deeply ingrained. She also remembered her experiences while in the United States; of being a foreigner herself and being an outsider where "everything is a question that you say, even though you are very educated, because you are a foreigner" and these were motivations for getting involved as well. It is still a challenge for Erla when she is abroad; the feeling that she doesn't belong is unsettling. However, this psychological discomfort and her experiences while in the United States also provides her with a significant source of empathy for those students who are in the cultural out-group, whether they are non-Icelandic students or diverse domestic students who appear, behave, or speak differently than those in the in-group. As is the case for many participants, this increasing diversity in the country, which includes not only these out-group students but also permanent immigrants, is one of the primary drivers for Erla's focus on practices related to IaH as part of her work.

Eyrún

When I interviewed her, Eyrún was adjunct faculty member working for the School of Education. She has been teaching and conducting research at UI for a number of years. Her research has led to several publications focusing primarily on intercultural education among youth and in primary schools. Her work in this area has recently generated significant interest from her colleagues as well as the public and media. Eyrún is completing her doctoral research at UI which explores the role of wellbeing in relation to cross-cultural friendships among immigrant adolescents in Iceland.

Eyrún's first steps toward exploring difference and intercultural learning came when she began the process of reflecting on her own position in life when she was still a young girl. She started recognizing her life was different than that many of her peers experienced in Iceland. She never knew her biological father and her mother was only 18 years old when Eyrún was born. Her grandparents played a more parental role and while she had strong family relationships with her extended family and a loving home, her parents provided only inadequate emotional support. There was not a specific moment or incident she could point to, but that she gradually started to understand that some her life circumstances were more "difficult" than others she knew. While these differences were in terms of limited connection with her parents, it was challenging for her, and it is something that she still carries with her into her adult life. The experience of this instability in her own nuclear family growing up added to her understanding of how challenging it can be for immigrant children who have additional factors that compound this instability.

Eyrún spent extended time abroad, face-to-face with difference daily in an unfamiliar culture and country. She lived in the United Kingdom for two and a half years from 2009-2011 and experienced what it was like to be an immigrant, an outsider. This was an experience she was consciously wanting to try and resulted in being an important part of her own intercultural development. There were two key aspects of her life in England that contributed to this abroad experience being transformative: The first was that Eyrún understood better the lack of control which immigrants often experience, by being an immigrant herself. This was particularly so because of the lack of social network:

> I think that was a very important experience for me to experience how to be powerless; to be nobody - how to be kind of somewhere where nobody knew who I was [...] you're a zero or you have to start anew.

Strong social networks are key a piece of cultural capital in the very tight-knit Icelandic society with its small population and where a variety of assumptions, judgments or goodwill are imparted to someone by their lineage. The complete lack of this social network then was a new experience for Eyrún and opened her eyes to the challenges of building a network from scratch.

The second key point of learning for her while she was in England was the recognition of the privilege she had by virtue of being White. She was treated differently because while Iceland was "exotic", she was still a college-educated, white person from a privileged region, whose husband ran a successful business in England hiring British workers. Eyrún commented about this experience, saying:

> I was in England and I lived in a relatively small town which was quite... multicultural itself. There were a lot of people from all over and what I, for example, experienced was that I was privileged. I was a privileged immigrant because I was from Northern Europe. And I found how people from other parts of the world were more marginalized.

Most of her connections and friends in England were also non-British and immigrants. One of her close friends was a Chinese woman who not only exposed her to a variety of new cultural differences, but also told Eyrún about the discrimination that she faced, which Eyrún had not directly experienced herself. In comparing stories and experiences about their interactions with the local British people, Eyrún realized how she had an easier time communicating with her children's teachers. In addition to her experiences while abroad, Eyrún also has interactions with cultural difference because of her family and her children's friends. Her sister is married to a man from Argentina and one of her son's close friends is Lithuanian and living in Iceland. She continues to have frequent interactions with people from other cultures.

Eyrún's motivation for getting involved in practices related to IaH was initially informed by her desire to help children have a more stable environment growing up. This, coupled with her recognition of the changing demographics in Iceland, formed an interest in wanting to understand and improve these children's' experiences:

> Yeah, I think when we started to see our society open up to the influx of immigrants. [...] it was kind of a discussion [that] started: What does this mean? What happens? We were [...] so naive. It was really underdeveloped in this area. We didn't really understand what was asked of us or what we were supposed to do with this new reality.

While she was completing her master's degree at the turn of the millennium, her mentor invited her to be part of a European research network which was focused on comparatively exploring issues of multiculturalism in European primary education systems. Through conferences and travel in this network, she was eventually hired as a researcher for the project Teacher Education Addressing Multiculturalism in Europe (TEAM) looking at Iceland before her full time faculty position in the School of Education. This project was designed to determine best practices in the field for teachers working with immigrant children and she was able to consider new perspectives about this work. This in turn led her to deciding to pursue a doctorate around these issues of children and multiculturalism and continues to inform her research at UI.

Hanna

Arguably one of the most strident voices on both the need for and the development of multicultural education in Iceland, Hanna has focused on the inclusion of children from immigrant backgrounds in the primary levels of the Icelandic education system. Hanna began her professional academic career as an assistant professor at the Iceland University of Education in 1998 prior to the merger of that institution with UI. She is now a full professor at UI and has extensive publications, teaching, and applied work around immigration, diversity, and multicultural education in Iceland. Much of her focus is on training and mentoring doctoral and graduate students who are now continuing the work she started over twenty years ago.

Hanna's experiences with cultural difference developed when she was young. She was born to Icelandic parents and raised in Iceland. Hanna states that in her early childhood, her father would frequently travel which ignited her interest in different cultures, languages, and religions. As she reached her late teenage years, Hanna herself went abroad as an exchange student and travelled throughout Europe with others and even by herself. She would use her own funds through working and saving for this travel. Ultimately, this path pushed her to pursue geography and anthropology at UI before going on to obtain a master's degree at the London School of Economics and Political Science and then her doctorate from the University of Oslo in Norway.

While her early life included important experiences through travel and living abroad, the most transformative moments came during her doctoral work. Through extended conversations with her participants, Hanna's dissertation which focused on the experiences of immigrants in Iceland, was one of her most transformative experiences with difference. She was conducting this research at a time when very little work was being done in this area:

> I think most sort of influential to my work was the experiences of my doctoral work which was a 3-year longitudinal study where I visited 10 families regularly and sort of interviewed them and observed and talked to them about their experiences of immigrating to Iceland. And the children were starting schools in Iceland and how they were doing and so on. So, I really got know these people well and I am forever grateful to

> them because they really opened my eyes to many issues that they were facing, and I learned so much.

Hanna credits the depth of the interviews in her study as the reason for understanding the challenges and barriers that immigrant families were dealing with in Iceland. She was able to connect with them and humanize them in ways she might not have been able to accomplish using an alternative research design. Although her participants were immigrants living in a different world, she could relate to them as she said, "[…] but still they're mothers […] like myself, you know similarities and differences." Hanna was able to cultivate empathy for their position and channel this into establishing herself in this field.

One example that was transformative to her assumptions about others occurred during one of her first interviews as a researcher. These interviews were conducted in the participants' homes, so she was entering their space without much sense of what she was walking into, but had expectations rooted in her own cultural assumptions:

> […] I entered a home where there was really a gathering of Muslims, this was like an extended family and they were praying there, and everyone was sort of included and I was just invited to sit with them. Well, I thought I was just coming for an interview, I was suddenly part of this ceremony, you know? It was a bit of a shock, but it was, at the same time, it was very nice because they invited me to be part of it and also observe; they were opening up their world for me, you know?

There was no indication from Hanna that she anticipated not being treated well, however, as an outsider she supposed a compartmentalized role as a researcher. For her study participants, the cultural importance of treating guests like their own was on display, and this is perhaps a dimension that Hanna had not expected because of her cultural norms of role separation in the professional/private life dichotomy.

While Hanna was already engaged in working with the experiences of immigrants in Iceland through her doctoral research, her focus began to shift toward supporting preschools. She was interested in the more applied work of developing teachers to be more intercultural in their thinking. This focus had its roots in a talk that she gave early in her career to preschool teachers as she discusses here:

> […] I decided to give a lecture about diversity in preschools and it was so well received. It was the first time

> they had ever heard about these issues in their training and they all recognized that the number of children from different backgrounds was growing in their preschools because most of them had part-time jobs at preschools. So just this, to feel the need and to get this very active and good response from this group of students. I always remember that because it really made me think "oh this is an area that I need to work on, I need to explore, and it's needed in the preschools.

Hanna's academic work has been very much driven by issues of social justice around immigrants and education. She saw a need in the field for support from who were experiencing their own challenges in teaching while also seeing what the schools' families and children were facing. Rather than narrowly following her own academic interests, she has adapted to her students' needs, which also fuels her broader attention to other practices related to IaH.

Terry

A well-known figure at UI, Terry was originally appointed as an assistant professor in Folkloristics in 1998 and now holds the rank of full professor, teaching a wide variety of courses including Old Norse religion, folk legends, folk games and festivals, Gaelic folklore, Nordic folklore, Performance Studies, and a course on Icelandic culture aimed at international students. In addition to his diverse scholarly activities, he is also active as a department administrator and frequently sits on committees, working on reports to move his unit, and the university, forward.

Born in the south of England, Terry spent young adult years working in several hotels in western Norway from 1974-1979, picking up Norwegian through daily conversation since that was the primary language being used at the hotel. This was a very pivotal time for Terry, interacting with people from Austria, Morocco, the United States, and Iceland, among others. This hotel had "all sorts of international people," which gave him significant exposure to live and interact with people from a wide range of cultures. This experience was so positive for him that he recalled wondering "what all the political mess is about between countries when people get on so well together." As a testament to his openness to difference, he noted during this interview that he enjoyed being a foreigner.

Apart from his experiences with other internationals in Norway, Terry pointed to his time in Birmingham in the United Kingdom as another pivotal experience. At the university there, he received his bachelor's degree in Drama and Theatre Arts and also a post-graduate certificate in Education. While this occurred within his home country, he recognized significant difference between peoples in different geographic regions of the United Kingdom:

> Going to Birmingham – University of Birmingham and teaching in Birmingham was a life-changing experience for me in the sense that I was coming from a, [...] I suppose, a middle-class, well, grandparents lower-middle-class; father works up to upper-middle-class – as a teacher you're middle-class – then you come from the south and go to an area where the people I came from saw them as a load of lazy bastards and couldn't understand why the grandparents, and the parents and the kids were out of work and it became more difficult to teach these kids and find ways of drawing - holding an education and then coming back down to the south where they had no sense of where they were coming from – it's partly why I came to Iceland. It became more like living a lie, the whole [...] privilege of going back down to a place by the sea where you can go and drive into the countryside. Upper-middle-class area, you're coming back up to a working-class area like Birmingham in the period of Thatcher when she was cutting everything off from the North – it was very, very difficult to live with.

Terry was able to experience the life of those in the north of the country. His assumptions and socialized viewpoints were challenged through new understandings of the role that certain privileges played in attaining education or steady employment. The stark difference between the north and south of Britain helped him internalize new perspectives about the challenging circumstances that those who were less privileged endure. Ultimately this meant that he looked for a more authentic life, away from Britain. Even while he still holds certain status there, he now feels that he is an outsider, no longer strongly connected to life there.

Terry met his Icelandic wife while working in Norway and credits her with some of the impetus for interaction across cultures as well. After his time in Birmingham, Terry and his partner moved to Iceland and his significant experiences with difference extended to this new home as well. The amount of contact he had with people of other cultures was reinforced by what he sees as a British cultural trait of separation and exploration without the need of reinforcing in-group identity:

> [T]he Brits and the Irish are a little bit similar: when we go abroad we don't hang out together naturally. We don't sort of get pulled together, we tend to all of us have our own people and then we'll meet in-between occasionally, but not as, not as a way of holding on to British identity. So, certainly I've had contact with a number of foreigners from the beginning, through learning Icelandic.

Rather than seeking out those from his home country who he would have more cultural similarity with, he spent his first summer in Iceland doing construction with Icelanders and learning about the people, language, and culture. Today, Terry is acutely aware of his status as a member of Icelandic society. Although as the spouse of an Icelander he was "immediately brought into a family," he is still a foreigner. Similar in this respect to Brynja, Terry is between, straddling both where he came from and where he is: yet not fully belonging to either, "as a sort of a foreigner wherever I am, even my own country now when I go back there." He underlined this point again later adding that being international is a foundational part of his life, "largely my whole background is international. I'm a foreigner wherever I go, so I bring internationalization to a certain extent."

An important avenue that gave Terry some of his initial motivation to engage in practices of IaH, came at the very start of his academic career at the UI. He spent a great deal of time and energy developing international relationships with other folklorists, demonstrating an international nature of his mindset from early in his career. Since Terry works across several disciplines, these scholars form his international community with whom he has very strong connections. In part, these connections were developed to gain a comparative and culturally different perspective on folklore and the other disciplines that he works in. These connections however, also afford him the opportunity to frequently interact with not only scholarly ideas from other perspectives, but also individuals from varied cultural backgrounds. He mentioned colleagues in the Scandinavian countries, the United States, and a connection in Kenya as some of the people who sparked his interest in exploring these comparative practices that he employs as practices of IaH. He still researches, teaches, plays music, and travels with many connections around the world and in this academic group in particular.

Summary

While each of the participants had unique experiences and moments which influenced their own interest in difference and concepts that inform IaH, there are several common threads in their backgrounds and initial motivations for being involved. All the participants mentioned that their time traveling or living abroad as a foreigner was an important part of their early interest and development. Many of the participants had direct experience with immigrants, racial differences, or privilege, which provided them with a worldview and framework for improving other's lives. These experiences also helped them increase their understanding and tolerance toward difference in their students and the greater Icelandic population.

Chapter V: Meaning Making through IaH

With participants' backgrounds in mind, this chapter considers how these five champions engage in the process of IaH. The analysis starts with participants' understanding of the concept, before considering their perceived roles, and then from those understandings, how they carry out their engagement in specific activities related to IaH. While the core of IaH is purported to be in integrating internationalized curriculum in on campus contexts, these goals require investment in and development of the academic faculty who create the content and instruction. Faculty member development needs to be considered a vital aspect of any successful effort. With participants' practices in mind, this section of this chapter draws on data from participant interviews illuminating how they construct their understanding of internationalization and IaH as concepts and then how they see their own role in this process.

Conceptualizations of internationalization and IaH

Despite several decades of increasing discussion and theorizing, generating some very broad agreement among scholars, the concept of internationalization in higher education and the more focused IaH are still often vaguely understood among most academic staff. The meaning of internationalization for the participants as outlined below provides the foundation for considering how these faculty members conceptualize the more focused IaH and then how they enact various practices of IaH in their roles at UI.

Constructing the meaning of internationalization

When participants were asked about what internationalization meant to them in the context of higher education, they reported a variety of understandings, often from the same individual – several noting the multiple dimensions of the concept. Despite this, there were points of agreement among the participants. One well-represented understanding was that internationalization broadly means intercultural or international education. Brynja notes that internationalization of higher education: "[...] means that faculty and students have an opportunity to operate [...] on an international level and receive students and faculty from abroad and sort of have this academic, cultural, intellectual exchange that's fairly broad." Here, internationalization of higher education is primarily the opportunity to engage on a more global scale through the exchange of people, ideas, and culture. For her it both going outside of the home institution or culture and then engaging with elements of "international", whether through connection with international colleagues who come on campus.

Other responses included a stated rationale for this sort of international education, to help students function or operate internationally outside of those only in Iceland. Brynja later continued by talking about helping students recognize their position and impact on the world:

> I think that as, as global citizens which we're, you know, rapidly becoming without necessarily being particularly aware of it in our daily dialogue, I think it's important for them to realize what this is and at the same time, understand the implications of what they do on a global scale and to understand; and I think it also sort of helps them understand who might be coming here and why.

Her second statement is a shift away from exchange and the experiences offered in higher education itself, to focusing on assisting students in mentally positioning themselves in the world and seeing the ramifications of their actions and choices. Through employing the term "global citizen" – though a contested term – Brynja invokes an ethical question about how students interact with or impact others.

Terry echoes this focus on internationalization meaning international education by talking about the preparation for future cross-cultural interactions with others, particularly outside of the island of Iceland. When I asked him what internationalization meant, he responded:

> I suppose there are different angles you can take on it. As part of the folkloristics job of course, it means getting students to be aware of other countries and other traditions outside their own, so that they can work out [pause] what is Icelandic and what is not. At the same time this is an island community and we have to - be able to prepare students and, especially graduates to function internationally. They certainly can't use Icelandic wherever they go and that means that university should be seen as a follow on from high school, upper high school, senior high where they're learning English, they're sort of reaching a higher level of use and it shouldn't stop at that level it should continue into the university environment where we're increasing their education, part of

> their education should be the ability to function and communicate in a much wider group.

In this statement, Terry speaks about internationalization in the context of UI and Icelanders specifically. He focuses on his discipline of folkloristics, which he sees as helping students understand their own culture. Moreover, Terry makes a strong connection between the use of English and the concept of internationalization as stated previously. However, he also explicitly notes that there is a wider aspect of learning multiple languages and being able to communicate in languages other than Icelandic. Terry places this understanding of what internationalization means in a very utilitarian frame of students gaining the skills and tools to interact with the wider world. This is evidenced by his direct linking of secondary and university education.

Beyond meaning international or intercultural education for students, Brynja, Eyrún, Terry, and Hanna also considered the internationalization of higher education to be a cooperation between universities in various countries, whether through communication and joint dialogue, research knowledge or exchanging students. Eyrún believes that internationalization "means communication, it means contact. It means research networks that are across countries. It can mean presenting what you're doing all over." Terry doesn't mention research directly but talks about internationalization as communication and cooperative learning: "it is a matter of bringing universities together and actually learning from each other in a positive fashion and an international dialogue." This could then include research and knowledge exchange, but also cooperative teaching efforts through distance learning or academic staff exchange. Hanna echoes Terry's belief that it is about bringing universities together, "So, in my mind, this is both about cooperation with other countries, other universities in other countries or internationalizing the university itself." This mindset of multi-layered cooperation stems from an intrinsic understanding of importance of international education and global learning. These three understandings are connected by focusing on dialogue and engagement across cultural and structural borders.

The participants also pointed to internationalization being about the academic staff as well. As reported above, Brynja said that internationalization means "[…] that faculty and students have an opportunity to operate both on an international level and receive students and faculty from abroad and sort of have this academic, cultural, intellectual exchange that's fairly broad." In her response, Hanna noted that in addition to cooperation, diversity and internationalized curriculum, internationalized staff was an important dimension of the process. Terry talked about this meaning of internationalization in more depth, stating:

> And then of course there's working, that all members of staff should be working and functioning going to conferences abroad as part of our duty and bringing, which gives us new insights into the way subjects are being taught abroad and gives our students insight into the way teaching is being done in other countries.

While Terry highlights faculty members crossing Iceland's political and geographic borders to attend conferences abroad, ultimately, he is also talking about these academic staff expanding their own learning, which in turn aids aspects and activities of internationalization on the home campus.

Erla points to internationalization meaning that the university, as an institution, is developing more intercultural and global perspectives. "So, being international, we need to welcome others who come from different cultures and help them learn also about our culture. So, internationalization is just being global and think more broadly. Not only narrow about Iceland or Scandinavia, much broader." While she does not explicitly mention faculty members, it is implicit that they are key constituent parts of the organization. Indeed, Erla uses the word "we" which includes herself as one of these academic staff who are developing. Just as Erla uses "we", Eyrún positions herself as assisting in developing the greater society to be global citizens:

> How we kind of challenge our people engaging in those discussions about what it means to be a citizen of the world or what it means to be part of humanity [laughs] or a global citizen. Or what it means to live in a country that welcomes residents from other countries to come and live here, which we have. We have of course obligations to that end. We are not a closed country, so we're supposed to welcome people from other places. So, it would mean, yeah, it would mean also our responsibility and our role and engage in that sort of discussion.

Like Erla, Eyrún does not address academic staff development directly, but speaks more about a responsibility of the faculty members to undertake this intercultural or international education for the betterment of society and those coming to Iceland from beyond its borders. Part of this responsibility then is to develop academic staff to be able to effectively teach these attitudes and skills. In this case, the intercultural and international development of academic staff is also included in what defines the internationalization of higher education by these participants either through explicit statement or through their recognition of the responsibility in such activities.

Constructing the Meaning of IaH

Unlike the broad term internationalization, not all the participants readily had an answer to the meaning of "Internationalization at Home." The question was occasionally rephrased to ask about their understanding of internationalization of the campus. While campus internationalization has been defined more vaguely and not the same concept as IaH (Beelen & Jones, 2015), there are significant overlaps. Using the words "campus internationalization" helped participants at times focus on the salient aspects when the term Internationalization at Home had less meaning for them. With this in mind, just as participants reported a variety of understandings of internationalization, they described a range of understandings about IaH as well many of which were informed by their own work.

Most of the participants discussed IaH in context of their own home campus, in very concrete ways whether the question was rephrased or not. Some of their understandings were similar to the broader concept of internationalization as a whole. A chief overlap was that IaH was also about teaching multiple perspectives on the home campus. After I asked about how he understands internationalization broadly, Terry for example said this about how he sees IaH:

> Education at this level should be comparatively international. Of course, that's students, it's a question of being foreign or international. I'm both a foreigner and an international. I think that it's important that they do learn about other countries. I think that it's important they're aware of what's going on in other countries [...].

IaH for Terry is still very much about international education, seeing new international perspectives in a comparative context. The commonalities here indicate that this aspect of internationalizing the curriculum, which maps well onto theoretical constructs of IaH, is not a peripheral component, but a core part of the more general concept of internationalization.

Other understandings were mentioned only in the context of IaH, however. Several participants understood IaH as embodying a more focused attention on creating cultural diversity and inclusion at the university itself. Erla spoke about a campus that was diverse with international populations, the cultural differences they bring with them, but also diverse in the abilities of staff and internationally-themed amenities:

> International is more different nations, but I look at maybe cultures more, so maybe nations will have many cultures and co-cultures. Well, internationalization would be where people can communicate in different languages I would see in campus here, students from all over, different colors, communicating in different languages. That would be international.

Again, an important aspect of IaH in this conception is a diversity of language on campus, not only for students, but also for the community working in a variety of languages. While the discussion about how much to use English or Icelandic, Erla posits that IaH would include a plethora of languages used for communication and work. This implies beyond limiting other language usage to the foreign language classroom and students, but also academic and non-academic staff and administrators.

Brynja also discusses understanding IaH to mean diversity, but specifically through a lens of inclusivity which translates as efforts to increase access to the university for immigrant population in Iceland. "Well here, very explicitly it means, really looking at and re-evaluating opening the doors to the immigrant population that's here. It really means looking at it from an inclusive perspective that everybody in the society has access." Rather than seeing IaH as solely program for those already in the institution, she posits that there is a strong need to create structures which allow others to gain entrance in the first place. She goes on to say, "As in elsewhere, class is slowly still there, but more people have access to higher education than ever before. But, that's not true for the immigrant populations. And when they do have access, they encounter enormous roadblocks." Brynja points out some of the continued issues with access to the university based on class as well but notes the compounded struggles that immigrant populations often face in thriving at the university even if they succeed in matriculating. Historically, there has been limited cultural diversity in Iceland and even fewer people in oppressed racial or ethnic minority groups. The terminology in Icelandic around concepts related to interculturalism is still in flux, with the word fjölmenning frequently being used for concepts of both "multicultural" and "intercultural." With the relatively modern immigration of diverse peoples to Iceland, concepts of social justice and access to the university, related strongly to theoretical constructs of multiculturalism, are still quite prominent in the minds of participants and administrators when discussing internationalization. This is echoed in Brynja's understanding of IaH and is close to the core of the initial impetus for the development of IaH as a focus.

When asked about what IaH meant to her, Hanna talked about diversity as well, providing a clear connection between the Icelandic society at large and how the university itself should mirror the changing population of the island:

> how do we make sure that the diversification of society is reflected in the university to make sure that we are including the people that live in this country, not only the Icelanders but also other groups or individuals. And also, to include diversity in our staff, so that would mean really looking at our own university and making sure that we are aware of all of these dimensions.

Just as in aspects of her understanding of Internationalization as a broader concept, Hanna includes the idea of diversity in the academic staff at the university to be an integral part of IaH. However, her focus is on academic staff being cognizant of the domestic diversity in Iceland itself, which prominently includes immigrant populations. Hanna sees IaH as a "more narrow concept", squarely focused on this project of including immigrant populations and other diversity in society at the university. This is through both access and internationalizing the curriculum in order to include these populations and present a variety of perspectives that speak to their cultural background and understanding. This concept that the university should reflect the greater Icelandic society ties Hanna's understanding of IaH back to UI being the national university, which for her, means including everyone in the nation.

Finally, Eyrún also provides an understanding of IaH that includes diversity. Like some of the other participants' understandings above, Eyrún talked about a certain community built around diversity:

> Maybe that would mean the community of the school of the campus, that it should be open and diverse and have room for diversity. But I think it would also mean that it supports opinions, it supports discussion, it supports yeah, open you know democratic discussion about such issues and about our position in the world as so on.

Broadly speaking, Eyrún understands IaH as creating a campus community that is positioned attitudinally as accepting and including diversity and difference. Eyrún also talks about diversity through a lens of a variety of opinions and a democratic classroom specifically. Through other conversations with Eyrún, her goal for the classroom includes creating space for a diversity of student voices from all of backgrounds, generating internationalized curriculum through the students' experiences and dialogue. Most participants believed IaH pertains to internationalized curriculum and creating a more diverse and inclusive campus community with an eye toward the immigrant population specifically.

Faculty Member Role in IaH

Conceptions of what IaH means to the participants helps inform how they see their own role in those activities. The changing demographics in Iceland were on the mind of the participants during data collection and this was made clear through discussion about the role of academic staff. For example, Brynja notes that the percentage of immigrants in Iceland has shifted dramatically in the past 20 years, and that because of this "[…] we have to do something - we have to be aware." Informed by their general view that IaH is related to issues of inclusion, many participants see one of the key roles of faculty members in IaH as developing increased awareness and knowledge of the issues of diversity, marginalization, and immigration. Hanna's statement about marginalization captures this awareness well:

> I don't expect this to be the one right view of things, but it's a belief that I have which has developed through the years and I think it's out of necessity because I see marginalization, as I told you about last time, and I see discrimination. And I think one way of counteracting that is developing international perspectives. Because it's a more open-minded view of things and it allows you to bring research and knowledge from different countries, from different areas and I think it's also related to general globalization which is happening whether we like it or not. I think this is necessary for our university as well as other universities to think about. If not, otherwise, it's the danger of becoming isolated in a way also.

While her statement could be considered reflexive, Hanna is talking about the international perspectives informing research and knowledge, which is the domain of faculty members. Stating that this is something that is necessary for the university to think about is then by extension something academic staff must consider as well. This awareness is of marginalization in the greater society, as well as awareness of the need for developing and then incorporating international perspectives to make faculty members' work more effective and relevant.

Erla also comments on the role of faculty members in developing and incorporating such awareness. While her focus in this statement does not have the focus of marginalization that Hanna discusses, she is addressing diversity directly:

> So, there are stressors because you want to be sort of a prestigious university, you need to follow international rules at least to compare ourselves to other universities. So, it's more demanding to be internationalized because we cannot only live here on this island. We need to look outside our island. So, I think it's more challenging but at the same time also more interesting. But it requires everybody to be more aware of how other things are done in other cultures both to different customs, different languages, rules, regulations, ethics, so it becomes more complex obviously because we are not all the same and we need to try first to embrace the diversity.

Erla speaks directly to the concept of awareness and provides a broader rationale by acknowledging that Iceland cannot escape the cultural effects of globalization.

Again, although her statement does not explicitly mention faculty members, it is clear when talking about stressors and international rules, she is talking about herself as a representative of the larger body of academic staff at the university. Moreover, Erla notes that internationalization "requires everybody to be more aware" of cultural differences and this includes the academic staff whose role includes teaching students this awareness as well.

My questions and the participants' responses centered on their perceived role in instruction as teaching is a core function of many academic staff and internationalized curriculum and co-curriculum are major components of IaH. A key question asked what responsibilities participants had in including diverse international perspectives or intercultural learning in their teaching. All responded that they believed they have a duty to incorporate such perspectives or learning into their teaching and they expressed this belief in a variety of ways. Although participants discussed the formal curriculum, answers also alluded to informal curriculum as well.

The participants see the responsibility of including such perspectives in their teaching as the core function of their work. As participants were identified based on their positions as being champions of IaH, this finding is not unexpected. Yet, it is worthwhile to note that teaching was evaluated as being of utmost importance even though participants have research obligations, which often overshadow teaching. While Eyrún has historically had less of a teaching load than the other participants in the study, teaching is still important to her, and she believes strongly in including multiple and diverse international perspectives in her instruction. When asked about what responsibility she felt toward this, she said:

> That's a good question. Maybe I'm one of those representatives of that, [I] contribute to kind of a discussion of what it means to be human or what it means to be part of a large world and what it means that the world is diverse and that our country is diverse and it's going to be and like something like that just being – keeping on, kind of giving out information that helps people understand and discuss and develop their own thinking about diversity and what it means and what it should mean.

Eyrún addressed teaching both inside and outside the classroom; formal and informal curriculum. This is evidenced by her answer using the word "people" broadly, rather than talking only about students. Throughout the data collection, she spoke of sharing with students, colleagues, and others in the community using such internationalized approaches and perspectives – including those perspectives she learned more about through the research network she was involved in.

Brynja was the most direct in her statement about her responsibility of including diverse and multiple perspectives. Her belief around this role is informed in part by the very specific nature of the position that she holds as the academic coordinator of the international education degree at the School of Education:

> I think that's my primary responsibility. I think the academic, theoretical, all that stuff comes along with it. I mean [colleague's name] has even said that to me "that's what you're supposed to be doing here in the classes isn't it? You were hired to bring this multicultural perspective into these classes and into this program and I just sort of go "oh, ok." So, I think if I weren't doing it some people would notice and it would be problematic for me professionally because [...] it's clear on my resume or CV that that's what I am, you know? And so, I think that unconsciously - consciously; probably both, is my primary objective.

Again, like Brynja states above, Hanna sees this responsibility of including diverse and multiple perspectives into her teaching as a core part of her work. For Hanna, this effort is in part due to her perception that so few others are engaged in this sort of work despite advancements and increased attention, "Well, I think because there are so few of us, [...] that are focusing on this area even though, the number is growing. I think, I feel that I have the responsibility to integrate these perspectives into all of my teaching and this is what I do." Hanna makes several statements around her understood responsibility of including such perspectives and learning into her teaching, but this is the most universal. It's not just pointing to a specific course or class where the content is on diversity or immigration, but rather indicating including multiple perspectives permeates all of her teaching regardless of subject. She sees her role then as filling gaps in the broader university or school curriculum, where students may not be exposed to such internationalized curriculum.

Terry also gives a universal response to this question, demonstrated by his reluctance to see including diverse perspectives or intercultural learning as something different or separate from any other responsibilities he has as a teacher. For him, these are one and the same, as he says here, "I do have a responsibility as a teacher to educate people, and educating them means for me, as I say, opening doors, opening understanding of different cultures and realizing their part of a global community, rather than just local." While some of the participants are more focused on including these perspectives in looking at immigrant populations and the communities within Iceland, Terry explicitly refers to educating others about their position in the global community. Again, like Eyrún, Terry speaks about people, rather than formal students only. This widens the scope of his understanding of his role in IaH to beyond his own classroom, which could include not only formal and informal curriculum, but also colleagues and the greater community. In his capacity as a teacher, he sees providing multiple perspectives from different cultures as a core responsibility.

Finally, Erla reiterates the idea that faculty members must be aware, but this awareness is of the role that they play in including international or intercultural learning. Erla speaks most directly to this core responsibility in her own teaching as well as taking coursework or learning beyond that received in electives which some students take, but most miss. Here, she talks about integrating intercultural and internationalized perspectives across the curriculum:

> This should be mandatory - they said in elementary and high school even, you know. Some of this stuff that I was teaching. So, I think that we as scholars, teachers, we need to be aware of that that we have a very important role by sharing our international, intercultural education. It's really important today in the education system.

> This not just – "nah this is just electives, you know, I'm just going to take it for fun." No, I think it should be mandatory this is part of this life you know. If you want to function in society and in the globe. You know? This is something that everybody needs to learn a little bit, at start to learn about it; think about those issues. So, I'll definitely try to work more on that, the modalities.

In this passage, Erla's understanding of the role that faculty have in IaH goes beyond the classroom. While she focuses on sharing international and intercultural education through faculty members' function as teacher, she also mentions the role of scholars. As we will see in the next section, which is concerned with faculty members' engagement in specific practices related to IaH, all the participants have been involved in researching immigrant populations, diversity education, or inclusive practices which sheds additional light on how they make IaH part of their work even outside of teaching. This then informs their teaching practices as they refer to examples and findings in their research, reinforcing this role of including such perspectives in the classroom.

Including perspectives beyond Western-based in teaching and curriculum

When asked about including perspectives beyond Western-based in the curriculum, several participants believed that it is their responsibility to include these viewpoints. They also stated however, that it was challenging to find enough material as a basis to teach broader perspectives. Brynja noted, "I mean that's a real struggle here especially because [...] the access to those [materials] are relatively limited." While she sees access to these broader perspectives as limited, she later stated that she feels that it is her responsibility to bring diverse scholarship into the classroom as few others are doing so. Much of the scholarship she pulls in originates from scholars who still come from Western societies but are from more diverse and non-hegemonic backgrounds.

Erla also believed that incorporating broader perspectives in the classroom is part of her role. Like Brynja above, Erla also noted the struggle in finding effective material or approaches to include in the classroom:

> This is actually challenging because I am constantly searching for relevant, appropriate textbooks, because, like you say, most of them have this focus on the – this part of the world, but not more other parts. I'm really,

> I'm struggling with that. So, I'm trying myself to take some research, so I have some articles, some research articles that show other perspectives and discuss it in the classroom. You know of course this, for example, Hofstede is very Westernized, and I discuss that when I do that. Because I'm more sort of a social constructed way to look at things, so I explain it in my classroom. "So just bear in mind that this research was done, were mostly men," you know Hofstede's [for] instance, mostly employees and mostly men, no women, that has an effect obviously on the research.

In this passage, Erla is speaking to both differences in research method and epistemology as well as the dominant Westernized modes of looking at intercultural research and teaching. To balance these Westernized approaches, she purposefully looks for research and resulting articles from other viewpoints to include in the classroom in addition to cautioning students about bias and monocultural viewpoints.

Hanna also noted her responsibility in including these broader perspectives specifically in the curriculum. She did not allude to any struggles with finding such material, rather she focused on the importance of helping her graduate students to recognize the need for culturally and geographically diverse perspectives. Hanna is responding to what she sees in some of her graduate students as a very Icelandic-centered worldview that will not always serve them or their students well:

> We I just feel it's important to open the students' eyes to something different because, I mean, first of all, when they start their teaching, or continue their teaching because some of these students are post-graduates of course, I mean, they are working with populations from all over the world. And even though we know many parts of the world are becoming sort of Westernized, it's important to realize there are civilizations all over the world that were there long before we existed. For example, the Icelandic society is very young, and we cannot claim to be you know, founders of this or that knowledge. It's all from older civilizations. So, I think it's so important to realize that there was a lot happening and so much thought and knowledge before these Westernized views appeared. And this is the knowledge that we are generally, teaching to our students or sharing with them. And of course, the history goes much

> further back. And I think we just need to open students' eyes to that; that there is so much else in the world that just our narrow Western knowledge.

In this passage, Hanna addresses a belief in her role as providing students with an internationalized curriculum and provides two rationales for such a curriculum.

She believes in the importance of providing students with diverse sources of knowledge, recognizing that many civilizations in the world pre-date Iceland. While Western cultures have been the source, or have incorporated some of this knowledge, much still exists which is relatively unexplored or unknown. The second rationale is that using multiple perspectives, including those from other cultures (ancient or not), will help her students to teach more effectively and inclusively in light of an increasingly globalized world and multicultural classrooms with students from all over the world. Hanna then sees her role as expanding this recognition of culture and knowledge base in her students.

Modeling attitudes and affective learning

Participants presented additional understandings how they understand their role in IaH through teaching. Erla and Terry both stated that they believe it is their responsibility to present principles or aspects of intercultural learning and multiple perspective taking through their actions; that is to say, leading by example through modeling these attitudes and behaviors. Erla for example said, "Well, I think one of my roles or responsibilities [is] just to be more tolerant. Like I said, less judgmental towards others." Terry also talks about exhibiting these perspectives. While he is referring less to increased tolerance, he wants students to be open to different opinions, think for themselves, and question what others assert:

> [...] I believe that teachers should be – should express opinions and be open to having them questioned. I want my students to vote; I want them to have, and certainly I don't want them to believe anything I believe. I say that all the time here, all the time here it's a questioning. But I want them to see I'm a thinking person too and that I don't feel any harm showing humanitarian, liberal, democratic views.

Terry's attention here is more on developing critical thinking in students, but also on bringing his own attitudes and actions into the classroom.

He understands his role as caring about humanity, being open to new opinions, beliefs, and behaviors. Showing that everyone should be appreciated. Both Erla and Terry embody values of withholding judgement and openness which are rooted in the intercultural education and multiple perspective taking implicit to IaH.

Another role mentioned was providing opportunities for affective learning. Erla's scholarship is in intercultural communication and she numerous entry points for affective learning because of course content. Erla talked directly about feeling that it is her role to help students build empathy toward others:

> Show them into some other people's worlds and let them in, and learn all about it and have them analyze and interpret whatever they say, discuss it and eventually they will be more open. I think that's my responsibility – not only to teach them something and get a grade, my goal is that [...] it will change them, it will touch them. Touch their hearts. Because that will make them, like I said before, it's like more than planting seeds because I want them to grow a little - start growing in my classroom.

All the participants discussed their role in teaching as helping students see and accept difference. However, Erla was the only participant to address the mode of learning through challenging and connecting with students' emotions. She implies that often students in the higher education classroom focus on grades and cognitive learning, while she considers her role as infusing emotional learning as well.

The participants all believed it is their responsibility to engage in these practices related to IaH and integrate them into the various aspects of their work. Several participants understood it as cultivating awareness of matters related to diversity and inclusivity both at UI and in the greater Icelandic community. Although there was some variation among participants in how they understood their role in IaH, they all believed that part of this role included a responsibility to incorporate diverse perspectives or intercultural learning in their teaching to help prepare graduates to be successful at navigating a globalized world as well as culturally sensitive and reflexive about their own positionality.

Chapter VI: Engaging in Teaching Practices of IaH

Beelen and Jones (2015) conceptualize IaH not as an aim or a goal in and of itself, but rather as a set of activities supporting the "integration of intercultural and international dimensions into the formal and informal curriculum" on the home campus (p. 69). While these activities are focused on delivering international and intercultural learning, this begs the question of how this set of activities relates to academic staff. What are the daily practices that these champions engage in? Participants' backgrounds, understanding and positioning, described in the previous chapter, provide a foundation for understanding the activities themselves. This chapter and the following investigate the ways these participants enact IaH, including the activities and actions that support the development and implementation of such activities on campus. The participants' practices are divided into four categories and this first chapter focuses on teaching. The next chapter will then cover building and maintaining networks; research; and connecting with Icelandic society.

Types of Teaching practices

The focus of IaH and Internationalization of the curriculum overlap significantly at the point of teaching. IaH narrows the scope of curriculum (which is both content and presentation) to the home campus and in the core curriculum, rather than the broader internationalization of the curriculum, which includes cross-border education as well. Beelen and Jones (2015) argue "the internationalization of learning outcomes, pedagogy and assessment are at the heart of Internationalization at Home" (p. 64). They also posit that "a variety of instruments can be used to internationalize teaching and learning" and then go on to list comparative international literature, guest speakers, international case studies, and online collaboration among others. What is missing from the broader conversation, however, is how IaH is carried out on a daily basis and what practices faculty members are actually engaging in on a granular level. This portion of the discussion then centers on specific practices and structure of the pedagogy rather than general approaches. While this account is by no means exhaustive, it highlights practices the participants themselves identify as important to their pursuit of the outcomes related to IaH as well as those evidenced in documents and observation.

As teaching is one of the central activities of IaH, the data on participants' teaching practices are particularly robust and rich. The practices of IaH through teaching are categorized into four clusters: Practices of cognitive engagement; practices of experiential or affective learning; practices of course design; and finally, practices of diversity and inclusion. Charts are provided for each of the clusters, denoting which participants demonstrated a given practice during the data collection. Key examples of each practice are then highlighted in the following discussion. While this organization is useful for clarity, the clusters of practices are not discrete; rather there are rich overlaps and intersections among clusters of practices.

Practices of cognitive engagement cluster

The first cluster is organized around participants' teaching practices that target multiple perspective taking, critical reflection, and critical thinking. These teaching practices are aimed at engaging students' cognitive skills in deepening their critical analysis of course material supporting IaH. The four practices in this cluster are: Including multiple and international perspectives; fostering critical thinking around issues of multiculturalism or difference; fostering critical reflection about self, bias, or assumptions; and finally, helping students understand global connections.

Table 2 Practices of cognitive engagement cluster

	Brynja	*Erla*	*Eyrún*	*Hanna*	*Terry*
Including multiple and international perspectives	x	x		x	x
Fostering critical thinking around issues of multiculturalism or difference	x	x	x	x	x
Fostering critical reflection about self, bias, or assumptions	x	x	x	x	x
Helping students understand global connections	x			x	x

Including multiple and international perspectives. There are several desired outcomes associated with activities of IaH including empathy building and improved intercultural communication to help students take multiple perspectives on the world. Several participants shared examples of how they used multiple perspectives or helped craft lessons incorporating these perspectives. In discussing multiple perspectives, it is important to acknowledge that they exist within any given site, as multicultural groups exist domestically as well as internationally. That said, presenting non-dominant perspectives is also a practice of inclusion as it can bring to light and elevate perspectives of those who do not have the power or position to do so.

In one of her syllabi, Brynja, for example, informed students that the objective of the course was the "understanding of dominant views and theories of psychology and philosophy about development of self in both Western and Eastern cultures." Erla brings her own international experiences and artifacts into her office space for the express purpose of leveraging them to expose students who visit her to international perspectives; similarly, Hanna addressed how readings and materials with multiple perspectives were included in the International Studies program, which she helped develop. One of the most interesting examples of teaching through multiple perspectives comes from Terry. He spoke of how he took part in developing an internationalized course out of Zurich that included multiple perspectives through short lectures given by experts from around the world, experts who would provide their own international perspectives on a given theme.

> [...] I took part – I think I talked about this before – I took part in a course from Zurich where Zurich brought in friends from all over the world to do short lectures, 10-15 minute lectures and I like the idea of doing that, which it's not examined at the end it, necessarily, but are courses which take up the theme of, what the role of Folkloristics for the world today, place and space, something like this. Old Norse religion. But we could pull on people from all over the world together and in a sense, a collection of materials you could actually have a course then which is then – the teaching is done by people all over the world and some of the best people, but then the discussion goes on in the local language within the country and that means that you get some very good academics who are just putting this material, which could be used again and again, offering readings and maybe some questions for an exam, but the actual mark discussion is done in the local country. So, you bring in voices from all over the world that you come to pick up through these networks; I think that can work quite effectively.

While Terry has not yet designed a course like this at UI, he spoke about adapting this method of course delivery to the UI, looking forward to what could be done around content in his areas. This is then both already a practice of teaching for Terry, as well as a foundation for designing such internationalized courses at UI in the future. The method of drawing international perspectives by a variety of experts from around the world is not necessarily unique, the idea that the course would be going on as a global class, with individual discussions in the local classroom is visionary. Moreover, he suggests that the assessment could even be internationalized.

Fostering critical thinking around issues of multiculturalism or difference. Scriven and Paul (1996) define critical thinking as "the intellectually disciplined process of actively and skillfully conceptualizing, applying, analyzing, synthesizing, and/or evaluating information gathered from, or generated by, observation, experience, reflection, reasoning, or communication, as a guide to belief and action" (para. 3). As a practice of teaching in the context of IaH, the act of fostering such thinking is accomplished through a variety of learning activities. For this cluster, evidence for this practice is both indirect and direct. Eyrún provides an example of feedback from students about their reaction to her learning activities engaging critical thinking about multicultural material in classes:

> There are some issues around those that they haven't really thought about. Of for example, what kind of processes or structures in the society can affect people coming from somewhere else and in the sense that it's a very complex, it's a complex world. And in the sense that how discrimination works and how it can affect you. I think that those are issues that many haven't really thought about [...] that some groups are privilege and others are not. And some groups have more access to resources while others have not.

Not only does she present students with new perspectives about difference, she also helps them think about the complexities of the world and how many layers interact. Gaining a sense of how discrimination works and the impact on individuals requires this sort of active analysis and synthesis of information. Eyrún does not specify which methods were used in class, but in this same conversation, she characterized the responses from students as an "eye-opener", a signal that students indeed engaged in critical thinking.

Another illuminating example comes from Erla who talks about how she makes critical thinking a core focus in learning objectives for students. While again she is not addressing methods used in the classroom, her approach to teaching is grounded in critical thinking:

> I focus on different critical approaches, so it's in my objectives, so you can probably see it. Because I want them to use critical thinking you know and I try to look at different ways of communicating, not only on a surface level because you have to think about the historical aspect and social political situation and things like that.

Erla provides evidence of both a broad underlying approach oriented toward critical thinking as well as specifics of methods. She points to encouraging students to think deeply about the complexities of historical and social-political realities and how they influence communication, which fosters complex analysis and synthesis.

Direct evidence for this practice comes through the syllabi and course exercise that participants provided as exemplars of their course design and material. One of Erla's assignments for students is a reaction paper on race, where she asks students to address questions like: "How do histories influence the process of identity formation? How do social positions influence individuals' attitudes toward history and what factors influence whether an individual sees history as an important element of identity? How does power influence the writing of history?" To answer these questions fully, students are required to skillfully analyze and evaluate the intersections of a variety of angles, perspectives, and information, including considering their own assumptions and constructions of reality.

Fostering critical reflection about self, bias, or assumptions. A third teaching practice of IaH in this cluster of cognitive engagement is the fostering of critical reflection. Critical reflection is different from the process of reflection, which can be about considering and improving procedural or mechanical improvements in learning. Instead, critical reflection can "refer to challenging the validity of presuppositions in prior learning" (Mezirow, 1990, p.4). Mezirow (1990) breaks down this concept further, stating:

> Critical reflection addresses the question of the justification for the very premises on which problems are posed or defined in the first place. We very commonly check our prior learning to confirm that we have correctly proceeded to solve problems but becoming critically aware of our own presuppositions involves challenging our established and habitual patterns of expectation, the meaning perspectives with which we have made sense out of our encounters with the world, others, and ourselves (p.4).

This critical reflection is different from only presenting new material; promoting such thinking requires shepherding students' thinking toward the explicit challenging of their previous assumptions. The critical aspect challenges dominant or accepted truths, and the reflection aspect locates the focus on the self. All the participants demonstrated this practice of fostering a continual challenging of what is previously learned among their students.

Eyrún noted that while her course content doesn't focus on identity, she invites students to challenge the hegemonic conception of what it means to be "Icelandic" and what this means as they consider their own identity:

> I've been reading about it, but it's not my focus: the identity issue. But it always comes up. You know, it always comes up in discussion because it's really a really big issue. So, it always comes up in discussion: who are you and what do you want to be? Are you Icelandic once you've settled here or are you not. And how do you want to see yourself?

In a similar way, Hanna asks students to be critically reflective: "Yeah it is about I think [pauses] basically all that we are, you know, talking about whatever that is. If it is [a] supervised meeting, or in the teachings maybe – what I point out, try to point out is being aware of your own views and being critical of yourself all of the time." Both participants encourage students to be more consistently aware of their perceptions and presuppositions from prior learning, and this gets at the heart of the teaching practice of critical reflection.

As an example of direct evidence, one of Brynja's syllabi has a section that assesses students' reflexivity and critical analysis. Erla also states in one of her syllabi that a course objective is to "[i]nvestigate or explore how your own cultural identity has been formed through communication." In a reaction paper which she assigns, Erla asks students to consider what personal experiences they may have had that intersect with issues of race and power, which may challenge previous assumptions about the significance of these aspects of identity. In addition to these documents, during the observations of teaching, many of the participants frequently ask students to connect the concepts discussed in class to their own experience. Hanna asks students in her master's-level teaching class to consider how culture impacts their classroom and the shifting societal demographics. These discussions challenge what the students previously understood about the "correct" methods for teaching pupils after learning about experiences and realities from the instructor but more importantly their peers.

Helping students understand global connections. Practices encouraging critical reflection discussed above are centered on helping students explore assumptions, identity, self and their own culture. The teaching practice of guiding students toward considering their global connection is an extension of such critical reflection. While this can also help students to reflect self critically, the primary focus of this practice is creating awareness with students about how they and their communities intersect with the wider world. Terry provides a grounding for this practice, asserting that his goal in teaching is to help students widen their perspectives, "I want more understanding in the world than there is in many cases. That people are not just thinking 'me' but they're realizing the role they have to play in the world as a whole." Participants provided some examples as to how this approach is translated as a specific practice in the classroom.

Brynja spoke about how she uses documentary films detailing world issues to situate her students' personal choices and actions into a wider context. In this example, the film she discusses presents some negative ramifications of globalization for peoples in parts of Ghana, where obsolete technology is dumped coming from mostly Western countries:

> I had then shown them - Journeyman Pictures does a whole series of them stuff around the world on a variety of different issues and one of them that they do is the [...] the technology dumps in Africa that are on fire and poisoning people and killing people and poisoning the ground water and people are trying to make livings off of this and I show them short video clips of these - very depressing things and, and they sit there and they're sort of stunned and they think well what can we do? And I say, well one of the things that you can do is not buy a phone every two years, you don't really need new phone every two years. Or you need to think about if you are going to get a new phone, what are you going to do your old phone?

Even while the material presented engages students cognitively, Brynja also highlights the affective impact of using such material in her classes. The content of the film paints a picture of life and the impact of consumerism that is new for many students. Using this film as part of her IaH teaching practice also creates space in the classroom to address intersections between intercultural competence, environmental sustainability, and human rights. Brynja notes that she takes such material and applies it to the students' daily existence by challenging students to consider their current behavior and future choices in concrete and tangible ways that could help reduce technological waste. She also teaches using other examples of negative impacts of particularly Western consumerism, including materials which depict the poor labor practices and conditions of technology companies in certain countries.

These teaching practices focus on engaging students primarily through cognitive modes of teaching. They support the development of international or intercultural competencies, including fostering critical thinking and reflection about themselves and the world around them. While many teaching practices in the remaining three clusters are also leveraging cognitive learning, these other clusters represent a reframing of teaching practices toward categories of specificity or aim.

Teaching practices of experiential or affective learning cluster

Some of the teaching practices in the second cluster pivot away from dominant cognitive modes of engagement in the classroom, toward modes and activities that attempt to provide experiential and affective learning. Others leverage cognitive processes to move students toward being able to emotionally engage with the material, such as understanding the global impact of their choices. They are all connected by the thread of bringing course material to life and helping students experience difference. The teaching practices of IaH in this cluster include using affective or experiential teaching methods and encouraging active intercultural engagement.

Table 3 Practices of Experiential or Affective Learning

	Brynja	*Erla*	*Eyrún*	*Hanna*	*Terry*
Using affective or experiential teaching methods	x	x		x	x
Encouraging active intercultural engagement	x	x		x	x

Using affective or experiential teaching methods. Many participants describe in-class exercises designed to elicit an emotional reaction from students, to then explore these reactions to challenge their perceptions, attitudes, or behaviors. Affective or experiential learning can be difficult work for students, and yet it is central in developing intercultural competence, an important part of any IaH effort. Brynja and Erla spoke about their use of simulations or activities meant to have students experience the frustrations that can come with miscommunications across cultures. These are intended to increased students' empathy and understanding. Brynja for example, uses the activity Barnga in her classes. This "card game" is designed for groups of students to play together, in silence after being given a rules sheet. They are required to use only non-verbal communication. After a short time of learning the rules and playing, a few students from each group are moved to another table and continue play but each original group learned using slightly rules. When participants change tables, students are playing with multiple sets of rules which leads to a breakdown in game play. Using this activity during my observation, Brynja drew the parallels to cultural rules at play during intercultural interactions. During the debrief, she later commented that her Icelandic students have a very difficult time with not being able to talk. It was clear as an observer that students found the exercise very challenging.

Erla spoke about another well-known intercultural simulation activity, Bafa Bafa, that she uses to help students experience challenges in cross-cultural communication and understanding. In the simulation, students are divided into two groups, with each group gathering in a different room. Here, the two groups of students are given cultural rules to follow when communicating which are significantly different. These rules may or may not be aligned with the students' own cultures, but the intent is to internalize, and role play with these new rules for the simulation. Each group then sends emissaries to the other group attempting to learn about that culture. However, the differences in cultural rules make ascertaining information challenging. When talking about the simulation, Erla focuses on the importance of students experiencing the uncertainly of communicating with those who are playing another "synthetic" culture, even though it is a controlled classroom exercise:

> It's always fun because students don't know what to expect you know. You divide the class into two different cultures: a & b, alpha, beta. And I had one student in my class to train the other half of the class, you know they go to a different classroom and you know the game. And I love that, and enjoy they enjoy it too, going through the uncertainty.

This simulation allows Erla to draw parallels between what happened during the activity and real-life cross-cultural communication. This simulation is designed to bring awareness to students about their own behaviors and lays a foundation for how to understand and navigate new cultural environments and interactions. The advantage of such simulations is that the cultural rules can be talked about explicitly in the debrief. While Erla teaches coursework in intercultural communication which lends itself to such activities, this simulation could be adopted in courses from a wide range of disciplines such as business or nursing to help others better understand culture.

Participants also mentioned teaching practices that get students to gain new perspectives through specific assignments or exercises that have students go out and purposefully observe the world around them through different lenses using concepts discussed in class. While these practices detailed below may also trigger affective learning, the experience itself is the primary focus rather than the emotions from the experience. Brynja, for example, has students go out an observe how Icelanders interact with immigrant populations in everyday situations:

> They opened my eyes to things I didn't even know where here. Even just very basic things like, what I mentioned yesterday about when you're talking to somebody that's not Icelandic. They either switch directly into English or raising your voice, which is a very simple example. Once I use it and then send them out and say "ok, now I want you to spend the rest of the week until you come back to me again and see how many times this happens to you" or that it happens around, the students will come back and they'll report "I never noticed this before," "this is amazing," "why do people do this?"

Brynja notes that she often uses this teaching practice of getting students to experience their surroundings in new ways. Through such directed investigations, students start questioning what else they might be missing around them. More in line with goals of IaH, these experiences also help students home in on challenges of cross-cultural interactions as well as issues of power and inclusion.

In a similar way, Terry talks about how his Performance Studies course challenges students to think about their identity and position in new ways. He talked about an assignment where he asks students to look at people's gestures and other behaviors as performance in everyday contexts:

> The Performance Studies course messes the way they look at the world up. I'll send them out and say, ok, we've been looking at gesture and everything now go up to the coffee place upstairs and analyze this lot and they'll say at the end of the course it just messed up their life; they can't go anywhere without looking at the performances that are taking on around them and the way adverts are using semiotic ways to get them to do things.

Encouraging students to look at the world as performance, provides a basis for comparative analysis of how culture impacts these daily performances which Terry often leverages in his classroom. For both examples above of experiential learning teaching practices of IaH, the heightened awareness of the role of culture can provide students with new perspectives on how it informs human interactions on moment-by-moment basis. Moreover, these teaching practices can help students gain insight on their own personal, often unconscious, behaviors.

Encouraging active intercultural engagement. One of the important aspects of intercultural learning is experiencing difference through interacting with cultural others. This practice could be considered an extension of experiential learning from above, but with a specific focus on the students' own personal interactions with people from other cultures. Jones and Killick (2013) note that cultural difference (broadly speaking) exists in all classrooms, even in domestic groups of students as they come from a variety of backgrounds and experiences. Erla noted how in her research methodology classes of 300-400 students, she often has students from different linguistic and cultural backgrounds which can create some communication issues during small group work:

> So, there are a lot of foreigners and now even more than ever before in this small tiny nation and a lot of immigrants so there are issues when they are working in groups because of the language barrier or miscommunication because of different backgrounds or things like that. So, I oftentimes call them together as a group into my office and let everybody a round-about fashion and discuss how do you feel about this and how do you feel, so one at a time. So, I think just my experience helps in a way because as I said before, if you experience something you learn it more.

Rather than addressing the entire class, or just asking students to work through the communication issues individually, Erla actively creates a learning space in her office for students in mixed small groups to discuss and reflect on their differences. Getting students to engage with each other in reflective discussion is a teaching practice that allows for facilitated conversation about intercultural dimensions that can affect group work.

Erla also spoke of teaching practices that she employs to get students to engage in intercultural interactions with culturally different people outside of the university. One such practice connects discussion points from class about cultural differences to the students' real-world interactions. Erla describes how she encourages or assigns students to visit various festivities or events and talk with people from those target cultures about their experiences and culture, as she explains here:

> Well, if we have been covering for example a specific country like we do in intercultural class and if they've been talking about verbal and non-verbal communication, I ask them if they can add something to that so when they go to those events, they talk to people who are maybe Japanese, ask them about it just so they can tie it into what I'm teaching, to make sense of the concepts I'm teaching so I try to bring them to life.

There are other examples in the data as well. Hanna and Erla encourage students to join conferences with a culturally diverse group of participants. Hanna noted, for example, that some of her students attended the Learning Spaces conference that brought together scholars and practitioners from a variety of countries and backgrounds to learn and discuss their findings. Based on observation data from the conference, many students from UI interacted with attendees from other countries and attended their sessions. Terry mentioned several times throughout the interviews how he tries to direct students toward conducting more research on immigrant populations in Iceland, which ostensibly would include direct interaction with members of those communities.

Experiential and affective learning are distinct from the dominate cognitive modes of learning as the primary goal is to experience difference itself rather than solely analyzing the experiences or perspectives of others. While cognitive processes are still an essential part of this learning in order to dissect and evaluate the experience or emotions, the learning entry point is unique.

Practices of course design cluster

The third cluster of IaH teaching practices includes those practices that relate to design elements in courses, specifically what categories and sorts of examples are used in the classroom. The overlap with previous clusters is palpable, as previous examples certainly included elements of course design, whether cognitive or affective in nature. However, this cluster is a reframing of the analysis of these practices, focusing on culture and internationalization as well as the different categories of comparative examples used in designing lessons or discussions. The practices included in this cluster are labeled: Using comparative international examples, events or phenomena; using local events, experiences or culture; using others' individual experience or stories; and bringing in authentic Self. The final practice discussed here of participants bringing in their authentic Self, is included here as they are presenting experiences from their own lives as examples.

Table 4 Practices of Course Design

	Brynja	*Erla*	*Eyrún*	*Hanna*	*Terry*
Using comparative international examples, events or phenomena	x	x	x	x	x
Using local events, experiences or culture	x		x	x	x
Using others' individual experience or stories	x	x	x	x	x
Bringing in authentic Self	x	x	x	x	x

Many of the elements of course design discussed below are intended to help students see beyond the confines of their own experience. Erla sums up this intension by commenting that not all students have lived abroad or have had the opportunity to go through the process of cultural adaptation:

> [...] But if you haven't been through the experience, you have to use a different approach, and you have to use more documentaries, more examples, more video clips, whatever. So, you have to work harder because you have to explain everything more specifically [...].

The experiential learning discussed in the previous section is not always available for students. Thus, in place of such real-life experience that cannot be replicated in the confines of a controlled classroom, the participants employ examples and stories as tools to encourage students to critically engage with what they haven't yet experienced. These categories of examples or narratives are used by participants then as starting points or context for discussing difference.

Using comparative international examples, events or phenomena. All the participants use comparative international examples in their teaching and often extensively. Some noted specifically how the perspectives on these examples come from non-Icelandic scholars or sources, rather than from the participants' own understanding. Syllabi from participants, for example, reveal a variety of reading material from various international sources. Erla uses issues of race in the United States and the intersections between race and intercultural communication. In the same way, Brynja discusses examples of race in the United States, but uses comparative examples from Scandinavia, France, United Kingdom and a variety of Southeast Asian countries as she finds strong stereotypes from her students about U.S. Americans, which makes the material harder to relate to even though her students expect U.S. comparisons.

Eyrún gave an example of how she discusses the child-rearing practices from different parts of the world with her students and how these practices are culturally informed. Hanna shows slides of Istanbul in the past and present as an example of multiculturalism in historical context and Terry brings into classroom discussions about folklore, performance, or religion from African, Sámi, Native American, Gaelic, or Russian traditions. In addition to these concrete examples, Terry provides a broader statement of how he includes such comparative examples in all his courses:

> Well, they do in the courses that I've taught which are all, which are all cross-, multicultural to a large extent. Yeah, I don't think there's any course that I teach which is purely Icelandic and even when I'm teaching an Icelandic course I'm comparing it to other countries and other cultures, I've had students noting this when I'm referring, in Old Norse the Sámi and Native American, Africa, things that I know of. So, of course, it has a role to play on the courses that I teach [...].

While it could be argued that Terry's academic disciplines lend themselves to comparative analysis, courses about Iceland itself, for example, could be taught with firmly domestic parameters where the focus is squarely on Icelanders. However, as he notes here, he intentionally brings in examples from other traditions to highlight the differences and international perspectives.

Other examples include the participants' use of current international events or phenomena as a context for discussing difference and international perspectives.

Brynja stated that she incorporates diverse perspectives through current events from the news into her class to help students make real-life connections with material in class:

> You know, but I always bring it back around or I or I will read the newspaper in the mornings or you know, I'll watch the news at night and I'll say, "hey did you read this, did you see this, you know this is connected to what this is" and then, you know, and then I'll bring it [. . .].

Brynja does not clarify whether the sources of her information are Icelandic or international, but the articles and stories are about international events and from a variety of sources. Given her multi-lingual background, it is likely that the sources are a mixture of both as many of her course readings are.

Using local events, experiences, or culture. Another practice in this cluster is when participants include aspects of Icelandic culture as examples in the classroom; examples from Icelandic society are meant to help students become more aware of behaviors and struggles in society. Again, Brynja spoke about how she uses examples of local culture in her classroom: "Yeah I use a lot of examples about Icelandic society if I can, you know, if I think they're relevant and stuff because, it helps these students understand where they're at. It also helps the students that live here and are maybe marginalized themselves." In presenting points about Icelandic society Brynja highlights aspects of Icelandic culture to the international students who are still learning how to navigate a new cultural context. She also notes that domestic students from recent immigrant backgrounds in her class may identify with the issues these examples raise as they themselves can marginalized in a cultural context they are already well aware of.

Hanna also brings in local culture as a discussion point. During the classroom observation, Hanna and her assistant instructor asked the graduate students in the class to discuss,"hverra manna ertu?", loosely translated as, "who are your people?" a very culturally layered question. This question has long been used among Icelanders to help identify each other's family heritage. As Iceland has historically been so homogenous and uses patronymics (and occasionally matronymics) in place of family names, detailing kin or which larger family one's ancestors are from, provides significant insight to someone's heritage and status.

The students reacted passionately to this question and what it means for questions of inclusivity and Icelandic culture. Those coming from recent immigrant backgrounds do not have this deep socio-cultural capital which creates another level of disadvantage and struggles for integrating into their new home. Bringing this question into the classroom then helps students reflect and be aware of Icelandic culture in new ways.

Using others' individual experience or stories. The teaching practice of using others' individual experiences or stories is another strategy for illuminating a difference or a different perspective. This practice centers on relating or eliciting more holistic stories and experiences from individuals, rather than isolated examples of a cultural behavior or action. For example, Brynja stated how she uses stories that she knows of which are about someone's experience with intercultural interactions. Other participants use this teaching method to create space for students to tell their own stories. Eyrún noted that she creates opportunities for discussion in the classroom. Her older students often recount experiences regarding their own bias or assumptions about multicultural issues or difference which "can be really valuable, that can really broaden the horizon, can really open up the discussion."

While each of the participants employ individuals' stories or experiences, Erla uses this practice most extensively. She spoke about using others' stories in the classroom as a tool for helping students see another perspective. Some of these stories Erla brings in from her research, transcripts from interviews with Palestinians who had come to Iceland and their experiences prior to arrival, presenting unique international perspectives of difference and experiences rather than her own interpretation. Other stories are through documentary films as she comments here:

> [...] so, in my teaching for example, I always try to bring like you in my classroom and I show documentaries or bring some real-life stories and have students study it and go in depth and learn something from that story or. And most of those documentaries are the truth - true stories. So, I think if you learn instead of teaching so many chapters in intercultural communication I think that's not as powerful as just taking a few real-life stories or people's experiences and go into, delve into them and have them take something and learn.

Here Erla presents a qualitative difference between textbooks and stories about actual experiences from the individual's own voice. Textbooks present material from a theoretical perspective, discussing approaches and categories of while in-depth stories can provide significant context, with the nuance and complexity that comes with real-life intercultural communication. Erla also comments how such stories are not just taken at face value, but that she has her students study them analytically and in-depth.

Bringing in authentic self. The final practice in this cluster is around the participants' authentic Self. The concept of authenticity in teaching is discussed in the next chapter as an aspect of participants' own growth and learning. However, such authenticity is also an IaH teaching practice. Data reveal that participants engage in this practice by bringing in their authentic Self into the classroom through stories from their own experiences. These personal examples are readily available to the instructors and present the students with a model to consider their own critical reflection. Brynja provided one of the more salient examples by talking with her students about her own assumptions have been challenged:

> If I'm gonna talk about racism and our implicit – our implicit biases, I usually start with myself because [...] I know that I come across as relatively open and cross-cultural and all of that, but I think that it's really important for them to understand that even people that are aware can automatically have biases and I use a very relevant example from my own data collection and my dissertation where I had this moment of awaking on how I was defining the study population that I was studying and I was realizing that the literature was wrong in how they talk about multi-ethnic, multi-racial students because most of it is focused on Black and White, or Asian and White and I go into a school and I had a conversation with one of the students and his cousin comes through the lunchroom and I - this is the example I give – and I say I really wish I could interview so and so because he's just an interesting person, and but he doesn't fit into the categorization of multi-racial. And the student looks at me funny and says "what do you mean, he's African-American and Native-American", but he looked so African-American to me, that I didn't make that connection and I sat there and I just sort of looked at him and I was I super embarrassed and it made me re-define how I looked at a population that I thought I knew something about.

Brynja purposefully includes her own experience in the classroom as a method of demonstrating how bias can impact perceptions. She also provides insight into the complexity of race and ethnicity in the United States, which her Icelandic students likely do not have access to. This sort of authenticity is often challenging to present because it creates a sense of vulnerability for the instructor. However, such openness on this topic can also impact students who may be more willing to actively question their own assumptions and bias around race, ethnicity, or culture. This is particularly important because these concepts are closely connected in Iceland, which does not traditionally have a diverse population in these areas.

Participants use various categories of examples in designing their courses to deliver intercultural or international learning. These practices detailed in this cluster range from the instructor's own personal and individual experiences to examples of local or international phenomena. While again, not all these categories are discrete, the data reveal that there are levels of specificity in the types and source of examples informing internationalized learning.

Practices of diversity and inclusion

This last cluster incorporates examples of teaching practices that intersect with previous clusters including cognitive engagement and experiential learning. This cluster brings together practices that are around a single theme of diversity and inclusion rather than a specific mode of learning or source of examples. Some of these practices are on intentionally including forms of diversity such as linguistic, cultural, cognitive, and ethnic or racial into teaching. The data reveal three different distinct teaching practices for this cluster including: Supporting and including non-dominant voices or identities; incorporating immigrant or multicultural issues; using multiple and diverse teaching methods; and finally, purposeful facilitation of interaction between diverse students.

Table 5 Practice of Diversity and Inclusion

	Brynja	*Erla*	*Eyrún*	*Hanna*	*Terry*
Supporting and including non-dominant voices or identities	x	x	x	x	x
Incorporating immigrant issues	x	x	x	x	x
Using multiple and diverse teaching methods and practices	x	x	x	x	x
Purposeful facilitation of interaction between diverse students	x	x			x

Supporting and including non-dominant voices or identities. The first teaching practice of IaH in this cluster is encapsulated in the phrase "inclusion of non-dominant voices or identities." One of the ways that this teaching practice is carried out is through supporting diverse identities that may not have the same access as dominant voices or identities. Another aspect of this practice is creating space for marginalized, non-dominant or diverse students for them to lend their own voices. Some examples of this practices come from participants who encourage diverse students in their classroom to engage in discussion or classroom activities. During the classroom observations, there were several examples of students from racially and ethnically diverse backgrounds sitting alone or on the margins of the classrooms. Participants made conscious and skillful efforts to elicit their input on discussions, without tokenizing or forcing their engagement. Eyrún purposefully supports international students or students from recent immigrant backgrounds through extra office time or similar accommodations. In another example, Brynja attempts to get diverse students from the International Education Studies program more connected at conferences and with social media groups to increase their involvement and reduce marginalization.

Terry explains how he creates space for students in his courses to comment on their own cultural norms or beliefs as well as their observations of Icelander's habits. In this passage, he talks about conversations in the classroom about identity and performance in a class that has a mixture of international and domestic students:

> What I mean for example just simply talking about the way people perform in daily life with their hands and their gestures and the foods that the present to people. Having, for example, Greeks when that [tilts head side to side] means "yes." And the problems that come up in communication physically. The way that we react as we move between countries, learn rules of behavior at the dinner table. So, you get more voices coming in. Which they quite like, and they also like watching hearing other students comment on how Icelanders perform, how they see themselves with the guest's eye, which is the Icelandic expression to see with the guest's eye that the guest tends to see things more objectively than the people at home.

Here, Terry points out how his goal is to bring more voices in, from diverse students about their own or other cultures or reflecting their own culture through artistic performance. Students from diverse backgrounds then can relate aspects of their own culture to a larger group of students, affirming their own identity and elevating voices that might not be heard otherwise.

In another example, Hanna purposefully structures group work so that students who may have different skills can still equally participate. She responded to a question about how she engages in international or multicultural activities by talking about cooperative learning as a device for inclusivity in the classroom. Hanna arranges roles in the group so that students who are international or come immigrant backgrounds still have an equal responsibility in the group work:

> Yeah, so that would mean for example, organizing group work that is well-structured so that everyone has an important role to play, so it's not only about group work

> it's about um, giving everyone a certain task and responsibility. So, it's really – we have developed a special way of doing this from a European project that I used to take part in where we organized cooperative learning particularly for multicultural groups as we called it then. So that was really to make sure that people that don't have for example, fluent knowledge in the language would be engaged anyway so they wouldn't be marginalized. So, when I can, I try to practice this. Especially when I know that there are some people that don't have the majority language, […] Icelandic, that we teach in. So, yeah. So, just keeping that in mind all of the time, how can I make sure that everyone is involved.

Hanna's master's-level classes in education are chiefly in Icelandic. As seen during the classroom observation, some students from recent immigrant backgrounds speak Icelandic well enough to be in the course but may not have the same fluency as native speakers. Therefore, students who feel less confident of active language skills in Icelandic, can take another role, which reduces marginalization.

Finally, although more of a practice of curriculum and program design, the very existence of the International Studies in Education program in the School of Education is also intended to encourage and give voice to the marginalized and non-dominant. Two of the participants are involved in this program: Hanna was one of the original founders of the program and Brynja is a key instructor. The curriculum, which informs daily teaching practices, is built around education in a globalized context and includes foundational coursework on education in multicultural societies with course titles such as: Comparative Education; Development and Self; Sociology and History of Education: Iceland in the Community of Nations; and, Globalisation and Education (University of Iceland, 2018).

There are several ways that this International Studies in Education program can be considered a practice of inclusivity. First, the program is the only bachelor's degree offered completely in English at the UI. This provides increased access to university for students from immigrant backgrounds who have sufficient skills in English, but not enough Icelandic to complete other coursework. Second, as a ramification of the coursework being offered in English, this program frequently includes domestic Icelandic students from non-immigrant backgrounds, Icelandic students from immigrant backgrounds, and international students. The classroom is then one of more diverse students, allowing for greater exposure to different student perspectives and voices. Finally, Brynja noted that for her, this program is related to supporting the growing immigrant population in Iceland, directly or indirectly.

Incorporating immigrant issues. As pointed out previously, there is a strong intersection between questions of inclusion and the immigrant population in Iceland. Many of the participants who are champions of IaH are strongly influenced by social justice which translates into incorporating immigrant issues into their coursework and classroom, even when the topic is not explicitly about those questions.

There are numerous examples of participants bringing in immigrant issues from Iceland into the classroom. Brynja, Erla, Eyrún and Hanna all bring in current research or knowledge on cross-cultural interactions between people of recent immigrant background and traditionally domestic Icelandic people or systems into the classroom. Brynja and Hanna for example talk about heritage language learners and what is being done to improve access in the schools, while Eyrún states that she brings research in how children from recent immigrant backgrounds in Iceland navigate the school system and the barriers to their social or economic advancement.

Pivoting away from examples of this teaching practice related to children and their education, Brynja and Erla also both talk with students about issues of brain waste for immigrants to Iceland. Erla even brings this research about immigrants and refugees into courses on other subjects, "Even in my Methodology class. I talk about, because it's research, I talk about what I do, what my object is, goal is to understand, now that we have a lot of refugees, not a lot compared to the U.S. but compared to a small nation, we are increasing number like 10% are immigrants." While not all courses lend themselves to discussing refuges, this intentional inclusion of such issues in a course exemplifies how intercultural learning and development can integrated and infused across disciplines along with more traditional content.

Not only does Brynja also include these issues in her classroom, she also leverages examples from current events to highlight the relevance and immediacy of the struggles refugees in Iceland face. In this quote, Brynja talks about how she purposefully chooses these examples so that she can create a dialogue in class where students feel like they have more context to discuss:

> We're all localized in our understanding of, of our reality until we start having those global experiences and thinking of them in that way. So, I try to draw that out of them and have them look at what's going on around them. I do it a lot with [...] dialogue around immigrants, because that's a big deal right now. I mean I don't know if you've

> been following the papers, but I mean I think every day for the last two weeks there's been something on the refugees situation. That Albanian family that didn't get refugee status and is being sent home. There was a Syrian family that came from Greece that is being sent back to Greece because it's "safe" in Greece. So, there's this whole very racialized dialogue that isn't racialized here.

Using current and local happenings as examples can magnify their struggles for some Icelandic students who may not understand the impact of the crisis on people in their own community. Brynja also attempts to generate a new conversation about the racialized nature of refugees and immigration that she believes is currently missing, raising awareness in these students about power and race.

As a final example of this teaching practice of incorporating immigrant issues, Terry talked about an article he wrote stemming from research on the Vietnamese community in Iceland. This article is now required reading for new students at the university, although he doesn't specify, likely in certain fields, "I know, in all the courses for the beginning students, that they all have to read this article on the Vietnamese. So, it's become sort of – and other courses I think it's being used as well. But as a way of teachers introducing the subject that this is an area of Iceland that needs to be known about."

The results of this research, attempting to humanize a marginalized population in Iceland, then impacts teaching practices of inclusion and diversity beyond his own classroom. This effort adds to the IaH activities on campus as other courses have incorporated this reading into their curriculum. It also provides some blueprint that other champions could emulate to help forge progress on IaH at UI through their own research.

Using multiple and diverse teaching methods and practices. Including multiple and diverse methods and practices is a teaching practice of diversity and inclusion related to IaH as such varieties of teaching methods may allow students from minoritized backgrounds to recognize their identities or cultures more readily when teachers present diverse perspectives. Additionally, multiple and diverse teaching methods and practices also allow for more engaged learning from those with cultural (Gay, 2013), linguistic or other forms of diversity (Brookfield, 2015) who may be less familiar or engaged with only traditional teacher-centered lectures. As an informant in CTL noted, the rationale for encouraging multiple and diverse teaching methods and practices was informed by the increasing awareness of student diversity in classrooms. Although there is still a culture of using teacher-centered lecture-based classes at UI, there is a growing shift away from this model because of greater inclusion of diverse students is represented by these participants. Several of the participants had illuminating statements during their interviews on their use of multiple methods in the classroom:

> Hanna: So, I think what I learned also was to try to use like multiple methods so that each student will find something suitable for them in each class. So I try to mix methods and I try to keep the students occupied with conversation and so on, because I mean, lecturing? I really finished lecturing a long time ago because very few people really think that this is useful.

> Eyrún: I think, well, because different students need different... Yeah, that's because, students are different, they have different needs, they learn in a different way, some people like to listen, some people just zone out and are gone in five minutes, so they like to do hands-on. So, I'm just trying to get everybody active in some way by using different methods.

Eyrún went on to state that she often uses two or three different methods or approaches in any given class, to make sure that students from diverse backgrounds have maximum opportunity to engage with the material.

As a more in-depth example, some of the use of multiple teaching methods comes in the form of incorporating multi-media in the classroom followed by class discussion. Terry talks about how he uses a lot of "YouTube moments from around the world" in his classes. Erla uses documentaries extensively. One film Promises (2003) is a documentary detailing the Israeli-Palestinian conflict through the eyes of a number of children from both groups. Hanna uses several short videos about race relations from a minority perspective. One of these videos, available on YouTube is titled "What Kind of Asian Are You" (2013), which is a comedic portrayal of how Asian-Americans in the United States are questioned about their heritage, often with little cultural sensitivity or understanding. Both examples of using multi-media occurred during the classroom observations and students.

Other examples from the data of using multiple or diverse methods include utilizing small group work, structured debates between groups of students, in-class reaction papers, student-driven discussions and student presentations. Some instructors noted that they will modify or update the syllabus based on student input and need. As discussed above, several instructors also use simulations or experiential learning. Eyrún, for example, provided a syllabus that includes details about the variety of formats the class period takes including: lectures, discussion, group project work or individual work on smaller projects.

The use of multiple methods extends to graded assignments as well. One of Brynja's syllabi included a group project, a group presentation, a final paper completed as individual work, and a final presentation in which the student has to present to the class in addition to the seminar and lecture style in-class format. While not all these methods were used in the same class period, data from classroom observations, syllabi, and interviews reveal that multiple methods are frequently used by the participants throughout their teaching and that most methods are not predominantly teacher-driven lectures.

Purposeful facilitation of interaction between diverse students. Participants provided several examples of practices of inclusion in their teaching. Some of these examples were about bridging the rural/urban divide in Iceland. UI is in the capital city and many post-secondary students living in more rural areas of the country have difficulty accessing educational opportunities in their home region. Both Terry and Hanna talked about their efforts around distance learning for those outside of the capital region, who are also often less privileged and have less access to resources. Hanna video tapes some lectures and Terry is looking into scaling up something akin to massive open online courses to reach these students.

Again, the reoccurring theme of language is also apparent in teaching, in this case, as a practice of inclusion and specifically, of facilitating interaction between diverse students. Brynja and Erla using language choice as a means to create spaces for offering classes in English, both to increase access and also to provide a space for international and domestic students to interact. Throughout the interviews, Terry was particularly attentive to how language is used in the university and the classrooms, specifically English and Icelandic. One of his practices is to encourage multilingualism in the classroom, letting Icelandic students speak in either Icelandic or English, even though he lectures in English:

> [...] my way of doing it, at least, is to allow them to ask questions in their own language so they don't feel any form of inferiority cause it's one thing communicating in a small group it's another thing speaking in English front of 50 people, this is uncomfortable it's embarrassing and people might even laugh at you. And the Icelanders are very, have a strong sense of shame and honor which goes back to Viking times and they don't like being made a fool of and they'd rather just shut up and do that. So, internationalization on that side is a

> matter of making them more able to function by understanding at least and having a few courses at least taught in English.

Although Terry teaches many classes in English as an important method of including certain international students who do not have the ability to speak Icelandic, he also allows for those who may not be able or comfortable with expressing themselves in English to the same degree they could in Icelandic. Terry also usually translates the question from Icelandic, into English for the benefit of the students who do not speak Icelandic. The syllabi for such courses are also bilingual. In this way, such courses benefit domestic and non-Icelandic speaking international students, increasing the inclusivity and raising the odds that domestic students will take a course in English which they may not consider otherwise because of the flexibility of language. This provides a more open venue for discussion and interaction between those who speak Icelandic and those who do not.

Another version of this teaching practice of facilitating interaction between diverse students is through cross-cultural collaborative distance learning. Erla teaches a course where her students were paired up with students at Arizona State University in the United States on a collaborative online international learning (COIL) virtual exchange course titled, "Culture and Workplace Conflict." The students are expected "to exchange at least 10 email messages with your partner and write a short paper together." Such virtual collaboration encourages cross-cultural engagement between students from Iceland and the United States around a structured assignment in purposeful ways that are often logistically challenging at the university itself because there is often not comparable numbers of students from different cultural backgrounds. Rather than small group work which also may include students from a mix of cultural backgrounds, pairing the students up one-to-one translates into more extended interaction between diverse students as well.

This cluster of teaching practices of diversity and inclusion highlights the intersection between IaH and social justice for the participants. Many of the teaching practices include considerations of the more marginalized, less privileged, or non-dominant students on campus, in Icelandic society or globally. The commonality with the other three clusters shows both that teaching practices are complex and can rarely be singularly defined. Clearly diversity and inclusion are an emerging core aspect of IaH and one that is less

Summary

These four clusters of teaching practices provide insight into the granular and everyday strategies that participants employ which are the foundations for IaH in the classroom. It is important to emphasize that not every teaching practice related to IaH could be captured, and it is likely that certain participants engaged in practices listed even if they were not demonstrated in the data collected for this project. Taken together, the clusters and individual practices detailed above present a picture of diverse methods and strategies in the classroom that are used by participants to teach international perspectives and intercultural learning.

Chapter VII: Engaging in Networking and Research Practices of IaH

Modes and content of teaching form a core aspect in the practices of IaH, but there are others which are vitally important. This chapter covers cognate categories of practice including building and maintaining networks, research, and connecting with Icelandic society. These practices connect more strongly with additional faculty roles that include responsibility to society, knowledge cultivation and professional development. After covering these areas, I also extend the discussion toward analyzing the more. This includes discussing the challenges and supports that faculty members find when engaging, what strategies they're using to advance their practices and development as well as what meaning or fulfillment, they gain from being engaged.

Practices of building and maintaining networks

Moving from practices of teaching, another of the key practices of IaH for the participants centers around building and maintaining networks with others. Such relationships should be considered part of faculty members' practices of IaH as their involvement in networks creates opportunities to inform other practices of IaH which more directly impact students and engage with diverse populations. Moreover, it supports continued development and investment in international learning. The examples from the data discussed below center around three different themes: relationships in which participants engage colleagues around learning or sharing about issues of multiculturalism and related practices, engaging in comparative international projects and research, or leveraging international connections to open doors for more student cross-cultural engagement. Often such relationships are with academic peers, but others are outside of the academy.

Some of this networking occurs on campus with peers. Brynja, Eyrún, and Erla all spoke about spending time interacting with colleagues in formal and informal settings where the conversations are on topics or issues of including international students, international education, or inclusivity. Brynja, for example, who is the coordinator for the international education undergraduate program, talked about how authentic engagement on personal and professional issues helps to create more trust with colleagues. This has led to more committee roles and input. She also had an interview with the student newspaper about a talk on brain waste and women during one of the Equality Days events. Erla and Eyrún spoke about how their work is resulting more invitations for lectures and recognition by others on campus of intercultural dimensions or issues. Terry has worked on a committee that concerns international students' access to coursework, and Hanna has been involved in a university-wide committee that is considering the university's response to the Syrian refugee crisis. These examples represent opportunities for participants to connect with others and influence policy and messaging around IaH.

Beyond this relationship work in Iceland, much of the networking is with international colleagues or other connections. Terry spoke about having a network of colleagues who help in marking graduate papers to ensure high quality programs and international perspectives on the academics that these students are producing:

> In the same way I go out of my way when I can with MA marking to get somebody from abroad to read over the essays rather than being done within the country so that we can ensure that the grading and the level of work is of international standard. I think that could be done more often; the trouble is of course when they're writing in Icelandic there aren't so many scholars who can read over this stuff, but I have a network of people that I make use of quite a lot just to keep ensuring that what we see as being as an 8 or 8.5 is higher than an 8.5 or above an 8.5 and the students can feel proud of this too, they know themselves that what they've done means something international.

Terry talks about using his network for quality assurance in the programs that are being taught and the resulting grading, but he frames it as something meaningful for graduate students because of the comparative international nature of this system. At the minimum, this encourages students to think beyond a local scope, to consider a more international mindset, in line with the aims of IaH.

All the participants spoke about networking and relationship building through conferences and research networks. Eyrún, for example, attributes a good deal of her understanding of international perspectives on issues of multiculturalism to her work in a European research network called Children's Identity and Citizenship in Europe. Through this network she was hired as a researcher in a five-country project about on multiculturalism and teacher education. More importantly however, this network focused primarily on improving inclusive pedagogies and developing teaching. The application to the university classroom, even while the focus the network was in primary education settings, is clear. Brynja spoke about a recent conference that she attended where she was able to make connections and gaining cross-cultural experiences that she was not able to when she was studying in the United States.

One particularly salient example of the intersection of IaH and such networks was the Learnings Spaces project, which three of the five participants attended. Hanna developed and led this international comparative project with a number of other researchers in various Nordic countries focused on inclusive pedagogies for multicultural schools. This conference was the culmination of only one of the network-based and collaborative projects she is involved in. As Hanna notes, "so, I mean I'm involved in projects in Nordic countries and European countries and new things keep coming up, so there is an ongoing dialogue all of the time." The importance of this statement is that the conversations stemming from this project are not isolated, but rather more holistic.

Finally, all the participants also mentioned other connections outside of the academy in a variety of countries around the world. Some of these connections were people who participants met while living or traveling abroad, others are former international students who they keep in contact with. A number of the participants stated that some of these people had significant impacts on their understanding of other cultures or difference. Eyrún pointed to her Chinese friend who she learned from while she lived in the UK and Terry noted that a friend in Africa opened his eyes to some of the cultural differences. Erla noted how she is still in contact with former students in Russia, Denmark, Norway, and the United States. While these relationships may not have a direct impact on current students, these continued connections to different people from diverse cultures provides ongoing opportunities for the participants to engage in reflecting about difference and practicing intercultural competence themselves which is necessary for effective engagement in IaH.

Practices of connecting with Icelandic society

Faculty members educating members of the greater public through disseminating research findings around issues of multiculturalism and inclusion can be considered a practice related to IaH. For those engaged in these practices of IaH, there is a reciprocal relationship with faculty members and the community informing and learning from each other. The community provides the context, cultural phenomena, and individual stories that these faculty draw from to inform their work which is often applied back to the community. Such practices ultimately improve both social climate for student learning and university goals around international education. To come back to the example of Terry's research on the Vietnamese population in Iceland, he used the findings as a vehicle to enlighten the greater Icelandic society. Terry leveraged this research to help increase cross-cultural understanding in the society through making his work available to the greater public, saying, "when I published the article, I deliberately published it in the most key Icelandic... cultural journal as a way of breaking down that wall." He went on to say that he was "arguing that these are Icelanders as [much as] anybody else." Not only did Terry publish the results in a venerated national journal for mass consumption, but he also gave public lectures about them, even when the audience was expecting another talk altogether. He related one story about how a community group in Iceland had asked him to talk about the Icelandic elves (often referred to as "the hidden people") and Terry recalled reacting strongly, "I was so pissed off with talking about elves that I said that I'll talk about the hidden people of Reykjavik I'm gonna to look at the Vietnamese. Because nobody knows anything about their culture, they've got community here."

Certain practices of connecting with Icelandic society are also rightly practices of building relationships, but the primary focus is more on providing assistance and help rather than networking. Some of the most significant connections related to IaH that participants have with the greater society are those with local primary and secondary school systems. All three of the participants from the School of Education have worked with local educators in the primary and secondary education system on practices related to multiculturalism and inclusion, whether formally or informally. Again, as IaH is concerned with inclusion and immigrant populations particularly, working in multiculturalism in Iceland This collaboration is in the form of project consulting or training with local teachers and administrators around inclusivity and multiculturalism in their schools or districts. For example, Eyrún related how she was working with teachers at an upper secondary school, talking about how to work with children of non-Icelandic origins. Hanna has worked with a Polish school, an NGO where heritage language is taught and with an association of women of immigrant backgrounds in Iceland. Much of her service work however, has been in the local non-specialized preschools and primary schools in Iceland. Here, Hanna explains how more people are seeing the need for multicultural support and then how she is involved in this work:

> I think for example, the awareness that we're seeing now of multilingual issues, you know. Supporting heritage languages; reaching out to parents and just opening the whole idea of you know, what's going on in the

> schools. How to build bridges between languages on an everyday basis. And I'm talking about real good schools that are developing this. I mean schools that have maybe 80% of children with other mother languages. You know. So, and I feel really, you know, honored to be able to support these schools because they're really doing such good work and many of the school leaders have been in our programs here.

For Hanna, this connection with Icelandic society impacts multiple groups of people, both the students and their parents who may be relying on their children to learn Icelandic to help the family communicate, as well as the teachers who are faced with a large population of non-native Icelandic speaking students. As many of the principals and administrators for these schools have been through the School of Education, this connection is reinforced with trust for the work Hanna and other colleagues are doing in the school system.

Brynja also gave examples of how she engages with local schools as part of service related to practices of IaH. Like Hanna, Brynja is involved in work at schools in an area around Reykjavík that has historically had challenging socio-economic issues with many students who do not speak Icelandic at home. She also gave another example of advising project where she is engaged in applied work with the local community:

> I'm an advisor on a project in a preschool that is doing a project of matching an immigrant family with an Icelandic family for you know, cultural adjustment purposes and when I first got onto it, one of the problems I was having with it and I sort of managed to get people to maneuver around it was that it was framed in the "look at how wonderful the Icelandic family can help this poor immigrant family make it here" and I was like well, there's something else going on there. The Icelandic family will have the opportunity to maybe practice a new language, learn about a new culture that they never knew anything about. It's a two-way street.

Brynja's assistance in this project gave her the opportunity to reorient the approach away from a deficit model for the immigrant families toward a balanced exchange of culture and perspectives that opened cultural doors for both immigrant families as well as Icelandic families. Without her guidance, the project may have been less effective and missed a significant opportunity for intercultural learning. Increases in such intercultural learning strengthens the universities position in the community and creates more opportunities for practices of IaH in the future.

More than any of the other participants, Hanna frequently talked about her work in the field. However, this work in the field also includes connecting with others around education including municipalities and the state government. She noted that this cooperation with the field is "always part of my work" and believes, "that's so important also to keep the relationship between the university and the field and so we don't get lost in publishing you know." She also talked about building relationships with the diverse populations that she writes and conducts research with and about in the field. Her focus is not to take the role of a detached academic, but rather to work collaboratively with others through applied work in the field which is ongoing and developmental. Indeed, Hanna states that she is still learning about:

> ...the importance of cooperating with the people; you know not working on or working, or writing about people, but working with and writing with the people I mean, for example in my case, these diverse populations. So, I think you know, right from the start I realized that you know I really needed to cooperate throughout and not be this isolated academic that many people tend to become. I've been resisting this from the beginning. So, this is both in research and also sort of international cooperation that it's about being involved all the time and not, not working in isolation or writing in isolation so.

Hanna is certainly referring to cooperation with practitioners and academics internationally in this passage. However, she starts by talking about "working and writing with the people" which is addressed to those communities she is investigating. Building relationships with and staying connected to these populations affords her the chance to continually be grounded in her work. It also gives her resources to bring into the classroom and as additional engagement opportunities for her students thus informing IaH.

A final mode of connecting with Icelandic society is through media and interviews. Erla and Eyrún spoke of media outlets that were becoming more interested in their research. Local television and print media organizations have increased their interest in hearing about refugees, immigration, and adaption in Iceland. A number of interviews were scheduled or had recently been conducted. Erla also spoke about her work with MARK as mentioned earlier giving more public lectures, creating yet another direct connection with Icelandic society.

Such connections with the public are aimed at reducing prejudice against marginalized immigrant populations or providing direct assistance in implementing practices toward improving inclusivity. This may help foster more equitable social and political conditions leading to greater access and inclusion in the university. These connections between engaged faculty engaged and the society at large demonstrate the impact and importance of a program of IaH which finds a locus at the institution and its members, but intentionally extends to make a broader impact through direct work with the community. This underscores the importance of institutions and individuals intentionally cultivating more faculty engagement, transforming personal and professional perspectives and efforts.

Practices of research

The section above on building and maintaining networks included examples and data about participants engagement in research networks. This section addresses research activities themselves as practices of IaH. When considering IaH broadly, research as an activity itself is rarely mentioned by scholars. This is mainly due to the focus on applied practices of developing intercultural competence and international perspectives in students, often undergraduates. However, when considering the role of faculty and their own practices it is necessary to consider how research may contribute to the development of IaH as a practice of building and maintaining relationships. All the participants are involved in some sort of research related to multiculturalism or international perspectives, through expanding the knowledge about culture, diversity, equity, inclusion, and immigrant populations. Such research is then arguably a practice of IaH itself for academic staff, being the foundation for other, more applied activities.

Eyrún, for example, has researched social adjustment of immigrant children and intercultural education programs. Her research has shown that adolescents from foreign-born parents benefit more from supportive parents than their Iceland-born peers. Erla has looked at cultural adaptation and issues of identity. Erla is expanding her research to look comparatively at those from immigrant populations with university degrees who struggle to find employment. This project focused on interviewing and centering the immigrants' voices in this work. Most of Hanna's work is around questions of diversity and education, recently as part of culturally inclusive learning environments. She has been the leading voice for inclusive education across Iceland's school system with her research leading to deep community connections. Additionally, Brynja has recently conducted research on social justice and democracy in Iceland through the historical lens of ethnic uniformity.

One of the most illuminating examples of participants' research as a practice of IaH is Terry's work on the Vietnamese immigrant population in Iceland. This example has been presented previously, demonstrating how multi-faceted and influential research can be to the various activities in IaH. Terry's goal was decidedly different than the anthropologists who were looking at how this population was adapting to Icelandic culture. He wanted to find out how they were negotiating identity and heritage in a new land asking questions such as, "What do you teach your kids, who teaches the kids, what's the role of this, how much do you keep, especially for people like the Vietnamese?" He went on to talk about his experience connecting with these people through his research:

> It was very revealing going home to these wonderful Vietnamese communities which are just so totally different to anything that I'd seen amongst Icelanders at least. And you realize why Icelanders are frightened. Because the number of peoples, for example, who are coming in and out of the door endlessly...which is so different to Icelanders when one or two come – who are these thirty people are they all staying there, what are they doing there? People are eating and gathering together in large numbers in very different way to the way Icelanders do.

Not only did Terry come to realize potential intercultural tensions between Icelandic and Vietnamese populations, but he also worked to bring others to this understanding through teaching informed by this research. Perhaps most importantly, Terry made sure that these transcripts and data were preserved in the national library, so that future students could continue conducting research using these archives. This additional step allows students and the public access to rigorously collected and recorded data and material about immigrant peoples and their heritage cultures in their own country. Terry continues to encourage more of his students to investigate research topics related to immigrant communities in Iceland.

Given that the participants were identified for this study because of their status as champions of IaH, it is not unexpected that some of their research would directly inform IaH. While academic staff who do not have research areas that align with these topics can still engage in many other practices of IaH, these participants have a more robust array of practices informed by their own research.

Challenges and Support

Although the major thrust of the present study was not focused on understanding the challenges or barriers that academic staff encounter while engaging in IaH, it is beneficial to know something about how they experience this as it is part of the process and important context for the cases. Indeed, while not asked about this explicitly, each of the participants expressed challenges in their work of promoting and engaging in IaH. However, the interviews did include questions about where participants find support when doing such work; what keeps them going. These challenges and supports are discussed below.

Some of the challenges the participants brought up included: logistic barriers within the system, having two physically separate campus, a general de-emphasis of teaching, a lack of awareness of the need for global and intercultural perspectives on campus, and explicit resistance by certain colleagues to adopt practices and activities related to IaH. Several participants, for example, noted that they did not have the power or status to be involved in directing curriculum or teaching to be able to assist in bringing these diverse and global perspectives and approaches into the classroom. Others stated that the had the ability to employ this sort of curriculum but felt very isolated in their work without much support.

One significant challenge that was evident in several responses was the looming specter of burnout. Burnout can be particularly prevalent when a small group of champions are attempting to shift a conversation and resulting action on such an expansive organizational and societal level. Some of the comments participants made were related to the daily work that most academic staff engage in, such as expectations to publish and struggles with balancing teaching and research, finding funding for projects, and similar struggles. However, it is important to remind the reader that these struggles are taking place against the backdrop of the continued effects of the economic collapse in 2008, which impacted faculty members' workload. Other comments were more directly related to raising awareness and making more substantive change. Brynja and Hanna made particularly salient statements regarding burnout. When asked this question about what keeps her from this burnout, Brynja responded:

> [laughter] I don't! I'm really tired! It's hard. I've been going through a really, I mean it's been really rough for the last 6 months. I kind of want to just get up and leave, because it's constant. I feel like I'm constantly fighting somewhere or trying to make sure that people are aware, "do you realize what you just said?" So, it gets pretty exhausting.

Brynja is noting the challenges of being a newer faculty member, but more specifically being one with expertise in areas of inequity and critical scholarship. She feels isolated in calling out the all too frequent spaces, situations and language that (re)produce inequitable environments.

For Hanna, this issue was less immediate, but she encapsulates this potential hazard well stating that:

> [T]he burnout is always just around the corner I can tell you because there's so many tasks and there's so many issues still to be resolved in Iceland and there's so much work and the feeling of drowning is there regularly. [...] I used to be on my own really focusing on this field even though I had colleagues that were interested. It was mostly me like 10-15 years ago.

Here Hanna laments that while the environment and support has improved at the university, burnout is always close by. While Brynja's focus was on shifting attitudes and perspectives in the university proper, Hanna points to her struggles with the burden of tackling issues facing the greater Icelandic society related to inclusion and immigration as well. These perspectives show the range of psychological burdens and challenges engaged faculty carry, from personal care to angst for humanity more broadly.

An important balancing question is then how these faculty members find support in continuing this work considering some of these challenges. When asked about who supports them in their work, answers varied considerably. Some pointed to professional colleagues, personal relationships or even self-reliance as sources.

Terry identifies his support as coming from other scholars outside of UI, rather than anyone internally. The support that he receives is less on logistics or direct questions about engaging in practices of IaH than on relationships fostered through his network:

> We've set up, at least in the Old Norse religion because I have several fields that I work in, one is Old Norse religion, and we meet up annual for small conferences that have come here at some point and we're traveling around - it's a sort of a rolling old Norse religion thunder review. Sounds a lot like Bob Dylan's never ending tour and we talk a lot in pubs when we travel around; we enjoy this, it's healthy and we've developed it in terms of not only meeting for those conferences, but also in guest teaching for each other's departments.

These connections with other scholars outside of Iceland offer Terry opportunities to operate in spaces outside of the university proper, develop working friendships and all the while engaging in internationalizing curriculum through hosting scholars from abroad. In addition, he engages in guest lecturing while abroad. He points specifically to these colleagues in Scandinavian countries and close friend from Kenya.

Others talked about support from internal sources at UI itself. Most of the responses did not point to individuals, but rather general groups of people in certain colleges or areas. Those in the School of Education (Brynja, Eyrún and Hanna) mentioned support from their unit the most. Hanna, for example, points to those people not only supporting her own work, but also coming along and helping to make changes:

> Well, I've been... very lucky to work with a group of enthusiastic people from different subjects within the School of Education, particularly. So, that has also affected me in that so many people from different subject areas are interested. I've worked with different groups but people that are really willing to make an effort to change things.

Her comments here about the willingness of others to create positive change reflect the general increased level of awareness around the university for issues of diversity and inclusion. In turn, this increased level of awareness provides some implicit support for the participants and others who are engaged in related work. Eyrún stated that she felt she had the support of many around the School of Education and those in the Social Science area particularly. Colleagues in the School of Education and Social Sciences ask her to come and present her research findings related to immigrant children. Their interest in her work is a more indirect form of support.

Erla also felt like there are some internal allies at UI supporting her in her work although she also didn't point out any individual. However, she noted that supporters of her work as a larger project were few. She felt that there is a significant amount of room for additional support, pointing to a general lack of support for intercultural learning. Much of this support comes from those people she interacts with already who are interested in such issues. They meet up at lectures and similar events on campus.

Some participants mentioned specific individual relationships as a source of encouragement for continuing this work. Brynja feels that she has support from a close colleague who acts as a sounding board for debriefing interactions with students and other faculty members around complex intercultural and multicultural incidents that arise on a regular basis. This colleague who supports Brynja has had a significant amount of international experience and is also bi-cultural herself. Consistent with the particularly strong impact of her family in her early life, Brynja's brother and son support her through keeping her motivated and authentic in pursing her work in international education. At the time of the interviews, this support was long-distance, as neither of them resided in Iceland.

Strategies to Advance

During the final interview, participants were asked what strategies they would ideally like to implement in the future to further their engagement in IaH-related activities. While the question leads to conjecture, it gave the participants the opportunity and space to consider how to deepen their practices and through this, provided some insight into their thought processes and goals regardless of their realization. Some key strategies participants pointed to were connecting with colleagues, improving or increasing teaching, connecting with student populations, engaging with the public, and increasing attention to research.

Connect with colleagues

The strategy participants most frequently cited to advance their engagement in practices or activities related to IaH was connecting with other colleagues. These connections that participants named included those through research cooperation, collaborations on policy and practice, and advocating. Eyrún and Erla spoke at length about their strategy of collaborating with other colleagues in research, both within and outside of UI. Eyrún was particularly interesting in working with scholars at the UI who were looking at similar issues around immigration and diversity. While she noted that it would be good for her professionally to undertake such collaborations, she also noted that this research would help "get things done" and move the conversation about issues related to multicultural inclusion further. Moreover, she spoke about then leveraging this research to make sure the findings and perspectives were somehow integrated into curriculum.

Hanna and Erla talked about looking for ways to raise the level of awareness and champion the importance of IaH with other academic staff in the university's various schools. Both mentioned that they would like to see colleagues around the university become more interested in engaging in practices of IaH. Neither of these participants however, felt that they had good mechanisms for evaluating whether other faculty members were interested in pushing IaH forward. Without knowing who is interested specifically, their strategy is focused mostly on keeping discussions going about the need for practices of IaH with the schools and other academic staff.

Terry, Erla, and Hanna spoke about connecting with senior administration to have more leverage in advancing larger related projects and policy. Hanna is continuing her strategy of formally commenting on policies and connecting with administrators on the main campus, while other colleagues have mentioned that she is approaching these conversations more openly than she has in the past. Erla commented about her desire to showcase her class as an example of the need for more IaH on campus:

> That's the next step, you know? How can I make them more aware of the importance because they are not in my classrooms. When they see others "ah ha, oh" in my classroom, but I sometimes wish they were there to experience it with me and people are really realizing how much they are taking away from it, the material in the class.

While she does not have a specific action plan of how to accomplish this this, she would like to bring decision makers into her classroom so that they can see the impact that internationalized teaching has on the students. She recognizes that some type of experiential and transformative experience may be a significant catalyst to bring more decision makers on board about the importance of intercultural learning and multiple perspectives on campus. Despite these efforts to make broader changes, Terry and Hanna, who have been in the system the longest, seemed more resigned in their comments about the effectiveness of shifting the culture of a university organization that was slow to change.

Terry and Brynja noted strategies of working with peer collaborators or other staff on campus to move non-research projects forward. These collaborations were more related to public good, whether on or off campus. Terry talked about collaboration with colleagues, but letting others take the lead on a project he started. He asserted that there are other capable academics to whom he could pass on the leadership of his "computers-to-African initiative," if they would be willing to "take the bat," though he would still be "ready to help out and do things with it." Brynja, looked across the entirety of university when considering this strategy of connecting with colleagues that was focused more on results for the home campus:

> I'd like to engage in a sort of multi-disciplinary, inter-disciplinary group that works on internationalization university wide. I mean I think that would be a really rewarding experience both personally and professionally as well as for the University itself.

While all the participants spoke of specific areas where they would like to see advancements, Brynja was the only participant to talk about a more comprehensive strategy for moving internationalization itself, as a bounded project, forward at the university. Again, while there is no specific set of actions to bring this strategy to fruition, the goal exists. As faculty members are the key drivers of internationalization, interest in working in an interdisciplinary group across the campus is a harbinger of advancement for IaH if such a strategy is realized.

Connecting with colleagues is also about advocating: encouraging action through deliberate conversations. One of Brynja's strategies for this is to continue to "show up," mentally and physically, to spaces where these conversations about intercultural issues may not be taking place, but where they are warranted:

> Just being there, being present, saying something, not pushing. Because if I look like I'm pushing an agenda I might get closed out. You know, and it's an important enough of an agenda that I'd rather take it slow.

This strategy calls for thoughtful navigation and interaction in a complex milieu with competing priorities and voices who may see IaH as what Brynja calls an "agenda." Connecting with colleagues in this way then is not the more obvious mutually beneficial collaborations that come from working on co-teaching a course or research. This is a strategy she hopes will continue to influence her colleagues in thinking about the importance of inclusivity, diversity, and intercultural education.

Increase and improve teaching

In addition to the strategy of connecting with colleagues, some participants stated that they intend to increase or improve the amount of teaching they do that includes internationalized perspectives. While many of his research and service projects are also international in their focus, Terry talked specifically about continuing teaching-related projects rather than investing in new efforts as he sees his academic profession winding down. He mentioned continuing teaching international students and taking part in the discussion around what courses his unit should be offering in English.

Other participants stated that they would like to build on current courses or even get more opportunities to teach content that intersects with intercultural communication, diversity, or immigration. Eyrún lamented that she did not have many opportunities yet to teach in the sorts of courses where she felt she could include multiple and diverse perspectives. She also mentioned that it was challenging to get new courses started that would allow her to incorporate her scholarly strengths. Instead, her strategy was then to co-teach or lecture in courses that already exist to add additional perspectives:

> [...] maybe the way is to come, to snuggle into some courses that are still there and change them a little. That's one way to do it. And to maybe implement new perspectives into, into those courses that are, yeah. And perhaps that's ok, I don't know. But I may need to do it, use several means to do this.

Hanna didn't talk about preparing new courses, but like Eyrún, discussed incorporating her research around diversity and culturally sensitive learning into her teaching going forward:

> We are in the process now of implementing the latest project, the Learning Spaces project and this will be implemented in, well in schools and we will try to open it up for our educational systems in all four of the countries, so this is a task that is waiting now, and also, I'll build on this in my teaching in the next years, definitely.

The international perspectives gained from the Learning Spaces project which Hanna headed up are quite significant regarding incorporating inclusive pedagogies for cultural difference. Bringing in their perspectives into her own classroom at UI would continue to add to her students gaining global perspectives in their field of education. Finally, Erla's strategy around her engagement in IaH through teaching was straightforward:

> And also I want to teach more of it because people don't think it's so important. That's really frustrating, I think. They say "Ok that would be interesting to teach intercultural, but we have other classes more important" you know. But if you're even going to be a manager, come on, you're going to have to be able to interact with people all over, even if you never – even if you leave Iceland you still interact with people across the globe. Via the internet, the phone, whatever. So, I think... they see this. That it is actually something that is important. So, I think that's one of my goals as well - or strategies.

Erla went on to say, "I want to change the way I teach, tell more stories, let that be the emphasis: take cases and have, even in the undergrad – undergraduate classes. I want to change it a little bit." While intercultural communication is Erla's area of scholarship, her strategy includes increasing the amount of teaching that she is doing in this area as she also teaches courses on research methods and other topics. Additionally, data from observations and class assignments reveal her courses on intercultural communication include multiple international perspectives as the content itself is not necessarily inherently internationalized. The data show a strong desire and intent to strengthen teaching toward incorporating more globally diverse perspectives and intercultural learning.

Connect with students

It is expected that academic staff who teach continue connecting with students as part of their regular work. However, several participants note that connecting with students outside of the classroom particularly is part of their strategy to advance IaH. Brynja's strategy for advancing her engagement in IaH comes through helping to organize and support multicultural students (many of whom are international). She stated that she has talked with students who would be interested in a multicultural student organization and has offered to be their faculty advisor and is still pushing for this outcome. Beyond this student organization, she also pointed to connecting international students with local students through co-curricular activities such as mixers, involving international students in the School of Education's current student organization or through an extended buddy program where domestic and international students are matched together. This buddy program could then benefit both paired students in intercultural development. She is particularly looking to have more events on the School of Education campus as most of the university-wide international events happen on the main campus.

While Brynja integrates domestic and international students, Eyrún's strategy of furthering her engagement in IaH included bringing more of her students into future research efforts. She is doing this in part to have a larger team working on projects to accomplish more, but also because it would be a significant learning experience for the students to become more aware of the challenges diverse populations face in Iceland. Hanna's strategy is to connect with students at all educational levels, from those in the primary and pre-schools where she does much of her research and consulting as well as students already in the university. While she didn't readily have specifics on what modes or methods she would use, her focus was squarely on students and working with them in teaching new perspectives to eventually move the society to a more tolerant and inclusive environment.

Engage the public

Three of the participants (Eyrún, Erla and Hanna) discussed interacting with the public as part of their strategy to advance their engagement in practices related to IaH. Although such external facing work does not directly focus on students at the university, there is value to support the activities and practices related to IaH. The potential impact of engaging the public is in building tolerance within the society, which could create a better experience for international students coming to campus. More directly, this public engagement may have a positive effect for immigrant and diverse populations in Iceland, helping to create social and economic conditions that lead to more students from these populations to attend the university. Such efforts may not have an immediate or even highly visible impact for IaH on the campus itself, but they are needed for future goals of developing and sustaining IaH in a meaningful and authentic way if we understand IaH to include engaging these populations.

Erla noted that she has been working with entities in the university, arranging more public lectures. These presentations by Erla are around her research topics in intercultural communication which are focused on populations in Iceland. Her goal is not just to conduct the research, but also ensure that the results are disseminated:

> Well I want to take many more interviews. Many – different groups in Iceland, that's one of my goals. I'm taking the two groups: Europe and outside Europe. I want to do more of this. Also, I'm doing um, working with a professor in London in England. And we want to take interviews with people from Africa who have university degree and have a difficult time negotiating with their employer or even getting a job in England, although they have PhDs. So, I'll look at that too. So, I'm not only here in Iceland but I'm there too. And then I want to maybe compare those, I'm doing several or groups of interviews here in Iceland and we're going to do something in London and then compare. So, I'm trying to spread my wings you know. So, work more with others and get more knowledge about it you know. And then I would like to go and discuss it in media as well when I have some research because I think people are now more open to it, more interested.

Erla is talking about research first and foremost. Future comparative studies can give new perspectives and is in and of itself part of developing practices of IaH. However, the piece of engaging with the public comes with increasing the connection with local media to share these results and raise awareness. Eyrún said this as well, saying that she hoped to engage with the media more in the future to draw attention to the issues she researches.

Hanna's strategies to interact with the public include continuing to partner and consult with the school systems in Iceland. This strategy is meant to help implement practices around inclusive pedagogies for diverse and immigrant students who may not have sufficient Icelandic languages skills.

> Well, of course it's very important to, to implement in the field you know, not only to publish or you know, or of course we know that because we know that the publishing world – I mean, we're publishing for each other, we're publishing for other academics. But it's so important to follow up in the schools and for example we can run courses for the teachers; we go into the schools and talk about the findings, discuss with them; support them if they want to develop something further. And we've already planned conference in Icelandic with Icelandic teachers in the Spring following up on the Learning Spaces - and that's another way to reach the field because not many teachers attended the Learning Spaces conference, so. And this we are doing with a teacher's organization so, they are more likely to come there but then also we need to go into the schools. And we have, I mean we have already contacts in many schools that we have been working with, so. That's an important next step is to continue that work. Try to disseminate in that way. And also cooperate. It's not only about disseminating the findings but cooperating and supporting.

This cooperation with local schools is a praxis: bridging theory and application with each informing the other. It involves engaging with the public by concentrating on supporting teachers who are instructing diverse and immigrant children. This ongoing integration with local schools, teachers and their students provide additional real-world examples and perspectives for internationalizing her own teaching further.

These examples of engaging with the public fall within the parameters of the holistic approach of IaH. Faculty development, including through their service expands the concept of faculty members' involvement in IaH beyond the formal classroom and into the field as well. Such engagement can foster better relations with diverse and immigrant communities and make those in the dominant group aware of issues leading to improvement for everyone.

Increase attention to research

The attention to research as a practice of IaH was already mentioned above regarding Erla's desire to undertake more research comparing student perspectives on the immigrant experience. Other participants also pointed to increasing their attention to research that focuses on diversity, inclusion, and similar aspects supported by IaH. Again, while such research is not part of IaH directly, it informs not only the public through mass media, but also the practices and understanding of faculty themselves who then incorporate this knowledge and learning into the campus and curriculum. Hanna talked about how she wanted to turn her work from the Learning Spaces research group and the resulting conference toward higher education:

> But I'm also thinking about new projects all of the time where I can, you know, where I should – what issues should be addressed now and what is, what is the most important way forward. So, my last application was about really taking the Learning Spaces project further and working in universities. So, looking at immigrant population in the universities and their experiences there, so. I mean I've already done some work on this, but it has not been very extensive, so. So, I've already applied for a grant for quite extensive research in higher education in Iceland. [...] I mean how the universities are adapting their teaching to these students and also, what services are available and, if there are any obstacles and all that.

Hanna's stated goal of conducting research in post-secondary institutions would bring attention to studying the higher education system, an area of study that is not receiving much attention in Iceland. There is no department at the School of Education devoted solely to studying higher education. While this would not be the first time she researched aspects of higher education (e.g. Books et al., 2010), it could mark a shift toward a more extensive academic investigation of internationalization proper. Eyrún and Erla also point specifically to conducting research projects around immigration and intercultural development as a strategy to deepen their work. Erla, for example, talked about this approach broadly:

> I think now by doing more research on the groups I want to learn more about, […] I can really interact with those people so I can tell real stories that are so powerful; real stories. So that's my goal: to do several of those, in different countries both in Europe and also in the US, I've planned that already. So that's one maybe one of my strategies; because then I can take it into my research and the classroom […].

Just as with Hanna's example about engaging the public, Erla also expects to take these future experiences through research and incorporate them back into the classroom. Although she does not explicitly discuss the impact beyond the classroom at the university, Erla is engaged in advocacy for intercultural learning at the university on a daily basis and it is more than plausible such findings could have a greater impact on policy and administration as well.

In addition to these concrete actions, some mentioned various elements that were needed to make these strategies successful. Four of the five participants cited time and space for development of their work as an important element needed to make their strategies for advancing practices related to IaH successful. It is worthwhile to remind the reader that since the economic crisis, academic staff have reported heavier workloads which leaves less time and space for innovating and integrating new practices or initiatives. In addition to time and space, some noted that increased resources were essential to make their work successful.

Just as there are a variety of practices and activities related to IaH, so are there a variety of strategies that participants are intending to use to develop or advance their engagement in IaH-related activities including connecting with colleagues, students and the public as well as further internationalizing their teaching and research. As these strategies may result in advancing their current work related to IaH or developing new directions, they can be understood as acts of developing the academic self as well. The increased attention from campus leadership toward practices related to IaH on campus may provide more support for the participants to realize these strategies in future years.

Meaning Making from IaH

The range of themes covered in this chapter so far include how participants understand Internationalization at Home, how they practice it, and what strategies they plan to use to advance their engagement in activities that support IaH. One final aspect of understanding the participants' practices and future plans is what meaning they derive from engaging in practices supporting and related to IaH. That is to say, what sort of personal or professional fulfillment do the gain from their engagement. This section then includes responses from participants on the personal meaning or rewards from being involved in these practices. Some of the data come from the direct question asked about meaning or rewards, while other data points come from other conversations where participants naturally brought up these topics. Their responses give some insight into certain motivations for undertaking this sort of work.

Development and learning

One meaning or reward participants cited from their engagement with practices of IaH is that of opening their students' eyes to different perspectives and other people. Brynja stated that she feels rewarded through hearing back from students who start to recognize how cultural issues play out in the real world after applying various lenses and perspectives they discuss in class. She gave the example of students sent out to observe how some other Icelanders interact with immigrants without much intercultural awareness. Hanna talked about the rewards she gleans from interactions with graduate students, "I enjoy learning about their experience and their developing practice." Similarly, Erla is encouraged by the increasing number of students becoming interested in researching and writing about intercultural issues. Two quotes from participants capture the reward of seeing others grow to understand difference through their teaching:

> Erla: Well, the most rewarding thing is when you can sort of open people's eyes towards differences. For example, the story I told you, people think "oh my god." You know, "why did I think this way?" I think that's the most rewarding thing I can ever think of. That's just everything to me. If I can make people, not make, but enabled them be, to grow and be more flexible, more open, understanding. You know, I think that's the best thing. That's the best salary and price, you know.

> Eyrún: Yeah. I find myself being rewarded most when I see changes in my students. When I see them grow. When I see [...] one student grow in how they work and how they, and their learning. If I can see them learn, if I can really see them change something in the way they work on these issues of application, I can see them really grow in what they're doing. That is really something that is rewarding to me.

Both participants talked about how meaningful student transformation is for them. For Erla, the reward is through the increased reflection students gain through her teaching in checking their own assumptions and prejudices which then results in more openness in accepting and understanding others. Eyrún spoke more specifically about how students come to apply their new understanding to broader issues around multiculturalism in Iceland. Her focus is on one individual student at a time. As Eyrún mentioned at another time, her goal is to not change the world, but to change the world of individuals. This is echoed in her focus in this passage on the reward of seeing just one student shift their perspective.

Benefit to society

Another important meaning for the participants gained through their engagement in practices of IaH is the benefit to society that results from their work. Terry, Hanna and Eyrún all made mention of these societal benefits through different lenses. Terry talked about how meaningful it is for him to see the individual transformation that comes from the experience of being part of a diverse international group and the understanding that perceptions and attitudes are not the same across cultures. He then relates this to how transformed individuals have a hand in the greater good to society:

> But the first time, when you become part of an international group, it's a [brief signal loss] for all of your thinking processes; your understanding of history and the world; that there are numerous perspectives, that there are numerous ways of behaving, that morality, attitudes to men and women differ. It's an overturning and it's and underlining of the [brief signal loss] that we have potential of understanding each other and working together and it's also a very good move in terms of, in terms of working against the things that caused world wars in the past and things of this kind.

This benefit to society then is global in scope. It is reasonable to believe that Terry sees this sort of IaH work that he is engaged in as a continuation of post-World War II intercultural education efforts initiated to avert another large-scale global conflict. Certainly, this meaning for Terry is part of his motivation for pursing activates and practices related to IaH as he frequently mentioned doing his part to bring about these changes as he can in his "corner of the world."

Hanna also sees this value to society as meaningful for her. This benefit comes through the progress made in implementing reform in the school systems that includes curriculum and teaching which are more inclusive and culturally sensitive. The reward for her is progression toward more human rights and equality through equal access and learning in education:

> Yeah, I mean just the, to see for example, as I talked about before, to see reform, to see school development, to include you know, equity perspectives and inclusion and so on. So, this a reward and just to see, more equality and human rights being taken into consideration in our society. So, you know, it's sort of the daily reward I'm getting and seeing people moving upwards in our education system, people from different countries that have been given a chance that maybe they didn't have before, you know? So, I think that's [...] what I'm aiming at seeing and it's very rewarding to see some of this happening because I know it's, it's - should not, it should not be taken for granted even though this is a society that claims to be, you know, aware of human rights and based on equality, so.

The benefits that Hanna sees for society is layered: First, the individual students benefit who gain from greater inclusivity and then in turn are more productive members of society, but second, there is also the benefit of increased consciousness in society toward such human rights. Understandably, Hanna does not state this directly, but much of her work in teaching master's students who are school instructors themselves and research initiatives have been important in creating the infrastructure and conditions for these education system reforms to move forward to where they are today.

Finally, Eyrún takes a similar approach in seeing meaning in her involvement in practices of IaH as a benefit to the country of Iceland. She understands the benefit as ultimately helping the society mature toward more inclusivity when engaging in challenging conversations around diversity. As these different groups are indeed part of the Icelandic society, the benefit is for everyone who make up the constituent parts:

> Well, [pause] in a maybe. Maybe it's self-centered attitude that it would benefit my country. You know, it would benefit the discussion here which is, we already talked about a little bit, immature and inexperienced, so I'm hoping what I can bring to the table helps us along in

> discussing and working through those issues and also how the world is today it's difficult to place regarding groups, different groups, so it's a really fragile circumstance and a fragile discussion.

While Hanna spoke about increasing awareness and human rights, Eyrún strikes a more urgent tone in describing the interactions between cultural groups as "fragile." This is particularly revealing as the Icelanders have had such little experience addressing these issues in their own backyard. She went on to talk about how the world is shifting and intercultural conflict is becoming more prevalent. The potential and actual benefit to society of her involvement in practices of IaH provides significant meaning for Eyrún.

Personal fulfillment

In addition to the rewards of seeing benefits for others, whether in an individual student's own growth and development or the progress that comes in society, a final meaning for the participants came in the form of fulfillment from their own experiences with cross-cultural interaction through their involvement in practices of IaH. Terry stated quite simply, "I enjoy being international". Erla and Hanna both talked about the enjoyment or sense of fulfillment derived from teaching diverse groups of students:

> Erla: So, you have to work harder because you have to explain everything more specifically which is ok, but I love teaching my more diverse group because they identify with more stories that I'm telling and it gives more reasons why I enjoy it more.

> Hanna: And also I've been teaching diverse groups of students for many years in the university and also in other countries, so these are all sort of experiences that have come together to well, how can I say, really sort of fulfill my need to work in this field, or in this international context. It's something that gives me a lot personally.

While some may perceive international or diverse groups of students in their classrooms only as added challenges to teaching, Erla and Hanna welcome these students in their classrooms and see their presence as a benefit.

Finally, Brynja moved from framing cross-cultural activities as providing personal enjoyment to focusing on the increased "wealth," as cultural capital, that multicultural experiences and relationships can bring. When asked about what rewards being involved in multicultural activities, through engaging in IaH, brings to her she replied, "The diversity makes you incredibly wealthy. I mean I feel like access to this diversity opens up all these others experiences for me." These cross-cultural interactions and contacts the participants have through their engagement in practices of IaH not only provides personal fulfillment, but also opens doors to new perspectives and knowledge.

The meaning for the participants' engagement in these practices of IaH exists in three different scopes: the first level is the personal fulfillment which is on the individual instructor; the second focuses on the development and learning primarily of their students; and the final, broadest scope, is the benefit to society. That participants brought out the meaning or rewards that their engagement in practices related to IaH throughout the interviews, suggests another piece of the motivation for the participants in undertaking such work.

Summary

Data presented above shows how these participants intend to further their involvement as well as what meaning or rewards their involvement in IaH engagement has for their lives which then in turn, inform and expand this process. These data describing the key aspects of the process of participants engaging in practices of IaH reveal that this process is neither non-linear nor static in nature, but rather is dynamic through shifting contexts and interplay between past histories and present events along with the ever-changing nature of participants' experiences and individual positions.

Chapter VIII: A Portrait of Adult Learning

External evidence, behaviors, and actions of participants only provides part of the picture. Engagement is a state of psychological investment, and it's important to consider the mindsets or tools participants employ which advance their own personal and professional development. It is scarcely a new concept that academics are not only experts in their given fields, but that they continue to develop as part of their professional work, and yet they are rarely characterized as adult learners. Framing the experiences of the participants in this study through a lens of adult learning allows for consideration of the developmental aspects of their engagement in practices of IaH and the skills, capacities, and tools they employ in this process. This development is often overlooked and underappreciated. This chapter then addresses this study's fourth research question, borrowing from Sanderson's (2008) language and approach: through a lens of adult learning, how do UI faculty members who engage in IaH develop their academic selves?

The cognitions and mindsets involved in such learning presented here are not discrete or sequential, but rather a fluid constellation of conditions, attitudes, and behaviors that ultimately work to develop the individual faculty member. While each of the theories or concepts which make up these components could be subject to extensive treatment, the goal in this chapter is rather to provide a solid foundation for a broader and multifaceted perspective on how the complex process of faculty development around IaH occurs, thereby establishing a basis for further exploration in future studies. Drawing from participant data, this chapter divides this portrait of learning into three main segments: disposition toward growth and development, collaborative learning, and authenticity in teaching.

Disposition Toward Growth and Development

Mindset for learning

Dweck's (2006) work on mindset and learning juxtaposes the so-called "fixed mindset" where intelligence is thought to be innate and a static entity against the "growth mindset" where intelligence is considered malleable, dynamic, and incremental. Undoubtedly, a growth mindset is the foundational internal condition necessary for development of the vast array of attitudes and behaviors needed for transformational internationalization. It could be argued that academics have a "growth mindset" based on their extensive formal education and continued scholarship as members of the academy, devoting much of their time to the enterprise of education and research. Undoubtably, academics as a group continue to gain more knowledge, but they may not reach for new challenges that stretch their own development beyond their area of expertise, and they may not see everyday interactions as moments for learning.

Participants in this study did however demonstrate a more growth-oriented mindset. For example, Terry shows a strong awareness of his own ongoing development. When asked about times when his biases or assumptions were challenged, he responded that he could not articulate any particular prejudice, but then went on to talk about where his global outlook came from, "Yeah maybe brought up, but also what I've sort of grown to experience I think. So, no, I don't have any radical sort of visions on the road to Damascus [...]. But again, we're always changing, we're always adapting, we're always learning. So, of course there are things that will change." Terry does not cite any moment of change assumptions but does provide a statement that places learning as central to the human experience. He recognizes that learning is a constant process that can include shifting of attitudes and adjustments based on new information and experiences – even if he is not always cognizant of every individual change. Transformative learning particularly is often associated with specific striking life-changing events, but people with a growth mindset are more aware of the incremental and daily nature of this process. The way Terry understands, by extrapolation experiences, this development reveals his reflexivity and awareness of continual learning and adapting.

Additional evidence of this growth mindset comes through genuine curiosity and interest in others. Participants reported a strong disposition toward learning about other peoples and cultures, the details of which are not squarely within their daily work – but broaden their horizons. This inclination toward exploring other peoples and cultures demonstrates not only motivations for engaging in work related to IaH, but also a disposition and desire toward gaining understanding about knowledge which may be outside of their specific academic disciplines or only indirectly related to their daily work.

Unlike Terry's awareness of inner adjustments in outlook, Erla said that she is often not aware of her learning about other cultures because it is so "normal" for her to engage in this on a daily basis. Later, she mentioned how some Icelanders believe refugees have a negative impact on the country. Her approach to this however, is to see the cultural differences as a learning opportunity. When asked about what motivates her to become more involved Erla noted that:

> I don't know this is just everywhere – we are now getting more refugees and more immigrants. So, the world has become more diverse with what's happening now with Syria and everywhere and it motivates me even more because it is increasing in importance of understanding, not talking, even intercultural communication. Just everywhere. So, I go to a lot of lectures and give lectures about diversity and those issues because I feel even here there are groups that are against taking more refugees into the country. So, I'm trying to see, look at the positive side, seeing how much we can learn from people from other cultures for example because so it is not only negative, it's a lot of positive things.

By noting that the presence of other cultures is "not only negative," Erla is acknowledging the frequent discourse in Iceland that recent immigration has created challenges for a culture and people not used to this diversity. These struggles in adapting are in the public consciousness where the focus tends to be on the challenges. Rather than isolating only the potential and actual benefits when advocating for multiculturalism in Iceland, this broader framing allows for a more inclusive mindset when talking with others who have had a range of experiences with cultural difference in Iceland.

For Eyrún, this disposition toward learning comes in the form of a certain humility, recognizing that there is so much yet to know and learn about those with cultural differences in the country. She notes that she is lacking in knowledge about the practical aspects of multiculturalism, saying "I still feel like a beginner in this process because I know that probably, well I feel like we need to be humble because we are new to this experience as a country as a nation." A growth mindset is revealed in the form of both recognizing the need for more knowledge in this area and then desiring to engage in learning more in the face of this perceived deficit. Rather than this collective positioning creating personal distance in ownership of this need, Eyrún positions herself as having only a nascent understanding in a society which is also just starting to grasp the complexities of improving cross-cultural existence. This is similar to what Erla says in the previous quote when she used the word "we" in talking about how much there is to learn from other people.

While the data pertaining to growth mindset is somewhat less robust than other areas of development, these important statements reveal that this mindset is evident and provide a foundation for the participants to be open to and engaged with various modes of learning. Such mindsets translate into their daily interaction with students, integrating their awareness and disposition toward learning and capacity. Moreover, internal conditions and attitudes toward human potential are factors in their engagement in practices of IaH.

Developing academic Self

The concept of developing the "academic Self" is strongly related to the concept of growth mindset. Both concepts focus on stretching the capacity to embrace learning something novel. Whereas the "growth mindset" provides the broad groundwork for a belief in their own ability to learn, tenants of developing the academic Self are more concerned with stretching professional development. Understandably, faculty members who are developing their academic selves are adapting and recreating their professional work and identities contending with new directions for their work and research, rather than only plumbing deeper into a single, focused topic. This expansion of intellectual interest and investigation is one of Hall's primary components in the concept of developing the academic Self.

Some evidence of participants developing their academic Selves comes from personal and academic libraries. Both Terry and Hanna for example, had large collections of books from a variety of disciplines in their office that were not part of their early academic scholarship. Hanna's library includes works on anthropology, religion, and philosophy which were not the focus of her early scholarship. Similarly, Terry's office contains a variety of works in addition to his doctoral work on drama and folklore, including visual arts, Celtic music, poetry, and classical mythology. While Brynja's office didn't have many books, she noted that her personal library at home contains a good number of diverse subjects from Russian to philosophy. These works are drawn on and incorporated into their broader understanding of cultural exchange and learning.

In addition to the bibliographic evidence of continued academic exploration, several participants reported during interviews that new research directions emerge out of their experiences. Even though Eyrún, for example, is still completing her doctorate, she is considering new research directions that have been called to her attention through other scholars and conferences. These are not necessarily direct offshoots from other work as she mentioned being interested in, "studying the experiences of, for example, exchange students or immigrants and that [are] trying to find their way through this system to see what can be done better." While Eyrún works in researching immigrant relationships in the school system, she has not yet worked on exchange students in a university setting, which is a new direction. Similarly, Erla stated that she was starting to do interviews with refugees who were settling in the small town of Akranes, which was not an area she had worked in before. Immigration as a focus for Erla has developed through her work in intercultural teaching and position at UI. While teaching in the U.S., her focus was more on questions of race relations.

Other participants, often reflectively, addressed their development of the academic Self directly. For example, Brynja talks about the continual re-imagining of her professional identity in ways she had not expected. However, she is increasingly passionate about these new directions:

> Yeah, [...] I mean, in my research, it just shifts and you don't realize its shifting – like I would have never thought of myself in this job as being their resident critical race theorist, but that's what I am. And so, [...] it's just weird how – I'd never thought I'd be a race theorist, that's not what I went in academia to be."

Hanna also detailed how engaging in practices of IaH has created new directions in her professional life, finding new areas to focus on in the education system by considering teachers and their practice rather than the immigrants or students and their experience which she had concentrated on previously:

> I mean [...] these experiences have led me to start new research projects on for example diverse teachers in schools – how they experience their work and their teaching and also research about really what's going on in the different classrooms or groups in preschools. Because before I didn't used to go that deep into the school practices so, I mean I think this is the influence of my own teaching through the years.

Not only has Hanna's research expanded into previously uncharted territory, such as working with diverse teachers rather than focusing on diverse students, it has also led her to situate herself in real world settings, with practical knowledge from the field. She goes on to say that she learns a lot from these experiences and that new knowledge is then translated back to the classroom for her graduate students in the way of concrete examples and stories of the challenges and opportunities that exist in the Icelandic school system.

This quote from Hanna then provides evidence of what Hall (2002) describes as a second key aspect of developing the academic Self: praxis. That is to say, the continual integration of theory and practice, which arguably includes integrating research findings into the classroom. Other participants also spoke about bringing their research into the classroom and integrating it into their daily practice rather than only relying on static lectures and examples recycled from previous terms. Erla for example, talked about how she brings her own research findings into all her classrooms, even those that are not directly about intercultural issues:

> And, so I think taking a story and I can actually - just yesterday in my methodology class – because I take all of my research into intercultural stuff into other classrooms since I've been teaching a whole lot here. So, I just use other opportunities, just sneak them in you know. And students really learn and enjoy it because I'm teaching research methods, but I take my research there.

While it is tempting to say that such a practice is not a function of engaging in IaH, but rather the foundational work of academic staff, the data reveal that undertaking research and teaching that intersects with intercultural or immigration issues has acted as a catalyst.

These concepts of growth mindset and developing the academic Self intersect around a continual stretching. This is a necessity for faculty members to grow from their work and expand their understanding, interests, and capacity beyond topics and issues they have investigated previously. While the evidence for a growth mindset supports a foundation for the motivation to learn broadly, the data addressing the development of the academic Self highlights the specific professional modes where this mindset plays out. Taken together, the data show support for the presence of this disposition among the participants.

Adult Cognition

While mindsets create the foundation for further development, other theories in the portrait focus on specific modes of understanding and learning. Brookfield (2000) argues that adult cognition, as an overarching category drawing on the work of a number of researchers, is not unique to adults, but that adult learners employ these capacities that make up adult cognition more often and more successfully than learners at other developmental stages. The four capacities in adult cognition include: critical reflection, thinking dialectically, practical logic, and knowing how we know what we know. Seen through the lens of adult learning, the data reveal that the participants are indeed utilizing these skills in their engagement in IaH broadly.

Critical reflection

Under the banner of adult cognition, Brookfield (2000) defines critical reflection as a form of challenging one's own assumptions or ideas that were formed from previous experiences in life. Evidence for this sort of critical reflection among the participants was the strongest of all of Brookfield's adult capacities. It comes, in part, from their awareness of assumptions and biases being challenged through their work related IaH. In one particularly salient story, Hanna shows how she recognizes her own process of learning and the assumptions she held about others:

> Oh yes, I think, I mean – they are constantly being challenged, you know, 'cause I'm constantly learning something new. [...] one example is, well this was a long time ago when I realized the difference of for example, [in] languages such as [...] some Asian languages were you have [...] the different meanings according to the sounds. [...] Tone-based languages – and I remember learning about these maybe 10-15 years ago and realizing the importance of the sound and sort of the, you know, how you use your voice and this is something that many, for example, teachers don't realize and they talk about these noisy students when they're speaking their languages [...]. So, things like that were a – many years ago – a real eye-opener to me because I didn't know about this before. And this is something that I want so, of course in teaching about but I'm not an expert on language, but this is something I think we need to include when we're talking about diverse students. It's one of the things we need to include and make teachers understand because there has been a lot of prejudice towards for example, Asian people and women are said to be "frekk" in Icelandic, maybe arrogant or loud because this is how it sounds to Icelanders. Some of the Asian languages they sound very loud and arrogant. So, and that has to do with the, the structure of the languages and how they are, the tones that they are using of course.

Hanna does not state directly what her attitude is toward language that others call "frekk", but we can infer that her own understanding shifted through this experience as she gained new explanations for difference. She learned both about the mechanics of language as the root of difference as well as a new appreciation for the general prejudice against these speakers. This moment of intercultural learning for Hanna led to a change in practice and was then translated into her own classroom, recognizing that other Icelandic teachers would need to know such information as well. Both her awareness that her assumptions are "constantly being challenged" as well as then her active incorporation of new truths she discovers from these challenges, demonstrate critical reflection.

Brynja also pointed to an assumption that was challenged while collecting data for her dissertation which took place at a secondary school setting in the United States, which was around issues of U.S. multiculturalism. Like Hanna, Brynja was able to gain a new understanding of a stereotype which she then actively investigated and incorporated into a new outlook through her own critical reflection:

> [...] we were sitting in class, one of the guys that was part of my dissertation, and we were sitting in his math class and I found out he smoked. And I said, "oh what do you smoke?" and he goes "well I smoke Kools" and I said "well, isn't that rather stereotypical" and he turned and he looked at me and he goes "that's so racist." And I was – shocked, I was so upset that I was being racist that I did two separate things: I went home and thought about it extensively until I went back to school the next time and then I checked with some of the others - they all knew each other – and I checked with some of the other students and said, you know I had this conversation and I said this and he said that this was racist. And they were like "oh he's just kind of – he's pulling your leg." And I mean [...] after [...] we had a conversation about it because if you look through magazines in the United States, Kools are marketed to Blacks. It's that - you see it in the glossy magazines it's mostly Black people smoking Kool cigarettes, so - so there was, for me there was a theoretical background to it and for him, I was stereotyping. And you know, he and I later had a conversation and actually [...] it sparked my thinking about what did it mean to say something that seemed relatively innocuous – I mean this, this actually went to the whole micro-aggressions piece that I've been working on since then.

This quote reveals something about the process of critical reflection for Brynja as she details not only her internal state of "shock", but also explains the concrete actions that she took including deep reflection and thinking as well as actively gathering more information from others. From the results of this interaction and her critical reflection of challenging previous assumptions, Brynja started to look at language differently and come to understand micro-aggressions more. Such shifts in understanding another person's perspective has carried over to the work that she does in Iceland as well, championing the challenges international students and immigrants face in Iceland. It is important to remember that multiculturalism in the United States often connotes meanings of social justice for historically oppressed peoples, which intersects with activities of IaH as multiple cultures in Iceland are almost entirely those from recent immigrant backgrounds, and therefore concepts of multiculturalism and interculturalism overlap greatly.

In addition to these challenged assumptions that participants experienced, Eyrún talks about how she learned about how others negotiated their identities:

> Some concepts we were using about our immigrants and now "immigrants" is not even a not always a positive word. But there are some concepts along the way that get some negative meanings over time. So, this is something I really hadn't given any thought and how that would happen, it came as a surprise to me how people negotiate identities. So, I really hadn't – because for me being raised and growing up in one country when homogenous culture and all that it didn't really, it wasn't really an issue. There wasn't an identity struggle around this issue. So, that was kind of a revelation for me, to hear about how people kind of differently express and differently negotiate their identities and that we shouldn't take anything for granted.

While it is significant that Eyrún learned about how others come to understand their own identity, this passage also shows that she was able to take this new knowledge and compare it to how her own upbringing, coming from a homogenous culture, was radically different. Such comparisons are the product of this critical reflection, being able to situate new information in contrast to previous experiences. Moreover, her statement that "we shouldn't take anything for granted" is an indicator that she has positioned herself to continue reflecting critically on questions of identity in the future.

While the participants' challenging of their assumptions demonstrates capacity for critical reflection, there is also evidence of active growth in this area. One aim of this research was to have participants think about their process and practice, for which they often have little time. Hanna summed up why this sort of reflective space is necessary when she was struggling with how to answer the questions that were provided to her in advance, "I was thinking when I was looking through this maybe the problem is that we never have the time to reflect on anything, it's like running a race all of the time." The mental room made possible through the interview and their involvement in the study led them to reflect quite profoundly at some points. Erla, Brynja and Eyrún explicitly noted that they had experienced some transformative moments during interviews in which they came to realize truths about themselves, personally or professionally, which were previously unconsidered.

> Erla. So, we talk about that and we have games about learning about some words, how you say hi and good-bye, and thank you in different languages so, I think our home is very international. I never really considered that but since you're asking, I think we are very international there. Brynja. I mean I come from a story telling family. Both cultures are; you know, Icelanders are story tellers, Irish are storytellers. I come from that kind of cultural background, so yeah it is sort of like that I guess. I've never really thought about that that way – thank you. That's kind of useful actually. Eyrún. For example, being aware that – you have to be active to learn. You have to be kind of, you have to or to be a good teacher you, you try to get your students active in the classroom, not just receiving. Yeah, probably. Cause through those conferences and through those texts that they were publishing, it was kind of the tone through it all. Yeah, this is one of the things I hadn't realized.

These thoughts, identities, or values around IaH that were previously unexplored, transformed into conscious awareness through the participants' engagement in this study and practices of IaH broadly. Moreover, all the participants stated that they were interested in reading the outcomes which could in turn lead to further critical reflection on their practice, that is analyzing and questioning the validity of their attitudes and effectiveness. Part of the intent of this study is to foster greater understanding and motivation among those doing this work and to provide the university insight into resources and champions already on campus. While not all impacts are traceable, one participant co-authored an article (Halldorsdottir and Gollifer, 2018) after the data collection which takes up some issues of IaH and immigration at the institution more intently.

Thinking dialectically

The ability to accept two contradictory truths simultaneously is one capacity that adult learners employ according to Brookfield (2000). This often takes the form of continual back and forth dialectical thinking between recognizing universal patterns and then also recognizing the contexts and specific situations that deviate from those rules requiring a disposition toward change as the opportunity to continue seeking an evolving understanding of truth. Erla demonstrates an example of this cognition when discussing her approach to teaching when she was in the United States, which changed based of the region she was teaching in:

> In Pensacola, Florida, there are a lot of African-Americans so they understood it pretty well when I was talking about it. In Arizona, they didn't [know] so much about African-Americans, more about Latinos so I use different stories. When I went to a small college in New York, close to Buffalo, it was completely homogenous, all white students. I had to talk to them like I do in Iceland, even though they live in America. I guess they never got out of their box. So, really you have to – depending on the context – it's what method you use. So, you need to be aware of that.

While she taught the same concepts and learning goals for each of these classes, she learned that there were differences, which ultimately impacted her choice of examples and approach in the classroom. Erla understands that there are methods and approaches to intercultural education that may or may not work – depending on the context and setting. This continued modification was not simply based on individual participant differences, which is frequently expected from instructors, but also was in recognition of regional contexts and related cultural implications less often considered. Rather than a one-time event, this is an example of the continued back and forth in her cognition at each university. She is synergistically creating a third way and new understanding, through being able to simultaneously hold the truths of both universal patterns and specific contexts.

Another example of this dialectical thinking came from Hanna when I asked her whether her attitudes about internationalization were ever challenged. She talked about actively challenging Iceland's historically parochial education system toward more inclusive and novel pedagogies which would take more global perspectives:

> Well, I regularly come across very narrow-minded opinions of people around me: both in my university and people in the field that talk as if we are an isolated community, that we will never develop, that we will never be teaching the way that we have been based on the same

> knowledge. So, when I come across this, of course I feel that these views need to be challenged, but then also my own views are challenged regularly because there are people in the university that believe that our language which is a minority language, of course, it's spoken by very few people, that it's in danger because of external influences - things like that and so we should really preserve the language and we should really make sure that the English doesn't sort of drown it and so on. And issues in relation to this, that challenge my opinions. So, this is like a constant dialogue. How do we find a balance between these points of view?

While Hanna continues to champion these pedagogies that are inclusive to immigrants and other marginalized groups as universal necessity, she also recognizes through being challenged by others, that the potential loss of Icelandic language and those cultural ramifications need to be considered. This back and forth in "constant dialogue" then plays out between various stakeholders within and outside of the university as well as in her own understanding. She recognizes and holds these contradictory beliefs with the universal pattern of inclusivity and the specific context of the Icelandic language. For Hanna, the challenges have led to her evolving understand of the truth of approaching questions of language usage in education.

Terry provides yet another example of this sort of back and forth between recognizing patterns and exceptions to those patterns when talking about opening students' understanding of their own position in the world. His desire is to create thoughtful approaches to difference and persevering the uniqueness in culture, rather than attempting to shape them into a monolithic "global" group:

> But certainly, what I haven't talked about is the element of not – I never want to create a sort of global – everybody's the same. This is what's so great about traveling, is that even within Europe – Europeans only become European when they're comparing themselves to America or Asians otherwise they're different and they'll look at other and certainly not – but at certain moments, they become French like now for example. So yeah, it's not something that's going to be lost, I don't think when we - the use of English, whatever, is not going to create a whole bunch of clones and I think we have a good reason to hang on to our differences.

Terry points out that Europe is comprised of significant differences and suggests that unifying identities such as being "European" only emerge in contexts that compare them against other large nations or regions. He notes this pattern of identifying broadly as European or whichever smaller unit (nation-state, ethnic group, etc.) one of these people adheres to and yet, he also recognizes there are deviations in this pattern. A new view materializes for him considering current events. This interview took place after the November 2015 Paris terrorist attacks in which 130 people were killed and another 368 were injured. He argues that this tragedy created a sense of unity around being "French" among those in Europe who would not otherwise identify this way. In this way, his involvement in this IaH practice of teaching global perspectives is informed by dialectal thinking about current events and identities.

Finally, for Brynja some of this dialectal thinking appears in how she understands her own position in Iceland and the work that she does. As a bi-cultural faculty member who spent significant time outside of Iceland, she is learning how to adapt to living in Iceland more permanently. This has been a significant learning experience for her:

> I never thought I'd have this kind of responsibility this early on in my academic career and so, the learning curve has just been huge for me and I probably should be writing about it. I probably should be taking this academic experience and this sort of idea of how to make a faculty that's white, middle-class, straight, mostly married understand what it means not to be that. In a culture that is so overwhelmingly homogenous. I've never, I don't think I've ever lived in a culture as homogenous as this culture cause it's so small, they can afford it. So yeah, I think I've learned a lot. I've learned a lot personally about myself as an individual and academically and professionally about what it means to be sort of stuck in the middle of this weird space.

The key phrase comes at the end of this quote when she talks about being "stuck in the middle" of what is seemingly a liminal space. While Brynja is compelled to understand and operate within homogenous cultural norms and dominant social identities of most of these colleagues, she comes from a divergent background that includes being bicultural and having a son who is biracial. Moreover, her academic experience in international education and critical race theory is not prevalent among most academic staff at UI. She is learning through her long-term residency in Icelandic daily life and how it differs from the patterns, norms, and behaviors of the more diverse societies she is accustom to. Going back and forth between prior experiences (universal patterns of understanding) and current experiences (specific contexts that create contradiction) helps her to gain new perspectives which then inform how she interacts with both students and other academic staff.

Practical Logic

Brookfield (2000) is careful to explain that the adult cognition "practical logic" is not what is colloquially referred to as common sense, but rather an ability to closely read situations and then adjust quickly based on this deep reading of the multiple contexts in a given space. That is to say, practical logic is breaking the rules of the dialectal thinking discussed above because of the immediate situation. For instructors, there is a clear application in classrooms where individual and cultural differences intersect with ever-changing discourse. There is ample opportunity to utilize practical logic because there are extremely challenging problems encountered daily in academia, and faculty members must rapidly seek new meanings through deep understanding of contexts to approach these problems in new ways.

Terry provides a unique insight into how he has learned to use this cognition in culturally diverse settings. He notes that he considers the audience and how to draw off them during a class:

> I think in terms of teaching, it's the same: any class, the more you do, if you're aware of the classes that you're teaching; [...] and in my case I've got a drama background – so you, you draw on the audience as any sort of comedy or tragedy. Comedy actors especially, draw audiences and the feeling that's out there before you get going. As teachers, we're all actors. And in a sense, if you've got any sense, you've got to draw off the audience. What works and what doesn't.

While Terry is pulling from his own experience and background in drama for his own approach, he also then broadened this out to teachers in general, that they need to be (re)acting in a similar way. Several participants employed such practical logic in their classrooms, playing off students' reactions, shifting and adapting to this "feeling." The extension for the participants then is also about "what works and what doesn't" toward both the individual and the cultural differences in the room. Brynja, Erla, Hanna and Terry were all teaching to multicultural groups of students during the observations for this research and navigated those cultural layers by understanding and adjusting based on what they knew previously of the students' backgrounds and reading their reactions during class.

Again, Terry shows another example of using practical logic when discussing how he was about to teach on the play Brand by Norwegian playwright Henrik Ibsen. Just prior to teaching, he heard about the events of the 9/11 terrorist attacks in the United States, which completely altered the meaning of the play for him. Terry again brings up human violence as an important and transformative catalyst to his worldview and understanding:

> That life changing thing of 9/11 when I was teaching the play by Ibsen, which I told you about, suddenly the play changed. It was this um, I think I mentioned it, [...] it's a play by Ibsen – it's a tragic hero who believes he's found a new form of God outside of the church and decides to lead his parish up into the mountains where they're probably all going to be killed by an avalanche to find God in danger and just as I was about to go up and teach this play, that's when I heard about – that's when I saw the footage of the planes flying into the buildings and I had to change, the whole play changed: it was about extremism. So, there are things I think, of course as you teach and things that happen, will change you're view completely. I've never seen that play again, but it underlined how everything that we read and do is shaped by the experiences of the world that we have.

The practical logic that Terry employs stemmed from his own understanding and contextualizing of this play in light of events that shifted the core meaning of the work. While this is not a rapid or close reading of the students, he reads the current environment moments before his lecture and addresses this. The basis for this class changed directions quickly, taking on new meaning in response to an emerging context that is now layered on top of the multiple contexts already in the classroom and on the play itself. His reflection and recognition that worldviews are ultimately the sum of experiences that individuals have and shift in light of new information is perhaps a good summary of this adult cognition of practical logic.

During the interviews, I asked Erla to provide an example of how she was able to bring mindfulness into her classroom, as she had mentioned this practice earlier. She told a story about a time during a class when her attitude and understanding were shifted during the discussion, which then ultimately altered her practice in the future:

> I remember once where we were talking about actually, we were showing "Promises" the video that I showed you about Palestinians and Israelis and there's one Jewish girl in the classroom. And people were really siding you know, want to side with the Palestinians and not the Israelis. So, I thought she was very quiet all of a sudden, she used to be very talkative in the classroom. But I knew she was Jewish, so I thought "oh my God, maybe I said something that hurt her" because I was, I don't know, I thought maybe I was too harsh or something when I was talking about Israelis, but I tried to be neutral.

While she noted that she attempted to present a balanced picture, Erla recognized some of the cultural layers in the room that were at work, specifically that one of the students was Jewish while screening a film about the complex Israeli-Palestinian relationship. While she may not have had this in her mind going into the class, she reflected in the moment, adjusting her mindset after recognizing that she may not have been as sensitive toward this student as she could have been. After relating this story, Erla later mentioned that she was still figuring out at the time of this story, how to deal with such sensitive topics. She stated that she had learned a great deal about such layers since and would approach the situation much differently if she were to encounter it again.

While the examples above discuss practical logic as it applies to teaching in the classroom, this capacity can also be seen in other academic work ultimately related to IaH. While Hanna was conducting research on immigrants in Iceland, she did not always have the tools and had to make adjustments as needed:

> For example, some cases when I expected to interview mothers and then I ended up interviewing the fathers. And in some cases, the mothers - we didn't have languages that we could share. These were mothers that had newly arrived in Iceland and they didn't have English and I couldn't speak their languages.

And she continued:

> some of this was related to the sort of man's role in the house, like the spokesman of the family. But the mothers were there and they took part in the interview, but it was like through the men. So, and this was a real challenge

> because I wanted to speak to the mothers, so. But you know, what can you do? And I had to also explain this when I was writing about it and this was criticized like, you know, the men not allowing the women to be part of the research, but it wasn't really like that. So, it was also challenged when I published. But what can you do in such a situation? Another thing is that you can have an interpreter, but I have very bad experiences of using interpreters in interviews. [...] So, sometimes there's a choice between an interpreter or using any other means that you have, and you know, and it brings you to this situation where you don't really have control, you just have to use the opportunities you have and try to figure out how to do things. So, this is something that, you know, I've learned a lot from this situation, where you have to just take what you get and just work your way through it.

Hanna had established methods for her research project and despite her plans, she was not able to carry it out as designed. She had to read the circumstances, consider new information and then adjust her methods both to be culturally appropriate toward her participants as well as to continue her project. Having to change and adapt methods while in the field is not unique to those engaged in research related to immigration or intercultural issues yet learning from this situation resulted in greater understanding for Hanna about the frame of mind and openness needed to enter the field. Even while she was criticized for her methods after publication, she used practical logic at the time and this new information changed the standard protocols and norms she expected to follow.

Knowing how we know what we know

Finally, the adult cognition of "knowing how we know what we know" is comprised of how adult learners understand themselves, their own learning, preferences, strengths, and how to compensate for areas where they have known weaknesses. To state it more succinctly, it is the capacity of learning to learn. Of the adult cognitions Brookfield (2000) presents, this was observed least among the interview data from the participants in part because participants tended not to talk about themselves in such meta ways, rather they focused on more concrete actions and behaviors.

One of the examples of this adult cognition came from Brynja who spoke and reflected on these personal and meta questions of learning more than most of the other participants. Brynja again brings in her bi-cultural identity and reflects on how she has learned about her own learning, approaches, techniques, and attitudes in the face of cultural and linguistic ambiguity:

> You just learn how to wait differently – being in different cultures. You learn how to sit back and watch. I was reading an article recently where somebody cites Jim Cummins and his stuff on the, the gap – there's a point in your language learning where children especially, multi-lingual children choose to be silent. People, adults tend to get really worry about that point and I get that gap all the time for me. I'll have moments where I don't know where the word is in one language and somebody will say, "well say it in your other language" and I'll be like, "but I don't know what it is in that one either" I can't think about it and it's just these slight moments – if you're working in that sort of cultural ambiguity situation. You just have to be willing to wait for it to come.

Here Brynja shows reflexivity and considers the modes of her own learning. In this example, she demonstrates that she has learned to be patient and wait for the answer because of the "cultural ambiguity", even when faced with questions from conversation partners that seem to demand a more immediate response. Brynja is also applying what she knows about multilingual development, recognizing that academic research is a method she can use to understand herself and own learning better. Brynja goes on to give another example of this "learning how to learn" by detailing how she processes information and what tools she uses to clarify:

> And sometimes it's just a matter of I'll go and have a conversation with somebody and it didn't quite turnout the way that I thought it was or it wasn't going where I thought it was going or I didn't get what I needed and I go home and I reflect on it and I go "oh wait a minute, but I said this or I was thinking this or he said this or she said" you know, at which point I'm like "I'm process, now I've processed what happened" and often if it's, if it's the opportunity presents itself, I'll go back and say "hey, you know when we were having this conversation, I think I misunderstood or maybe there was something I didn't get" and I'll ask, but that took a long time to develop, maturity-wise.

Brynja's comment illustrates how she has learned to know herself and her own needs in the context of cultural difference and points to how she is working in culturally diverse contexts. She recognizes that she has a process to how she learns which includes engaging in a conversation, taking mental and physical space for reflection and then coming back to the conversation partner asking clarifying questions.

The other key example of this adult cognition of knowing how we know what we know is from Terry, who talks broadly about his ability to adapt to other cultural norms and behaviors. He often employs this through his travel to various other countries, frequently as part of his academic work:

> Yeah, you realize – we adapt in all these places, in my case as an actor I start picking up the accent. You adapt behaviors to all those areas, it's a chameleon element. And you learn, from the chameleon element, you learn by becoming the other character and blending in with their way of behaving and buying drinks, you're feeling what it is to be something else.

Terry has learned about his own learning through being involved in drama as an actor, which he then uses in intercultural interactions while abroad. He knows that by actively and consciously stepping into someone else's proverbial skin and experiencing the "other" as what he calls a "character," he can adapt and use behaviors, accents, and norms that are not his own. These are skills and experiences that can translate back into his work in IaH, whether in the classroom or in research that ultimately informs teaching of the value in adapting to others to better navigate intercultural experiences and highlight differences between cultures.

These four capacities that Brookfield (2000) put forward are ways of learning that are not exclusive to adult learners but are more frequently employed by them. While not every participant is going to display each of these cognitions, there is support for each.

Collaborative Learning

Two of the components of this portrait presented so far (growth mindset and adult cognitions) are concepts that can apply to adult learners broadly, whereas the third, development of the academic Self, falls squarely into the more specific professional context. Collaborative learning (Coffield, 2008) straddles the line between these adult learners in generalized contexts, and the professional specific attitudes and behaviors that relate primarily to academic staff (in roles both as teachers and researchers). Again, this sort of learning stems from a mindset that foregrounds curiosity, openness and humility in educational spaces where the teacher flattens traditional power hierarchies, recognizing that knowledge and learning is co-constructed with everyone present. There are two primary aspects to this type of "collaborative learning": The first concerns seeing instructors as learners themselves of both new perspectives on material and the craft of teaching, and the second focuses on viewing instructors as members of communities of practice.

Instructors as learners

For Hanna and Erla, collaborative learning can be seen through statements showing a mindset of willingness and openness to learn from others. This is an extension of the mindset for learning discussed previously, but specifically in the context of being open to learning through interactions with others in a collaborative manner. Hanna reveals this sort of mindset in this quote about her continual process of learning:

> I mean I'm learning all the time, basically. You know? I'm learning from every person I work with, something new. It's been very important to keep an open mind and not suppose anything or, or you know, expect anything in particular. And that's a challenge you know? Something you think you know things but, you know, you keep learning something new and just to take every person and individual, as a new person and new cooperation and not to expect anything from, from certain populations. Because it's all about the individuals, really. It's not so much about groups or populations and this is something that – some of the mistakes that many people in this area are making you know? That they are generalizing about populations or groups or people.

Hanna sees every individual as a potential partner in collaboration, from whom she can learn. This is a mindset she applies not only to those she is working with in research, but also extends to the classroom and other interactions on campus – every person she works with. This mindset is paired with a recognition that she holds certain assumptions, as humans tend to do, and so she makes continual conscious efforts to challenge herself when it seems she already knows certain aspects of people.

Erla gives evidence of this collaborative mindset in talking about her experience. When I asked whether she had incorporated her reflections on previously held assumptions that were challenged during a class back into the classroom, she agreed that she did and noted that she always brings it back to the classroom. When I probed further on whether this was then a continual process she responded, "Oh absolutely. It's very dynamic. It never stops because you can always learn more about myself and other people obviously. That's why I think it's important when you're teaching that you take stories, real-life stories for example now it's a lot about the refugees from Syria so I bring that into the classroom." While Erla connects her learning to incorporating personal and other relevant stories and experiences into the classroom, she positions her own learning as dynamic and thus always changing based on new information and contexts. Rather than taking a position of maturity and expertise where there is little to gain from introspection or others' experiences, Erla embraces the attitude that she can always learn more about herself and others. Additionally, she confirmed that this learning "never stops." This reflective and long-term oriented mindset creates a foundation and openness for collaborative learning with others whether students, peers, research participants or those in daily life.

Learning from Students

Within this aspect collaborative learning, that is seeing instructors as learners, an important thread deconstructs a traditional teaching model where the instructor holds the information and the students are only receptacles passively taking information in. This approach is part of what Freire (1993) identified as the "banking" concept of education. While learning from others in the concept of collaborative learning can include colleagues and research participants, it more importantly includes students in co-constructed formal and informal learning spaces. Brynja encapsulates this approach well, through her comments about how she thinks about this teacher/student relationship when asked about what she learns from her students, "That it's not – you know, that it's not just a matter of me or the teacher having all this information to share, but there's a great deal that teacher, in the process of teaching if they're a responsive teacher learns in the process, that you know that and another piece of it is that you're not perfect."

Brynja positions herself as an instructor who is fallible and may not have all the information or answers, despite having a significant knowledge base.

The theme of students contributing to the discussion and providing valuable insights or experiences to the conversation is repeated by all the participants. While these responses are taken from different parts of the interviews, they provide significant data that the participants are engaging in collaborative learning through their practices of IaH:

> Erla: I enjoy having international students because I get to hear from them, get their experiences, also maybe explain, give an example with stories and they can

> maybe sort of identify with some of the examples I'm giving. I love it. It helps me also learn more about their background.

> Hanna: It can be what material I choose, but also how I organize the course as a whole. What sort of components I bring in and it can be both examples I provide or I ask the students to provide examples and they bring in material to the class or the course. I often do that. So, they contribute also to what the class is doing or what's going on in the course. And it's also about how I organize the setting, the sort of cooperative learning or different ways of trying to engage all students.
> Terry: But simply they [the students] come in with a different background than the background I came with, and they have – they'll see things from a different perspective. So, I'll learn things as it goes along, and this is what it should be when, in the performance studies class that we go out and we, they come back with insights that maybe I've never considered before. And the same thing even with Old Norse religion, which has been written endlessly about. But people have new things to say and it should be that way [...] But then the teacher should also be ready to say, "yeah that doesn't work exactly, that's a really good, that's a new approach; I've never thought about that, good" and to give a reward to somebody for trying something out. It doesn't have to be somebody who has all the answers.

> Eyrún: So, I usually what I try to do there then, well I stop and I try to start some conversation you know, by asking questions about what they think if they have experienced something like that themselves, what they've seen around themselves you know. Something or how they, if they are, if they agree with, with studies – if they, is there something that they would find they could criticize the approaches or somehow what I'm telling about.

All the participants state that they engage students in a collaborative way by providing their own background and experiences which add to the class conversation and learning. In her quote, Erla talks about learning from her students' heritage and background, where she actively seeks out additional information about the culture of those in her classroom. She talks about investing time in the international students in her class to expand her own understanding of where these students are from. While Erla notes that this is for her own learning and knowledge, spending time learning about students' backgrounds will also help her to connect with those students in the classroom as well make the relationship more authentic.

When asked about what teaching methods she employs as part of IaH, Eyrún spoke about how she encourages students to share their own experiences that might challenge her current ideas and positions. She tends not to lecture in her classes when she teaches, but rather encourages group work and discussion which facilitates this. While she does not make the explicit connection between what she does with new information from her students, she wants to know about students' experiences. Additionally, she encourages them to challenge the veracity of material she presents in teaching by testing it against their own experience.

Hanna and Terry talk more explicitly about asking students to bring in not only their personal background, but also knowledge about the course content and material. For Hanna, many of her students are graduate students who are working professionals in the field with examples from their daily work to bring into the learning space. This collaborative teaching and approach in how Hanna runs her class was demonstrated during the observations as well, where she actively solicited experiences from her master's students with genuine interest. She takes and incorporates the stories, knowledge, and experiences of these students into her future teaching as well. Terry echoes Erla's recognition that students come with diverse backgrounds and that this gives them perspectives different than his own. He went on in that interview talking about students stating, "what they have to say is as valuable as anything I have to say," which moves this collaboration beyond learning from experiences of the students, and demonstrates he is also learning from them intellectually and academically. He empowers students and positions himself to be open to learning from their intellectual abilities which also encourages multiple perspectives in the classroom integrating IaH.

Some data show, however, this collaborative learning does not translate in all contexts for the participants. Despite Eyrún's comments about getting students to give their own perspectives, she did not always see the same opportunities to learn from her students in the same way. When asked at another point in the interview directly about what she learns from students in the classroom, Eyrún noted that she didn't feel like she learned as much from student experiences and attributed this in part to the limited types of courses that she is able to teach at UI. Her focus throughout the interviews was also strongly through a research lens where she had the mindset of learning about gathering data and learning about experiences of other populations interacting in the community. Notwithstanding this divergence, the majority of statements from the participants demonstrate collaborative learning through encouraging students to share and being open to learning from them.

Learning about craft of teaching

Beyond learning new information and knowledge from others, in this sort of collaborative learning, teachers learn about the art of teaching itself which may include aspects such as how to improve their methods, approaches or understanding of dynamics in the classroom. While the evidence from participants in this study is somewhat limited, there are some indications that they learn about the craft of teaching through engaging in these practices related to IaH. Hanna discusses how she has learned about teaching and the classroom setting while abandoning the lecture format:

> So, I mean, people pointed out to me quite early on that you know, we really need to look at these diversities also in Iceland. And that's one thing, and another thing is that you will never find a teaching method that fits or suits everyone. So, I think what I learned also was to try to use like multiple methods so that each student will find something suitable for them in each class. So, I try to mix methods and I try to keep the students occupied with conversation and so on, because I mean, lecturing? I really finished lecturing a long time ago because very few people really think that this is useful. So, I always try to talk to the students about what they prefer as the method.

In recognizing the various kinds of diversity in Iceland, including differentiations in social class and access, Hanna learned the importance of employing mixed methods in teaching which is itself a practice of IaH. Moreover, this quote shows that she also collaborates with the students by directly inquiring on what works for them, moving toward a more student-centered learning environment. Not only is she valuing the students' own knowledge of self and learning, but she has also learned that part of productive and effective teaching for such students comes from structuring the class around their needs and expectations rather than her own conceptions of how that classroom should operate.

Like Hanna above, Erla also talked about teaching methods in the classroom and abandoning the strict lecture format. Rather than focusing on how diversity of students influences the classroom, she focused more on incorporating new methods that she has learned are more emotionally powerful for reaching students in ways that will likely have a greater long-term impact. Here, Erla is responding about the process of incorporating real stories from others into her classrooms:

> Well, when I was in the U.S. I started to do it there. You know, I taught like the thirteen chapters because we had thirteen weeks or whatever. But I was starting teach more like the African American stories, but I do it more now, I think it's more powerful to take – to do more of that, to use that method. I think because if people can; if it's something emotion and you can put yourself in other people's shoes and it's something that you will take it away from the classroom and remember it and it touches you and think "oh my god, how would I feel if I were him" I think that's more powerful. Because if you just read about it and learn it, you take an exam you forget it. Ok that's, it was a fun class, but I don't remember anything. But if you really live it and analyze and discuss it, I think that's more powerful.

Erla used to teach directly from a textbook week by week, though not stated explicitly, likely through lecturing and assessing cognitive knowledge. Certainly, she was sticking to a prescribed format. However, through working and living in cultures different than her own, she began investigating and incorporating real stories from others which she found to be influential tools in the classroom to help students build empathy for others. Erla recognized the importance of affective learning and is both learning herself through the stories themselves and from the students' reactions to the material which she commented on in a previous quote. This sort of affective learning is at the heart of intercultural education and in turn, IaH.

Finally, while talking about a course he and others developed for international students to learn about Icelandic culture, Terry asks about what it means to be Icelandic. This rhetorical question is particularly interesting in this time of changing demographics in the comparatively small island nation. Terry comments about not only his own learning about Icelanders, but also about learning from other people from a variety of cultures and peoples in his classroom who are taking these courses:

> What it's like being here for a while and becoming Icelandic. What is it that makes you Icelandic? When does somebody decide that you're Icelandic and that's, it's almost more – I'm learning more from Icelanders as time goes along and the inherent class system for example. From teaching courses with people, you realize the breadth of – the more people from different places the – the breadth of world, global, worldviews that you have to bear in mind.

Learning about the craft of teaching in Terry's quote is not about specific methods, dynamics, or student interactions. Although he talks here about knowing more about Icelandic culture and identity, his ultimate point in this statement is about his own developmental process of expanding his own perspectives through connections with various peoples in his classes. Terry's wording about having to "bear in mind" different worldviews shows the cyclical nature of this process, how he applies this mindset to his teaching and then learns more through that application.

Communities of practice

The second major aspect in Coffield's (2008) concept of collaborative learning centers around teachers (re)negotiating both meaning of practice and identities as they come into communities of practice. As Wenger and Snyder (2000) state, these communities of practice are "groups of people informally bound by shared experiences and a passion for a joint enterprise" (p. 139). The community of practice evidenced here is with other academics engaging in practices of IaH. The evidence that supports the notion of these communities of practice around IaH is derived from participants' collaborative efforts and active learning from peers who are also in these communities. Eyrún and Terry provide important examples of collaborative learning as coming into communities of practice.

Eyrún, for example, when asked about how she is involved in helping students work better across cultures, commented on her participation in a collaborative group of teachers who are working in part toward this aim at UI, "[…] we have this collaboration, maybe Brynja has mentioned it to you, it's a collaboration among the teachers at the undergraduate level, level in educational students. And that's of course a venue – and we discuss all kinds of stuff there around teaching mainly." Later she went on to talk about an international network that she is also learning from:

> Funny that you should mention because when I was, I told you about how I first came into contact with

> those issues. It was through this European network. Children's identity and citizenship. I always struggled to begin with. I struggled with the fact that those were, I thought I was going into research network. [...] They were not very ambitious [in the] research – [...] why I am spending my time on this? So to speak. And then I realized after a while it isn't a research network, it's a [...] network of higher education professionals. And they're talking about practice, and it doesn't need to be this ambitious research. Just to present and share practice. So, then I got more relaxed about it. And I also realized after a while of being in this network, that the network wasn't necessarily about developing ideas or studies or research, it was about us coming together and getting to know each other and learning about each other. It was about us as people expanding our views, going to all those different places and countries which we've never been to. And so, in a way it had to do with more relations across cultures more than anything else.

Eyrún talks about coming into two different communities of practice in these quotes, both of which intersect with practices of IaH. The first community is local, made up of colleagues in her own organization at the university who have come together to share and learn from each other around improving teaching and learning across cultures. This collaboration then exposes her to a greater number of ideas and practices to take with her. She also has increased opportunities to share her own insight with others, forming stronger connections between her research and practice as well as among this group's members in this community. The second community of practice she talks about is an international network of practitioners. While this international group comes together less frequently in person, there is a greater diversity of views and experiences within a variety of contexts from the participants who are all focused on teaching and multiculturalism. Eyrún's shift in understanding of the purpose and usefulness of this international network resulted in continual efforts to engage in other practitioners around topics related to IaH, both strengthening current communities of practice around teaching and becoming part of new ones as she learns more.

While Eyrún also noted that she is not able to teach directly on content related to multiculturalism in the classroom very often, she stated her desire to do so and undoubtedly participation in this network would help translate ideas of working across cultures into the classroom. Later she talks about ways in which this network has impacted her teaching, "This network of course has [...] had quite a strong emphasis on discussions in the classroom, for example. And actually, that was my research topic in my master's Thesis. I was studying discussions in the classroom. So, of course that affected me as well. So, democracy all those discussions, about the democracy and citizenship and those issues." The direct impact of this specific community is impacting her teaching methods and engagement, but also the content of her classes.

Terry pointed to learning from a community of practice of other teachers as well. For him, participating in this community comes from his learning through observing others in the classroom when he visits or hosts colleagues from other universities:

> And that's probably one or two courses a year of this kind and of course we had to learn from them, I love going in to watch other people's teaching, I'm trying to encourage people to do it more with our own teaching within the university here, but I know a lot of friends who are also very effective teachers and I think I have a good sense of who can teach and who can't just from my own experience as time goes on, so yeah you learn from this.

While Terry is speaking broadly about learning from watching others teach and his ability in evaluating their effectiveness, he is doing so in the context of questions on being involved in practices of IaH – specifically learning from international peers. He does not explicitly state that these hosts and guests are observing his teaching but based on other data in the interviews about his relationships and exchange of teaching, this practice of observing is likely reciprocal from many members of this community. While he does not specify all the aspects he may be learning about during observation, he does state that he believes he has a "good sense" of who teaches well, which has likely been enhanced through this consistent practice. Not only is he actively participating in this community of practice, but he is also encouraging others to join this community at UI.

A final source of evidence for the participants coming into communities of practice around IaH is their engagement with various committees, working groups, and networks on campus discussed previously. In these activities, there is shared expertise and interest, if not passion, for education among the participants and the other members of these groups working with issues and practices related IaH. While there are more readily discernable benefits of participation such as gaining new information, or performing service as faculty members, this is not the only learning. It is important to emphasize that their participation in these groups is not only outwardly benefiting others but is also translating into individual learning and development for the participants themselves as shown here. The participants come to engage with these groups often voluntarily, finding new meaning and re(negotiating) identities based on their sharing with and learning from colleagues which bring the participants into new communities of practice.

Collaborative learning is a multi-faceted concept that positions instructors, here the participants, as co-learners in the enterprise of education. A vital aspect of this collaboration is coming into communities of practice which inform practices of IaH in teaching and around those communities related to multiculturalism, social justice, and international perspectives. The data show that participants not only have a disposition toward collaborative learning, but also believe that they learn through interaction with students and peers as well as about their own craft of teaching.

There are two interesting intersections of collaborative learning with other aspects of the study: the first is that this sort of collaborative learning discussed by the participants, especially learning about the craft of teaching, strongly relates to the efforts by the university to focus more on student-centered classrooms. While the evidence is not demonstrated by all the participants, several of them mention how they learned about using new or multiple methods that allow for more student voices and more affective learning. The second intersection is with the concept of authenticity in teaching, which, as discussed below, focuses not only on teachers' learning in the classroom and through their teaching itself, but also does so expressly in areas of interpersonal communication and empathy rather than about the craft itself.

Authenticity in Teaching

The adult cognition capacity of "knowing how we know what we know" discussed previously in this same chapter was used to analyze how participants become aware of and leverage their own preferences, strengths, and weaknesses in their personal learning processes. The concept of authenticity in teaching also concerns teachers' self-awareness, but specifically in knowing themselves as teachers. According to Cranton and Carusetta (2004), the core critical reflection of the teacher-student relationship occurs in the intersecting space of the critical reflection of themselves as teachers and the critical reflection of the "other" – here learning about students' characteristics, personalities, and cultural layers. As awareness through these critical reflections develops alongside an understanding of the contexts in which they occur, so does authenticity. This results in bringing increased personal congruence (e.g. beliefs, values, passions, and genuine care) into teaching spaces which ultimately improves teaching and learning for everyone involved. Cranton and

Carusetta (2004) argue that this authenticity in teaching is an ongoing developmental process, like many of the other components of this portrait.

Some of these aspects of authenticity in teaching map onto and support other components of the portrait of learning already discussed above. For example, aspects of participants' critical reflection are treated in the section on adult cognition, while aspects of learning about the "other" (e.g. students) is discussed in the section on collaborative learning. While those data and analyses will not be revisited here, it is important to bear in mind that this portrait of learning is a fluid constellation of concepts which have numerous intersecting threads, therefore previously analyzed data also provide some of the foundational evidence for authenticity in teaching.

In addition to those already discussed data, there are several aspects of authenticity of teaching that could be explored, but the focus of this section will be primarily on data that demonstrate how participants are bringing their own experiences, values, and beliefs into their teaching and workspaces. All participants revealed that they bring their genuine selves into the educational spaces and work through incorporating overlapping personal and professional values, beliefs, and goals. Some participants gave specific examples within the context of teaching. When asked generally about connections between personal and professional values and beliefs, several participants responded with statements which reveal this aspect of authenticity in teaching.

> Hanna: Yeah, of course I try to share what I think is important of what I do. I try to share that with friends and family you know, because I think this, my profession is so much a part of me, you know? It's very difficult to keep it separate, you know? Because I'm really doing what I believe in every day and what I think is important in life generally and I'm applying that to my work. And again, this is coming back to issues, like values like human rights and equity and so on […].

> Terry: […] I do believe very strongly in the value of bringing education to places like Africa; I believe in equal rights; I believe in understanding other cultures. So of course, the psyche of the global community is something that I feel very strongly about and I'm ready then to take part in building up interpretation here understanding what's going on with the Icelanders.

> Eyrún: [...] the reason I went into educational studies and research, was to allow everybody to self-actualize. Or you know, to be able to develop all their potential. So, we have an education system that really allows people to fulfill their dreams and ambitions and so on – the potentials of people, children, young people. This is the personal value that drives me into this direction, and I think that it has only been strengthened [...] through these issues, these perspectives [...].

Hanna makes the more poignant statement here about bringing her authentic self into her work. This is not necessarily a conscious effort, rather she notes that it is just difficult to keep them separate because they are so deeply intertwined. While not as explicit, we can infer this from the other two statements from Terry and Eyrún about the overlap between these areas, as they discuss how personal beliefs inform and drive their work. These participants offer a strong perspective of equality and social justice, which supports the conceptual overlap between multiculturalism and interculturalism in an Icelandic context. Eyrún's statement about allowing "everybody" to develop their potential was in the context of being engaged in multicultural education, while Terry and Hanna talk about equality and equal rights. This value of inclusivity exists both in personal and professional contexts with each informing the other.

Along with these broad statements, the participants provide more specific examples as well. When Terry responded to questions about personal values playing a role in his teaching specifically, his answer positioned diverse and comparative international perspectives as a personal belief which becomes congruent with his actions in the classroom:

> Well, they do in the courses that I've taught which are all multicultural to a large extent. I don't think there's any course that a teach which is purely Icelandic and even when I'm teaching an Icelandic course, I'm comparing it to other countries and other cultures, I've had students noting this when I'm referring, in Old Norse the Sami and Native American, Africa, things that I know of. So, of course, it has a role to play in the courses that I teach, that I used to teach. The way that the Icelandic, the Nationalism functioned and why it came to exist in the 19th century, all of that is an international movement. The big project now on the Grimm ripples, the way Romantic Nationalism drives across Europe. So,

> everything I've done – the Masks and Mumming project was also international. So, I don't think there is anything that I've done that is not. So, it's not a deliberate ploy, it's more that I simply like seeing things in this global perspective I suppose.

Terry feels like a foreigner everywhere and is driven by his values embodied in his term the "global psyche." He brings this authentic Self into his teaching practice in the form of examples from a variety of cultures and peoples in order to provide multiple perspectives in his classroom. While he also talks of research projects which take comparative perspectives, the incorporation of these into a conversation about teaching implies that the learning and knowledge derived from these projects informs teaching in the classroom as well.

During the class observation, Brynja told personal and detailed stories about her experiences in Minnesota and in Iceland, family history regarding her own relationships and her bi-racial son and some of the cultural barriers and discrimination they faced. She also related stories about her own social media use and her love of science fiction. This was brought up in interviews as well and she stated that her personal beliefs and values are incorporated into professional contexts. Both during personal and professional conversations, she says, "it just sort of seeps out all the time from me. This just sort of constant thought process that I talk about multiculturalism [...]." She gave a specific example of how this works in her classroom: "[...] if somebody says something – I may agree with them on whatever opinion they've just voiced – I try really hard to then say, "right ok, but have you thought about it from this perspective, because somebody else may understand it this way, and that can be just as valid." And that's a personal belief."

Guiding students toward seeing alternative perspectives is used by many instructors at the post-secondary level – but this is far from universal. Brynja explicitly connects this didactic method with her own personal beliefs. Getting others to see the validity and value in another person's perspective is important in her daily life. Brynja referred to several conversations with others in challenging them to see other viewpoints and spoke of frequently reflecting with friends who help challenge her own perspectives on topics and interactions.

Erla echoed the general attitude that these values and beliefs pervade both personal and professional life. When asked about who pushes her to continue pursing activities related to IaH, she responded with, "it's just a way of life." She also provided more specific evidence supporting authenticity in teaching by addressing how she brings personal stories and experiences – one aspect of this authentic self – into her classroom:

> [...] I love telling stories in my classroom so I'm not shy to tell people that this is how I've perceived it before but now after I learned about people's lives or got share it with my students and also it helps because I'm doing research, taking interviews, with both refugees and immigrants and also people in business because you have biases and some prejudice there as well in business.

Not only is Erla taking personal stories into the classroom, but she also specifically talks about her learning process in tackling her own prejudice which models for students how to engage in reflexivity and challenge personal unexamined biases. While the concept of authenticity in teaching focuses on the student/instructor relationship as mentioned above, Erla stated that she brings her authentic self into discussions in the workplace with her colleagues as well – which is a still a space for information exchange and learning in a more informal context:

> So, we start here at the core at the home. So, I take it in my office and people who come in can see that I have traveled because I bring some stuff in from other countries and I talk about it in meetings. You know, this is how this is done in this country and that country and so I think consciously am bringing these notions into my meetings, staff meetings, because this is part of who I am so I think the more we do, the more we travel, the more we learn about other cultures, it becomes so natural to be together and be in peace and harmony despite the differences and I think that's what we all want right?

Like Brynja previously who mentioned that conversations about multiculturalism "seeps out" of her all the time, Erla notes that talking about her own learning of other peoples and cultures is just part of her daily conversations and life at work. Sharing these experiences in direct interactions with colleagues demonstrates that promoting intercultural learning is not limited to students but extends to other faculty members who may then, in turn, incorporate this into their own work with students. In this way, Erla is impacting and developing IaH beyond her own classroom.

Finally, in addition to bringing this authenticity into the classroom and extending to workplaces, there is evidence from three participants (Terry, Erla, and Hanna) that demonstrates that they explicitly and consciously bring such authenticity into their work office space as well – which often transform into informal learning spaces. These spaces then represent both a practice of teaching, as well as part of the participants' own ongoing development. The photographic data (figures 3, 4, 5, 6, and 7) below illustrate some of the specific ways participants enact this sort of authenticity.

While it is common practice for many to fill individual workspaces with artifacts that are meaningful (in one way or another), these items are to a greater or lesser degree, authentic. As Terry noted during the interviews, the choice of office décor is a type of performance which is establishing and relaying a deliberate narrative. Through a lens of practices informing IaH,

Figure 3 Erla's bookshelves

these are physical representations of issues, frameworks, or values that are important to participants in their lives. Erla's office includes paintings and figurines from various places where she has traveled. She stated that she purposefully includes these items so that others can see their importance, not the least of which is the importance to her personally. One figurine of Nelson Mandela is particularly meaningful to Erla, as she considers him one of her heroes because of his work to end apartheid in South Africa. Terry's office includes items with personal meaning beyond those which correspond to his scholarship. Two prime examples include a photo of Jerry Garcia of the band The Grateful Dead, which gives clues to Terry's international musical influences and a photo of Terry himself playing

Figure 4 A figurine of Nelson Mandela sits on Erla's bookshelf

Figure 5 One of Terry's office walls

Figure 6 A photo in Terry's office of he and colleagues playing music together

Figure 7 Figurines from China on Hanna's bookshelf in her office

music with some academic friends. In congruence with his belief in exploring global perspectives, Terry also has several international posters, art, and books in his office. Hanna's bookshelves are also filled with books on topics from religion to anthropology in many languages. She also has some objects such as two figurines, gifts from China, which not only show her international connections, but also act as an embodiment of her stated desire to continue learning from other cultures.

Authenticity in teaching has numerous dimensions, including empathy and deep care for students and their learning. Data presented here focused on how these participants bring in personal experiences as illustrative examples in the classroom as well as incorporating their beliefs and values (often explicitly) about education, social justice, and utilizing global perspectives. The growth for participants as seen through a lens of authenticity in teaching is not about the craft of learning and the resulting communities of practice, which is important to the concept of collaborative learning, rather it is the transformative learning that Cranton and King (2003) promote of a communicative and emancipatory nature. This learning is a recursive process by which participants incorporate their authentic Self into the classroom and workspaces, resulting in stronger relationships with students (and even colleagues) and creating authentic spaces to better critically reflect about practice and Self.

Summary

Each of the components of the portrait of learning discussed above (from adult learning to collaborative learning to authenticity in teaching) allows for unique insights into how the participants develop from their engagement in practices of IaH. The divergence of these components provides a complex picture of faculty members as adult learners while the uniting concept is the shared thread of critical reflection. Each of these components are present in the data as shown above, but not every participant learner (much less every adult learner) displays each of these as strongly or even at all at a given time. As the focus of this study is to report on this cohort, there is more to uncover in future research reporting on both the individual and a larger sample group. Nevertheless, the data provided here supports the notion that academic staff continue to grow through engaging in such mindsets, some of which are fundamental to adult learners broadly, while others are specific to teachers and academics working in higher education.

Chapter IX: Conclusions and Looking Forward

There is mounting evidence that Internationalization at Home needs to be a cornerstone of student-centered internationalization efforts at institutions of higher education to engage all students. Faculty members continue to be key drivers in internationalization, and their importance in bringing about transformative IaH is even greater as they have control over the formal curriculum. This study starts to fill the gap in literature on how faculty members both go about enacting and practicing IaH in a day-to-day way, and how they further develop their academic self through these practices. Furthermore, the study considers IaH from the perspective of the faculty member by using an exploratory methodology that relies on the participants' own voices and understanding. The threads woven together here establish an intricate tapestry of how champions engage in IaH activities and how they work toward developing more transformative internationalization.

Exploring Engagement in IaH

The goal of this study was to determine how faculty members make sense of IaH and then how their understanding is implemented and experienced. During the analysis of the data, it became evident that the concept of a process of engagement should be understood as a specific phenomenon that undergoes gradual changes leading toward a certain end, rather than a lock-step movement from one discrete category to the next. Findings about the components of this process are discussed below.

Understanding of internationalization and IaH

Participant histories provide context for individual cases informing this process of engagement in IaH. Contextual data show that all the participants spent time living abroad which resulted in particularly formative experiences with difference. These experiences provided significant motivation for their interest in international education and also provide insight into foundational rationales for their engagement. These motivations were primarily individual and intrinsic, which align with literature about what drives faculty to participate in internationalization broadly (Calikoglu, Lee & Arslan, 2020; Li & Tu, 2016).

An important starting point for gaining clarity of the participants' engagement is by exploring how the participants make sense of internationalization and IaH in their own academic and institutional contexts. Participants recognized the multi-dimensional nature of internationalization which resulted in a variety of conceptualizations, which is not uncommon among faculty members (e.g. Friesen, 2011). Despite this variety, three common understandings developed from the data analysis: the first is that participants understand internationalization to mean intercultural or international education through providing students with the opportunity and tools to operate in a globalized world. The second conceptualization was that internationalization means cooperation between universities. Examples from the data include sharing knowledge through research or joint educational projects as well as student exchange partnerships. Finally, a third common understanding is that internationalization means faculty member participation in and development from international interactions such as, participating in international conferences, conducting research utilizing multiple perspectives and being open to and welcoming of diverse global perspectives and peoples. All three of these understandings center on building capacity - whether in students, faculty members or institutions. Overall, the participants universally viewed internationalization as a positive force, which has been shown impact the level of faculty member involvement in internationalization (Schwietz, 2006).

Notably, participants did not voice more marketized understandings of internationalization such as raising international prestige, profile or rankings which are frequently mentioned as institutional rationales (Seeber et al., 2016). However, participants acknowledged that rankings were important institutional goals for UI. They also noted that questions of language use in the classroom and the sheer numbers of international students dominated much of the discussion about internationalization across the campus. As these participants were purposefully selected because they are champions of IaH, it is unsurprising that they hold robust and learning-centered understandings of internationalization as a concept.

In regard to IaH itself, the term was more challenging and opaque. However, there were overlaps between internationalization and IaH particularly around internationalizing the formal curriculum. Most participants believe that IaH pertains to designing and delivering curriculum through student-centered teaching which supports developing multiple and international perspectives on the home campus. This understanding of IaH by faculty members is corroborated elsewhere in the literature (Robson et al., 2017). The changing demographics in Iceland and the challenges faced by diverse populations strongly informs another important aspect of the participants' understanding of IaH as a project in creating and integrating cultural diversity at the university. This stems from a belief that the diversification of society, particularly those from immigrant backgrounds, should be reflected in the population, values, and programs of the university, including diversity in both students and staff. In this way, participants understood IaH to be more relational.

Understanding of role in IaH

The participants' understandings of IaH provided a foundation for asking about what responsibilities faculty members had in those activities. As participants understood IaH to be delivering and supporting diverse perspectives through the curriculum, broadly speaking, they saw their role as academics central to IaH. Findings reveal that all the participants believed that they had an obligation to incorporate diverse and international perspectives or intercultural learning into their teaching, including those from non-Western sources or perspectives. While they also acknowledged the need for administrative support in messaging, this was more in relation to getting other faculty members involved.

There were also close connections between participants' understanding of IaH around diversity and inclusion on campus and in the classroom, and what they believe about their own responsibilities. Participants saw their role in IaH as promoters of increased awareness of diversity through research, building and maintaining networks, service, and teaching. Issues of social justice and immigration were central to their ideas of this work. For many participants, their experiences with marginalized populations or social inequities motivated their engagement in this sort of education in the first place. Ultimately, this understanding of role in IaH links to the core intercultural learning which these activities support, as Bennett (2010) contends, "intercultural competence expresses the essences of social justice: equal humanity" (p. 1). This conception of a faculty member's role highlights the underlying purpose of IaH as developing global citizens, rather than providing students with instrumentalist framework of training the global worker. However, these are often competing paradigms (Harrison, 2015), and participants cite both rationales when making sense of their roles in IaH: that they need to help prepare graduates to be successful at navigating a globalized world, but also that they must be culturally inclusive and reflexive about their own position.

Enacting practices of IaH

As the participants believe that their role is essential to IaH efforts as they understand them, it is important to investigate how they enact this belief through various practices they engage in as part of their work. Participants were asked about practices of IaH with prompts about their role as faculty members. Their practices of IaH ranged from larger on-going projects in the community to granular classroom activities.

Teaching

Practices related to teaching were particularly rich and showed that participants employ a variety of practices in internationalizing their curriculum which is part of IaH in the formal classroom aimed at developing intercultural competence and multiple perspective-taking in a global context. While the four categories of teaching that emerged from the data overlap and are therefore not discrete, they all center around a particular aspect or facet. One of the overarching categories to emerge from the data was practices of course design. These practices are built around comparative examples that participants used to illuminate concepts from a variety of sources such as international or local events, as well as examples from the participants' own experiences. Practices in this category had the strongest representation from participants.

Two other categories of teaching practices coalesced around emphasizing modes of learning. Teaching practices in the group "cognitive engagement" include those intended to cultivate higher order thinking processes such as fostering critical thinking about issues of difference as well as encouraging critical reflection on self, bias, and assumptions. These two practices were found frequently among all of the participants. Affective modes of learning were also demonstrated as a practice of teaching. These included cultural simulations and interactive activities aimed at helping students experience the emotions that arise from intercultural misunderstandings. Even while not all participants explicitly stated such learning outcomes as part of syllabi, these sorts of teaching practices emphasizing cognitive and affective modes of learning assist the development of intercultural and internationalized attributes which are increasingly both needed and expected from graduates (Association of American Colleges and Universities, 2009; Jones & Killick, 2013), including those from UI.

In keeping with the participants' understanding of IaH, a fourth category of teaching practices emerged around enhancing diversity and inclusion in the classroom. All the participants engage in teaching practices such as supporting and including non-dominant voices or identities and incorporating immigrant issues. While the data provide insight into the daily and even moment-by-moment practices, the variety of practices employed supports the notion that the use of multiple methods of instruction is as an overarching teaching practice of IaH. This approach is more student-centered, providing space and opportunity for not only including those with cultural and learning differences striving for a more equal learning environment, but also how to highlight and leverage those differences in the classroom as an instrument of intercultural learning.

Practices outside of the classroom

Practices of IaH emerged around interacting with on-campus peers, as well as with off-campus colleagues and Icelandic communities. While faculty member activities not directed at students on the home campus may seem ancillary to internationalizing the formal or informal curriculum, they inform integral components of IaH efforts. Consequently, this study examined those related activities that support the development of an international outlook or understanding (Robson et al., 2017, p. 30), not only for the participants themselves, but also for others on campus or those in the greater community.

One of the practices outside of the classroom to emerge from the data is research, particularly on issues of multiculturalism or comparative international perspectives. Much of this research is focused on populations in Iceland, which also provides researchers with a connection to the society. In addition to publishing, participants incorporate such research data and findings into their classrooms work, which then has a direct impact on specific teaching practices of IaH. Moreover, it also increases awareness on campus of such issues.

Other activities emerged from the data around maintaining networks, where participants frequently engaged with colleagues from the home campus as well as those abroad to share research or practices related to multiculturalism or inclusion often through conferences, research networks or projects. Participants actively form relationships with others, creating networks to leverage; additionally, these opportunities to gain international and comparative perspectives on topics in their discipline advances the participants' IaH research capacity and teaching effectiveness. Conversely, these individuals and broader networks that the UI participants engage with benefit from the interacting with peers whose views, scholarship and practices which promote the outcomes associated with IaH. Findings reveal that participants actively engage with senior and unit-level administrators and faculty colleagues through individual interactions, sitting on committees or tasks forces, and through creating spaces on campus for discussion on how to make progress on issues related to IaH.

These more relational practices extended beyond influencing IaH at the university, as they also influence Icelandic society, both to the public and more targeted entities or organizations. Although it has become somewhat marginal in recent literature (e.g. Beelen & Jones, 2015), connecting with the local community has historically been related to IaH in regard to connecting with local immigrant and diverse populations. The extension of this (and this was the case for Bengt Nilsson working in Malmö) is that through a framework of IaH, the university can invest in and incorporate more local students from immigrant and diverse communities to infuse more diversity into classrooms, creating opportunities for intercultural learning and exchange. Moreover, such practices constitute an ethical position: to decolonize higher education by purposefully improving access for those populations. As Crowther et al. (2000) contend when discussing the institutional implications of IaH: "Recognition that the network of external stakeholders is wider than students, their parents and others (in particular, public bodies) who sponsor the system, but extends to society in general and to the employment market in particular, leads one to the conclusion that higher education must serve the needs of more than just the academic community itself" (p. 39).

Findings from the study show a variety of practices connecting with Icelandic society in formal roles as consultants or disseminating information about research to the wider public. These sorts of practices increase awareness of multicultural and international issues to the benefit of the entire country. In this way IaH is a foundational component of the burgeoning Internationalization of Higher Education for Society (IHES) which "explicitly aims to benefit the wider community, at home or abroad, through international or intercultural education, research, service and engagement" (Brandenburg, de Wit, Jones, & Leask, 2019)

These practices outside of the classroom, provide some answer to the final research question: How do UI faculty members who engage in IaH in and beyond the classroom influence campus and disciplinary colleagues? As vocal champions of IaH, the work and conversations that these faculty members undertake daily impacts their own spheres of influence, starting within their local faculties and extending on to impacting IaH at the institutional level. Thus, the participants function as champions by taking on important roles in shaping and advancing IaH at UI, growing a sphere influence even while the work remains institutionally decentralized. All the participants discussed strategies about continuing to cultivate their engagement, much of which included continuing to influence campus community members through teaching, research, and service, by advocating for increased attention to IaH. They cited support from colleagues and friends in this work, but burnout was a significant concern for some. Two other participants noted that retirement was on the horizon. Taken together, these challenges signal the need for others to take up the mantel to share the work around IaH among more faculty members at UI.

Faculty engagement in IaH as adult learning

As noted at the beginning of this book, engagement is defined as a psychological presence in which faculty members devote their attention toward activities of finding purpose, congruence, and challenge. Therefore, using a constellation of five theories related to learning as lenses to interpret data, findings in this study highlight ways the participants then develop as part of their engagement in IaH.

Growth mindset and development of the academic self

The theories of a growth mindset (Dweck, 2006) and the development of the academic self (Hall, 2002) converge on an openness of new directions in learning and understanding. Seen through these theories, findings indicate that participants are continually seeking to stretch their understanding and knowledge about the world around them. Participants displayed a growth mindset, some by recognizing a constant flux and need to adapt to a shifting globalized world. There was an especially strong disposition among participants to learn about other peoples and cultures supported by a level of humility and willingness. This growth mindset forms a foundation of self-directed learning (Dweck, 2006) which then translates to participants' research as well, where they re-imagine their professional identities through new avenues of thought or inquiry emerging from their engagement in issues and practices of IaH. Often these new directions were only tangentially related to their initial academic pursuits. Participants also then brought this research informing IaH into their classrooms, which supports the second major aspect of development of the academic self of praxis, bring theory and practice into teaching (Hall, 2002). While data supporting a growth mindset was the most limited of the portrait of learning, taken together with data supporting the related theory of development of the academic Self, it is clear there is a willingness and desire to expand understanding around IaH.

Adult cognition

Brookfield (2000) contends that adult learners employ four distinct capacities in their learning more frequently than children or adolescents. The adult cognitions of critical reflection and thinking dialectically were particularly salient, while the other two were evidenced by only a few participants. The participants frequently discussed self-reflection of their own biases or assumptions in their practices of IaH and adjusted their approach accordingly. Participants also showed their learning from thinking dialectically, recognizing that different environments require different approaches to teaching because of cultural differences. Taken as a whole, data reveal that the faculty members in this study utilize these capacities of adult learning regularly in their engagement of IaH.

Collaborative learning

In addition to the specific learning capacitates, participants demonstrated a disposition toward collaborative learning (Coffield, 2008) as they approached the classroom as learners themselves through encouraging diverse student populations to share their experiences, thoughts, and stories. With this disposition toward collaborative learning, participants also were able to develop their craft of teaching through this inclusive approach. Data also revealed that participants came into new communities of practice through engaging in IaH, which generated new understandings and shared meaning around advancing international and intercultural learning on campus. These communities of practice are particularly important because as Otten (2009) contends, such a "community has much better potential than a single person to explore different views and arguments" (p. 415) within the domain of IaH which will provide more unified efforts among faculty members.

Authenticity in teaching

This growth also occurs through participants' authenticity in their teaching; the on-going process of gaining self-awareness in their professional roles as teachers (Cranton & Carusetta, 2004) engaging in practices of IaH. Data show that participants became more mindful of their practice as teachers through authentic interactions with their students This authenticity in teaching was particularly demonstrated by participants bringing in their own experiences into learning spaces through artifacts and personal stories. Evidenced by data showing the meshing of personal goals, values and beliefs into teaching contexts and spaces, this authenticity is one indicator that participants are indeed engaging by investing their compete selves into their professional roles.

Informed by their understanding of concept and role in IaH, this growth stemming from participants' engagement then increases, develops, and expands their individual practices of IaH. The participants' own learning through engaging in these practices is neither linear nor sequential, but rather it is dynamic as growth occurs at various points in the process, informing and recasting the process itself in new directions. Practice informs their individual learning which in turn, informs practice.

Evidence from this study then adds support to the assertion that these participants should be regarded as adult learners and that such lenses are useful to exploring their experience in engaging in IaH, leading to a more transformative internationalization.

Implications

It has long been asserted that faculty members are principal agents in internationalizing higher education (Altbach, 2002; Brewer, 2010; Finkelstein et al., 2013) and yet, their voices are underrepresented in the literature (Jones & de Wit, 2012). While the findings from this study confirm their centrality to IaH in this context specifically, it also orients the conversation toward amplifying faculty perspectives by providing participant-generated descriptions of their own conceptions and practices. This adds needed voices to the literature from those who are in the vanguard of implementing IaH in the formal curriculum, shaping the concept itself, shifting and adding to its meaning for peers within the participants' institution, but also for scholars studying IaH. Moreover, this study redirects attention back to the individual and the relational aspects of IaH, offering insight as to how faculty members can advance on the continuum of internationalization more transformatively.

Refining practices of IaH

Jones & de Wit (2012) note there is also a gap in the literature detailing the actual practices of IaH, stating that "research, the curriculum, and the teaching and learning process, which should be at the core of internationalization, as expressed by movements such as Internationalization at Home, often receive little attention" (p. 38). The results of this study then contribute the understanding of what constitutes practices of IaH by exploring the work of faculty champions. While some of the practices detailed here coincide with those identified previously (Beelen & Leask, 2011; Hanson & McNeil, 2012) as the tools which define IaH, others are novel. Perhaps more importantly, this study expands the scope and detail of practices by including specific modes of teaching and classroom activities, which have largely been unexamined. Evidence defining what constitutes a practice then supports what Beelen and Leask (2011) posit about IaH, that "as a concept it will continue to evolve in response to the local, regional, and global contexts within which it operates – it will continue to be 'on the move'" (p. 20). The incarnation in the context of UI supports this assertion. Ultimately, the participants' engagement which informs the study helps in understanding faculty members' daily activities which can aid in translating the theoretical positions of IaH into specific approaches or actions.

Growth from engagement

This study provides evidence that these faculty members who are engaged in practices of IaH develop their academics selves toward an orientation of transformative internationalization rather than only symbolic efforts. These practices then result in professional and personal development, fleshing out the framework and certain characteristics proposed by Sanderson (2011) for the "ideal and authentic teacher for contemporary higher education" (p. 161). The growth participants experience is ongoing as they continue to learn from their engagement, finding new depths of understanding. This reinforces the notion that there is not a final level of attainment, much like intercultural development itself, which is the core of IaH. It is clear from the data that this development of the self extends beyond the participants' teaching role, to the research and service roles as well. Importantly, this growth from the practices, mindsets and cognitions detailed in the portrait of learning provides insight into intrinsic motivators which keep these participants engaged in all these roles. Viewing faculty members as adult learners then has implications for identifying those characteristics which are salient in each faculty member already, and those which may need further attention. Making them explicitly aware of these mindsets and modes of learning can help faculty members understand how they can increase the depth of their engagement. It can also help them by orienting their attention away from additive ideas of simply "being involved" in more and more activities. This sort of activity-based approach can lead to engagement fatigue. The data from this work exemplifies a more integrated and transformative approach exemplifies a more sustainable model toward engagement.

Faculty champions as leaders

The participants in this study invest their internationalized self into their entire professional role on the home campus, thus making them champions of IaH. This adds to Childress' (2010) definition of champions as having "vast knowledge of international issues in their own areas of expertise and strong cross-communication skills" (p. 28). Several of the champions involved in this study were primarily concerned with improving their own practices rather than making changes to the institution as echoed in the literature (Anderson et al., 2008). However, others spoke about shifting the orientation of their units toward thinking about IaH. Ultimately, they are providing grassroots-leadership (Kezar & Lester, 2009) through designing and incorporating innovative practices of IaH. The participants' engagement has an impact on their colleagues' understanding which may result in more involvement, allowing the leveraging of collective action toward internationalizing their entire departments (Bogotch & Maslin-Ostrowski, 2010). These champions then can be considered transformational leaders who look to develop others (whether students or staff) to their fullest potential with concern for the greater good and by doing so, continue to change themselves in the process (Northouse, 2010).

Prioritizing IaH

UI is not alone. There are institutions of higher education in various locations around the world that are expected to be at the vanguard of research, professional development, and an educational bedrock for the progress of their societies. Many institutions have relatively disconnected pockets of IaH efforts around campus in addition to the division between international and domestic students (Alexiadou, Kefala & Rönnberg, 2021; Crawford & Bethell, 2012; Robson et al., 2017).

While the focus of this study is on clarifying the internationalizing of certain individual faculty members, there must be a more organized and systematic approach to make IaH effective. The rationales and motives expressed by administrators and the participants for engaging in IaH varied but did not conflict. This implies space for agreement in the foundational approach between the top-down and bottom-up efforts to implement IaH, particularly around the concept of inclusive education for diverse populations. The participants' connection between inclusivity and internationalized teaching and learning confirmed by this study, aligns with scholars who contend that "responding to the diversity of international students and responding to the diversity of home students are in fact not two agendas but one" (Jones & Killick, 2007, p. 110). This response comes via IaH, implemented throughout the core curriculum so that all students have access to the same internationalized learning outcomes. It is not sufficient to internationalize a single course, experience or even program; rather participants highlight that faculty must develop a global mindset that pervades their entire role. This development must be part of a cultural shift on campus toward valuing intercultural learning and increased empathy among faculty members across the institution. To bring this about however, it will ultimately require investment and action from both faculty members and administrators in co-constructing a campus climate conducive to IaH and then the initiatives that support its continued development. As Robson et al. (2017) contend, "opportunities for the academic community to develop an international outlook need to be driven from the bottom-up and supported top-down, offering opportunities for personal and academic development to students and staff alike" (p. 30). Ultimately, successfully implementing IaH efforts requires a relational approach with focused qualitative attention on internationalizing the individual agents. There is a need for champions, as important individual agents, to continue building communities of practice across the university as many others on campus are unfamiliar with practices of IaH or the status of these participants as champions of these practices.

Supporting faculty members engagement in IaH

Of the five participants, three are from the same school, and most of the participants were concerned about burnout. While there are likely other champions on campus, it is clear there is a limited number. The need for developing a broader selection of faculty members' capacity to internationalize teaching is central to IaH (Robson et al., 2017) to "engage with, model and deliver" (p. 30) internationalized and inclusive learning across the entire campus and in the compulsory curriculum (Beelen & Jones, 2015).

Childress (2010) contends that there are different levels of faculty engagement in the internationalization process, including the highly engaged champions and the advocates who support specific aspects of internationalization. While faculty members from all levels should be incorporated into the discussion, examining the participants' path of development toward the champions they now are in this study suggests that those latent champions or advocates who may be willing to participate in certain IaH activities are more likely to become engaged as they continue finding and learning from new practices. These first steps might come through connecting and collaborating with established champions. However, there are other important tools to encourage engagement. A program of intentionality, individual support, investments, institutional networks, and infrastructure which help faculty members to engage in internationalization broadly (Childress, 2010). Mestenhauser (2003) identifies structured faculty development opportunities as an important tool for engagement in IaH specifically. Achieving this broad engagement requires tapping into intrinsic motivations which align an institutional strategy, messaging, and goals for IaH toward internationalist values and not competitive approaches (Turner & Robson, 2007).

While one participant noted that there are others now trained to continue their scholarship, new teachers often lack the clout or experience to significantly influence programing or education within their own units much less the university. Moreover, it is unclear whether the same amount of interest will exist in developing intercultural competence among other academic staff. While these participants are champions of IaH with intrinsic motivations which inform their research, service and especially teaching, scaling engagement in IaH at UI likely requires institutional systems of recognition and reward (Robson, 2017) which can incentivize other faculty members to seek out their own development, both for internationalizing curricula, but also for transforming their own beliefs and values through internationalization of the self (Sanderson, 2011). Central and unit-level administrators who recognize the importance of IaH can also assist by creating time, space, and the climate for such professional and personal development opportunities. Support must also come in the form of providing monetary and non-monetary resources as well as strategically prioritizing faculty development.

Campus diversity

Actively recruiting and supporting domestic students from immigrant and diverse backgrounds to come to the university will also increase the university's connection to local diverse populations, which is currently being supported through efforts by faculty champions. Additionally, proactive methods for engaging these diverse students will help create an environment inclusive of all students by strengthening the diversity in the classrooms and on-campus. This then increases exposure to difference and opportunities for leveraging alternate perspectives and new forms of knowledge, which may challenge long-standing parochial understandings on campus. There will be greater opportunity for inclusivity if the university culture can extend this emerging paradigm to understand that traditional domestic students come from diverse backgrounds in terms of class, gender, ability, learning styles and life experiences that include cultural, racial and ethnic identities. This can then be leveraged to challenge the false dichotomy between domestic and international students (Jones, 2017). Despite this opportunity, Harrison (2015) reminds us that IaH is a problematic endeavor in terms of power, especially in international classrooms where there is frequently resistance to intercultural group work; a challenge which was confirmed by data in this study. Therefore, issues of power must be openly and explicitly addressed moving forward.

Icelandic society

There is a need for intercultural skills and capacities across the globe, and Iceland is no different. The 2014 Intercultural Cities report by the Council of Europe (Intercultural Cities Secretariat Council of Europe, 2014), Reykjavik ranked as one of the lowest in the sample of cities in terms of commitment to interculturality – which is to say, commitment to inclusion of people from diverse cultural backgrounds as part of the city. Significant efforts have been made in recent years, including the city's Multicultural Council, which have improved the city's score to now being average among cities in the report (Intercultural Cities Secretariat Council of Europe, 2020). While this is a step forward, the country must commit to supporting diverse peoples and perspectives, not least for reasons of inclusion and equity in country, but also because Iceland will need an interculturally capable society to work toward solving the ever-increasing complexity of global problems.

Page (2007) finds that groups comprised of diverse individuals consistently outperform homogenous groups in high-level problem solving, noting that "two people with different perspectives test different potential improvements and increase the probability of an innovation" (p. 7). As Iceland is not immune to global climate change, increasing economic disparity, and food and water security, the citizens will need diverse perspectives and knowledge bases to have a productive and healthy population in the future. They must leverage the resources and capital of their strongest institutions to build a citizenry capable of tackling significant changes occurring in the modern world. This study provides evidence as to how participants are providing the groundwork for this change not only through their teaching of students, but also in their direct work in supporting, and championing inclusion of diverse populations across the society.

Lastly, the impact that participants have demonstrated in advancing practices of IaH underscore the need for further incentivizing and supporting their efforts. While the university continues to have funding restored by the government, they are still not at the levels necessary to develop and carry out the necessary institution-wide goals of IaH.

This means that the government ought to look carefully at the benefits of fully reinvesting in the national university and consider additional avenues for expanding opportunities for intercultural training. This is because IaH is not solely about giving students opportunities to engage such populations solely for the students' own growth. Rather, activities of IaH such as those highlighted by the participants look toward mutually beneficial projects, activities and interactions that create equity and opportunities for marginalized communities, translating principles into inclusive action. As more directly conceptualized in internationalization of higher education for society, early descriptions of IaH outline the impacts must extend to the greater community as well (Crowther et al., 2000), especially those which align with promote inclusivity for local culturally diverse populations (Mestenhauser, 2003; Wächter, 2003).

Recommendations

For IaH to succeed it must be embedded in all areas of an institution through an ongoing process. One recommendation to accomplish this is to establish a centrally supported IaH strategy through engaging a variety of stakeholders (Robson et al., 2017). This would include both academic and non-academic staff, engaged faculty members, the office of diversity, the international office, and the Center for Teaching and Learning among others. This strategy aligns with points already stated in many universities' current strategic documents and could inform such documents in future incarnations. Given that faculty members develop from involvement in these IaH processes, it behooves administrators to invest through creating messaging and environments supporting IaH as well as monetary resources to embed intercultural and global learning into their courses.

Leveraging champions

The participants were identified to be part of the study because they are champions of IaH demonstrated by their engagement in and support of related activities. Their very participation in these practices can be understood as leadership: innovating and pushing forward IaH in their own areas of influence, which will be crucial for the success of the university's students and ultimately, Icelandic society. Leveraging such champions ought to begin with clarifying the constellation of their practice and leveraging their leadership while incentivizing them to mentor others and be good "organizational citizens" (Kezar & Lester, 2009) in supporting and increasing the development of practices of IaH. More specifically, the institution's leadership can draw on the theories presented in the portrait of learning in this study to deepen the engagement for faculty members who are involved in practices of IaH. It is through such ongoing development for the individual that the university can shift toward an institutional orientation of transformative internationalization.

UI would also benefit from creating space, rationale, and opportunity to building more communities of practice among faculty members. One important way this can be established is through an internal network of faculty members who are interested in various aspects of IaH. This network could be coordinated via listserv, to communicate amongst various champions without requiring structured meetings until enough of a base is established to move into more formal spaces. This network would serve to build internal capacity, especially in areas of teaching and internationalizing of the curriculum. While it is clearly necessary to maintain the Icelandic cultural and linguistic identity of the university, this network could be strengthened by strategically hiring additional non-native faculty members who would bring new resources to an IaH agenda (Hoffman, 2003).

In addition to building capacity through these established champions presented in this study, more resources could be directed toward the Center for Teaching and Learning to specifically develop more seminars and workshops to assist faculty members in sustained efforts to internationalize the formal curriculum. Additionally, each school could leverage a dedicated professional teaching and learning specialist with core training in internationalizing the curriculum tailored to each discipline (Leask & Bridge, 2013). This could be facilitated together with advancing diverse teaching methods and strategies. Advancing this initiative could increase the number of experts on campus who focus on improving teaching for faculty members to better understand, establish, and implement global learning and related outcomes. Multiple and diverse methods of instruction are gaining traction within the university and should continue being developed, enhanced, and delivered throughout programs at UI as part of an ongoing IaH agenda.

Finally, the university could establish a standing committee that is charged with planning IaH efforts across the university, focusing on both the formal and informal curriculum. Of note, this committee could establish a protocol for assessing the development of intercultural competence and international perspectives across campus. As in many institutions, most efforts focus on data required for rankings and compliance with the state government and supra-national organizations. This committee could also help university create and implement cultural diversity and inclusion goals established as part of the Bologna Process.

Significance to Iceland and the University

The Icelandic public as well as the government and public institutions must traverse the challenges associated with transitioning from a highly homogenous population to one with significant racial, ethnic, religious, and cultural diversity. This research is intended to help spur conversations about the place of intercultural and international education in Icelandic higher education. As Iceland's largest comprehensive research and educational university, the University of Iceland is undoubtedly an important site at which these dialogues must take place. By homing in on the experiences of faculty members rather than administrators as the point of entry, such conversations encourage a bottom-up or grassroots approach, even while both top-down and bottom-up approaches are necessarily for successful IaH (Robson et al., 2017). Indeed, efforts led by members of faculty, rather than administrator-driven directives, have greater impact on mobilizing other faculty members to participate in internationalization (Turner & Robson, 2007). So, while the results of this study may be useful for senior administrators in engaging faculty and formulating the necessary strategic plans for internationalization, it may be even more beneficial for faculty members to hear from their fellow colleagues, in their own voices, how they both interpret the meaning of internationalization as well act to create it.

As part of an increasingly interconnected world, faculty at UI must be invested in the daily task of developing students' sense of empathy and equity, global mindset, intercultural sensitivity to be ethically engaged members of a larger society, especially as the realities of global challenges and disparities are emerging in their own backyard. Realizing these outcomes requires faculty members themselves to cultivate these perspectives and embrace a more inclusive and equity-minded outlook. Additionally, many faculty members at UI are recognized in the greater Icelandic society with an amount of influence on government, business, social and cultural institutions. Results of this study may then aid faculty development and institutional opportunities meant to move the institution toward organizational change (Bond & Blevins, 2020) through transformative internationalization, beginning at an individual level, that could ultimately have a significant impact on the entire country and beyond.

Looking Ahead

While this study offers some foundational perspectives on building global mindsets in faculty members and how they may transform both the university and its graduates, the way forward is complex. There is significant space for investigating how this can be accomplished through taking institutions from a more symbolic end of the continuum to the more transformative orientation. Even as the concept of IaH is still being parsed and shaped (e.g. Beelen & Jones, 2015; Robson, Almeida, & Schartner, 2017), the minimal amount of literature investigating faculty member development is of concern. As discussed above, faculty members are key agents in advancing internationalization as a whole and particularly in internationalizing curriculum, which is central to the IaH framework – and yet not enough attention is paid to investigating their intercultural and international development. Further work needs to be done around issues of growth and change to understand more fully the ways that faculty become engaged in the often challenging and under-appreciated work of IaH. This research in turn could be applied to support current champions through their engagement in these processes as well as formulating strategies for developing new champions. If the key to IaH is to integrate such approaches throughout the entirety of the curriculum, more attention must be paid to faculty members in these areas – they will not be able to teach what they do not know.

Turning to the conceptual and theoretical, Bengt's contextual explicit connections with local cultural groups and communities needs to be revisited. Beelen and Jones (2015) note that while such partnerships with diverse and international communities cannot be made in all contexts, such activities represent a "distinctive element" of IaH as opposed to other conceptualizations of internationalization. Not all universities are geographically located in diverse communities. However, as the global movement of peoples and expansion of globally connected classrooms through virtual exchange and collaborative online international learning continues, there will be fewer and fewer universities that operate in anything that could be deemed a culturally homogenous context.

Integrating diverse communities into the fabric of local institutions of higher education is undervalued in practice and under investigated in research. Indeed, Bengt Nilsson's approach at Malmö was intended to benefit university students as well as local immigrants. This perspective of including and bringing local diversity into institutional spaces for the benefit of both has been minimized in much of the literature and in some cases altogether forgotten. Increased efforts in exploring how institutions connect with, assist, and integrate these diverse communities will further global and intercultural learning.

Positioning IaH as a concept built on inclusivity through praxis calls for incorporating peoples from diverse communities as students and as drivers or co-creators of research— enacting the very concept of intercultural competence in an authentic way. This authentic modeling comes through actively engaging and co-learning with these populations as part of the mission of universities who engage in IaH; revolutionizing the power structures of the university (Freire, 1993). Questions of power can never fully be removed from intercultural communication (Martin & Nakayama, 2014), and they should arguably be centered in the very core of intercultural education.

While there is progress in researching diversity in the greater society and particularly in the primary schools, there is a need for developing intercultural competence and international perspectives in Icelandic universities and society. For UI specifically, there is fertile ground for conducting exploratory studies around aspects of IaH. Several questions ought to be examined, such as: In what ways are conversations shifting around how the university defines what it means to be Icelandic? How will the university respond to the country's rapidly changing demographics? To what degree is the formal and informal curriculum internationalized across the university? Even more importantly, research establishing the level of intercultural competence of the wider academic staff will be an important step in determining the strategies and development needed to develop curricula that can deliver global learning for the student body. In turn, studies should further investigate the intercultural impact of the various initiatives meant to integrate international students on campus and particularly whether international and students from immigrant backgrounds are changing the way traditional domestic students approach difference.

As demographics continue to shift, institutions of higher education will increasingly need to play a central role in societal development. The intentional cultivation of intercultural capabilities and global mindsets for sustainable development, inclusion and equity are among the most crucial tasks for higher education in our increasingly globalized world. Finding any measurable movement forward is challenging and complex. For higher education, it requires thoughtful investment an intentional transformative, rather than symbolic, orientation through programs of IaH which permeate all aspects of institutions. Faculty are the key to realizing this program and there is an ever-present need for them to embrace practices of IaH and intercultural pedagogies. Administrators must invest in and support faculty in tangible ways to help them develop and grow in their teaching and engagement.

This book illuminates the kinds of faculty leaders who form a foundation from which to advance a more transformative internationalization. Academics, who are so often cited as being resistant to change, can and do experience growth in critical thinking and feeling that then positively impacts their practice and students through their engagement. Such faculty champions embody the ethos of IaH that Terry so aptly stated, "we're always changing, we're always adapting, we're always learning."

Appendix

Research Design and Methodology

Merriam (1998) asserts that case study design has become the fundamental way of doing educational research. This is in part because this research design allows for researchers to gain an understanding of the complexities of the case itself in a real-world context without reducing it to predefined narrow categories. As Merriam (1998) notes, "the interest is in process rather than outcomes, in context rather than a specific variable, in discovery rather than confirmation" (p. 19). While Stake (1995) distinguishes between intrinsic (interest in the case on its own merit) and instrumental (interest in gaining broader understanding of a phenomenon) case studies, the first goal is to understand the bounded entity.

There are no requisite methods of data collection in a case study (Merriam & Tisdell, 2016). Rather, methods are chosen based on the data needs established by the research question; a strength of case study, more than other forms of qualitative research, is the freedom to use whatever methods are necessary to understand the case (Yin, 2018). However, as stated in the definition above, researchers using a case study research design in the field of education employ multiple methods of data collection which are frequently qualitative in nature (Merriam, 1998; Stake, 1995). Along with multiple methods and aspects of emergent design, research questions are refined and progressively focused as a study becomes more sophisticated through ongoing data collection and analysis.

A descriptive, instrumental, and exploratory case study research design is appropriate for this study for several reasons: First, the cases in this study are bounded or "fenced-in" (Merriam & Tisdell, 2016; Stake, 1995) as individuals who are contained in a single institution and within a specific population. Although the aim of the research is not to understand the entity of the university as a whole, the phenomenon of faculty engaging in internationalization and the context cannot be easily separated (Yin, 2018) and the study therefore also includes a description of the unique setting in which the cases operate. Second, case study design is particularly well-suited to explore processes of human experience and understanding of the world they live in and thus allows for in-depth inquiry (Merriam, 1998) which aligns with the focus of the study. Third, this study conforms to conditions that Yin (2018) advances that support the appropriateness of using a case study research design, including when there are more variables of interest than data points and there is no control over behavioral events. Fourth, case study is particularly suited to answering research questions of "how", "why" and exploratory "what" (Yin, 2018). Fifth, based on a review of the literature, there are currently no studies on faculty and internationalization and an exploratory approach that considers multiple cases to understand the phenomenon is warranted. Sixth, and finally, there is an increasing need to gain a deep understanding of faculty engagement in internationalization to assist in the development of a transformational orientation both within the institution and in the greater society surrounding it.

Role of the Researcher

Research is inherently subjectively informed. Regardless of whether the methods are quantitative or qualitative, researchers bring their own background, assumptions, and experiences into their scholarly work. Consistent with the theoretical framework utilized to analyze the data in this study, which considers the "Self," it is relevant and important to include a reflexive account of my values and experiences that underpin the work. My interest in adult learning is driven by a deep belief that faculty members are critical agents of change as they educate the next generation of thinkers, scholars and citizens. Indeed, faculty members can (and frequently do) make lasting and significant impacts on those they teach and society broadly. While there is a body of literature on how faculty members are supported, there is less about how faculty members themselves engage in their own learning. Examining this process regarding IaH is intended to have an impact on supporting faculty members through their work.

Selecting the research site

The cases, or individual faculty members, in this study exist within single institution. The University of Iceland is the country's flagship research institution with approximately 14,000 students and 755 academic staff (University of Iceland, 2016b). The main campus is situated in the heart of the capital city Reykjavik, which is also primary urban center with a population of approximately 170,000 in an island-nation in the North Atlantic of a little over 330,000 total inhabitants.

Sampling strategies in qualitative research are deliberate and purposeful, including selecting the cases that best answer the research questions (Creswell & Creswell, 2018; Merriam & Tisdell, 2016). Case study research specifically, often requires a two-step process in selecting this nonrandomized sample (Merriam & Tisdell, 2016). The first layer of purposeful sampling is the site at which the cases exist. Creswell & Creswell (2018) considers these as "with-in site cases" because the cases as manifestations of the phenomenon are contained within one institution. The selection of UI was not because it is illustrative or typical, rather because it is unique and unlikely to be found elsewhere (Stake, 1995). This is in large part due to the broader social, political and geographic contexts in which the cases exist that are of particular interest and unique.

Sampling the cases

The case study is instrumental as the goal is to learn about something beyond the units of analysis which requires a second layer of sampling, the cases themselves. Purposeful sampling (Patton, 2015) allows the researcher to deliberately select participants precisely because they are information-rich and can best inform the phenomenon under inquiry. For this study, participants who represent the individual cases were selected because they are particularly or significantly involved in practices of IaH. Patton (2015) refers to such a sampling technique as extreme sampling, where the cases have success or attributes beyond the typical or norm. A case for this study then is defined as an individual faculty member who is a teaching faculty member at UI and engaging in practices of IaH. In initial contacts with potential participants only tenure or tenure-track faculty were considered, but as it became clear that there were non-tenure track faculty significantly engaged in this work, the definition was expanded to include all categories of faculty members.

Defined selection criteria were used in determining which faculty members qualified as "significantly engaged." These faculty members were then invited to participate. Merriam and Tisdell (2016) note that selection criteria do not need to be overly explicit, but include guiding parameters, which may develop once in the field. The guiding criteria based in a review of the literature for selecting participants to interview and observe included 1) being a teaching faculty member, and 2) a demonstrated interest in international activities through a combination of the following: significant travel abroad; scholarly or applied work with immigrant, diverse or multicultural populations; well-networked internationally; and employing an internationalized curriculum. Furthermore, the case selection is small so that the particularities and complexities of the process emerge from in-depth focus rather than a broad and shallow understanding resulting from a large selection of cases. Five cases then were the focus of data collection throughout the entire research process.

In addition to the participants, key administrators and staff were also interviewed to provide important contextual information. These key administrators and staff spoke to the current state of the university as well as broad internationalization efforts and activities on campus, which aided in understanding the context and provided access to institutional documents. The administrators were informed that neither their names nor titles would be used in the final report to promote candid conversation. Beyond these formal interviews, ad hoc conversations took place with various members of the university community for added context.

Data Collection, Analysis and Verification Strategies

Beyond the data collection methods described earlier, methods scholars generally agree (Merriam & Tisdell, 2016; Stake, 1995) that data analysis in case study is inductive, meaning that collection, analysis and report writing are at times concurrent activities which often inform each other. Interpretation of data stems from the researcher, starting with particulars and moving toward constructing a small number of general and broad themes (Creswell & Creswell, 2018). This is accomplished by organizing and coding the raw data and then building categories into patterns (Merriam & Tisdell, 2016) using Nvivo 11 software. Codes emerge from the collected data, but I also employ some pre-determined codes based on the theories of adult learning and the broader conceptual framework of the study. In the same way, I was sensitive during the process toward themes found during the literature review, but also reactive to new themes that may have been poorly documented.

This study follows verification constructs originally put forward by Guba (1981) which have been further developed by Shenton (2004). Triangulation of data (Merriam & Tisdell, 2016; Stake, 1995), member checks (Creswell & Poth, 2018; Shenton, 2004; Stake, 1995), and a report written as a thick description (Creswell & Poth, 2018) were used to ensure credibility or truth value. For confirmability or neutrality, qualitative researchers attempt to find an emic view and insider status. It is important that the researcher includes a reflective commentary throughout the process, both on the development of the research itself and on the researcher's own shifting self-reflexivity. This was accomplished through journaling, being mindful of my own positionality in the process and using a software package for coding. Dependability or consistency, comes through the research design and implementation, and particularly the specific details of the data collection (Shenton, 2004) which are laid out above in the section on data collection. Finally, for transferability or applicability the report is a thick and rich description of this "sending context" allowing the reader to decide whether and how the results transfer to other cases (Shenton, 2004).

References

Agnew, M., & Kahn, H. E. (2014). Internationalization-at-home: Grounded practices to promote intercultural, international, and global learning. *Metropolitan Universities, 25*(3), 31–46.

Albrecht, S. L., Bakker, A. B., Gruman, J. A., Macey, W. H., & Saks, A. M. (2015). Employee engagement, human resource management practices and competitive advantage: An integrated approach. *Journal of Organizational Effectiveness, 2*(1), 7–35. http://doi.org/10536/DRO/DU:30071114

Alexiadou, N., Kefala, Z., & Rönnberg, L. (2021). Preparing Education Students for an International Future? Connecting Students' Experience to Institutional Contexts. *Journal of Studies in International Education,* 1028315321998498.

Allen, E. (2004). Role of faculty in international education. Retrieved from http://www.aplu.org/NetCommunity/Document.Doc?id=64

Altbach, P. G. (2002). Perspectives on international higher education. Change: *The Magazine of Higher Learning, 34*(3), 29–31. http://doi.org/10.1080/00091380209601852

Altbach, P. G., & de Wit, H. (2017). The new nationalism and internationalisation of HE. *University World News.* http://www.universityworldnews.com/article.php? story=20170914073027157

Anderson, J., Dickens, A., Hyland, F., & Trahar, S. (2008). A changing world: The internationalisation experiences of staff and students (home and international) in UK higher education. http://dera.ioe.ac.uk/13074/

Andrews, T. (2017, April 24). Digital devices snub Icelandic language, which is a problem for Iceland. The Washington Post. https://www.washingtonpost.com/news/morning-mix/wp/2017/04/24/digital-devices-snub-icelandic-language-which-is-a-problem-for-iceland/?utm_term=.deb9564f0f26

Appadurai, A. (2001). Grassroots globalization and the research imagination. In A. Appadurai (Ed.), *Globalization* (pp. 1–20). Duke University Press.

Association of American Colleges and Universities. (2009). Intercultural knowledge and competence VALUE rubric. https://www.aacu.org/value/rubrics/intercultural-knowledge

Badley, G. (2000). Developing globally-competent university teachers. *Innovations in Education & Training International, 37*(3), 244–253. http://doi.org/10.1080/13558000050138489

Bartell, M. (2003). Internationalization of universities: A university culture-based framework. *Higher Education, 45*(1), 43–70.

Beatty, M. (2013). *Factors influencing faculty participation in internationalization at the University of Minnesota's schools of nursing and public health: A case study.* (Doctoral Dissertation). University of Minnesota.

Bedenlier, S., & Zawacki-Richter, O. (2015). Internationalization of higher education and the impacts on academic faculty members. *Research in Comparative and International Education, 10*(2), 185–201. http://doi.org/10.1177/1745499915571707

Beelen, J. (2011). Internationalisation at Home in a global perspective: A critical survey of the 3rd global survey report of IAU. *International Journal of Education Technology in Higher Education, 8*(2), 249–264. http://doi.org/10.7238/rusc.v8i2.1094

Beelen, J., & Jones, E. (2015). Redefining internationalization at home. In A. Curaj, L. Matei, R. Pricopie, J. Salmi, & P. Scott (Eds.), *The European Higher Education Area* (pp. 59–72). Springer. http://doi.org/10.1007/978-3-319-20877-0

Beelen, J., & Leask, B. (2011). Internationalisation at home on the move. In *Internationalisation of European Higher Education* (pp. 1–24). Raabe.

Bennett, J. (2008). On becoming a global soul. In V. Savicki (Ed.), *Developing Intercultural Competence and Transformation* (pp. 13–32). Stylus.

Bennett, M. J. (2004). Becoming interculturally competent. In J. Wurzel (Ed.), *Toward multiculturalism: A reader in multicultural education* (2nd ed., pp. 62–77). Intercultural Resource Corporation.

Bennett, M. J. (2010). Creating an interculturally competent campus to educate global citizens. In Proceedings of the Universidad 2010 7th International Congress on Higher Education: The University for a Better World. The university for a Better World. Havana, Cuba.

Bentao, Y. (2011). Internationalization at home. *Chinese Education & Society, 44*(5), 84–96. http://doi.org/10.2753/CED1061-1932440507

Bertrand, C., & Bourdeau, L. (2010). Research interviews by Skype: A new data colection method. Academic Conferences Proceedings of the 9th European Conference of Research Methodology for Business and Management Studies, 70–79.

Beuckelaer, A. De, Lievens, F., & Bucker, J. (2012). The role of faculty members ' cross-cultural competencies in their perceived teaching quality: Evidence from culturally-diverse classes in four European countries. *Journal of Higher Education, 83*(2).

Bhat, C. S., & McMahon, M. (2016). Internationalization at home for counseling students: Utilizing technology to expand global and multicultural horizons. *International Journal for the Advancement of Counselling, 38*(4), 319–329. http://doi.org/10.1007/s10447-016-9274-7

Bogotch, I., & Maslin-Ostrowski, P. (2010). Internationalizing educational leadership: How a university department jumps the curve from local to international. *Educational Administration Quarterly, 46*(2), 210–240. http://doi.org/10.1177/1094670510361746

Bond, S., Qian, J., & Huang, J. (2003). *The role of faculty in internationalizaing the undergraduate curriculum and classroom experience*. CIBE.

Bond, M. A., & Blevins, S. J. (2020). Using faculty professional development to foster organizational change: A social learning framework. *TechTrends, 64*(2), 229-237.

Books, S., Ragnarsdóttir, H., Jónsson, Ó., & Macdonald, A. (2010). A university program with "the whole world as a focus": An Icelandic response to globalization. *Innovative Higher Education, 36*(2), 125–139. http://doi.org/10.1007/s10755-010-9163-7

Boyer, E. (1990). *Scholarship reconsidered: Practices of the professoriate.* Princeton University Press.

Brandenburg, U., de Wit, H., Jones, E., & Leask, B. (2019). Defining internationalisation in HE for society. *University World News.*

Brandenburg, U., & de Wit, H. (2011). The end of internationalization. *International Higher Education,* (62), 15–17.

Brewer, E. (2010). Leveraging partnerships to internationalize the liberal arts college: Campus internationalization and the faculty. *New Directions for Higher Education, (150),* 83–96. http://doi.org/10.1002/he

Brookfield, S. (1995). *Becoming a critically reflective teacher.* Jossey-Bass.

Brookfield, S. (2000). Adult cognition as a dimension of lifelong learning. In J. Field & M. Leicester (Ed.), *Lifelong learning: Education across the lifespan.* Routledge.

Brookfield, S. (2009). The concept of critical reflection: promises and contradictions. *European Journal of Social Work, 12(*3), 293–304. http://doi.org/10.1080/13691450902945215

Brookfield, S. (2015). *The skillful teacher: On technique, trust, and responsiveness in the classroom* (3rd ed.). Jossey-Bass.

Brown, S., & Jones, E. (2007). Contextualising international Higher Education. In S. Brown & E. Jones (Eds.), *Internationalising higher education* (pp. 194–200). Routledge.

Buckner, E., & Stein, S. (2020). What counts as internationalization? Deconstructing the internationalization imperative. *Journal of Studies in International Education, 24*(2), 151-166.

Cai, Y., & Kivisto, J. (2011). Tuition fees for international students in Finland: Where to go from here? *Journal of Studies in International Education, 17*(1), 55–78. http://doi.org/10.1177/1028315311429001

Calikoglu, A., Lee, J. J., & Arslan, H. (2020). Faculty International Engagement: Examining Rationales, Strategies, and Barriers in Institutional Settings. *Journal of Studies in International Education,* 1028315320963508.

Caniëls, M. C. J., Semeijn, J. H., & Renders, I. H. M. (2018). Mind the mindset! The interaction of proactive personality, transformational leadership and growth mindset for engagement at work. *Career Development International, 23*(1), 48–66. http://doi.org/10.1108/CDI-11-2016-0194

Childress, L. K. (2009). Planning for internationalization by investing in faculty. *Journal of International & Global Studies, 1*(1), 30–49.

Childress, L. K. (2010). *The twenty-first century university: Developing faculty engagement in internationalization.* Peter Lang.

Clark, B. (2013). *Faculty perceptions of the importance of internationalizing the general education curriculum in the Florida college system.* (Doctoral

Dissertation). University of South Florida. ProQuest Dissertations & Theses. (Order No. 3558998).

Clarke, M., & Hui Yang, L. (2021). Internationalization: Perspectives from university faculty in the Republic of Ireland. *Journal of Studies in International Education, 25*(2), 136-151.

Clifford, V. A. (2009). Engaging the disciplines in internationalising the curriculum. International *Journal for Academic Development, 14*(2), 133–143. http://doi.org/10.1080/13601440902970122

Coffield, F. (2008*). Just suppose teaching and learning became the first priority.* Learning and Skills Network. http://tlp.excellencegateway.org.uk/ecpd/ecpd_modules/downloads/coffield_if_only.pdf

Coffield, F., & Williamson, B. (2011). *From exam factories to communities of discovery: The democratic route.* IOE Publications.

Colbeck, C., & Michael, P. (2006). The public scholarship: Reintegrating Boyer's four domains. *New Directions for Institutional Research, (129*), 7. http://doi.org/10.1002/ir

Cooper, J., & Mitsunaga, R. (2010). Faculty perspectives on international education: The nested realities of faculty collaborations. *New Directions for Higher Education,(150*), 69–81. http://doi.org/10.1002/he

Cranton, P. (2002). Teaching for transformation. *New Directions for Adult and Continuing Education, (*93), 63–72. http://doi.org/10.1002/ace.50

Cranton, P. (2006). Fostering authentic relationships in the transformative classroom. New *Directions for Adult and Continuing Education,* (109), 5–13. http://doi.org/10.1002/ace

Cranton, P., & Carusetta, E. (2004). Perspectives on authenticity in teaching. *Adult Education Quarterly, 55*(1), 5–22. http://doi.org/10.1177/0741713604268894

Cranton, P., & King, K. P. (2003). Transformative learning as a professional development goal. New *Directions for Adult and Continuing Education,* (98), 31–38. http://doi.org/10.1002/ace.97

Crawford, B., & Bethell, L. (2012). Internationalized campuses just don't happen: Intercultural learning requires facilitation and institutional support. In S. Ahola & D. M. Hoffman (Eds.), *Higher education research in Finland: Emerging structures and contemporary issues* (p. 442). Jyväskylä University Press.

Creswell, J. W., & Creswell, J. D. (2018). *Research design: Qualitative, quantitative, and mixed methods approache*s (5th ed.). Sage.

Creswell, J. W., & Poth, C. N. (2018). *Qualitative inquiry and research design: Choosing among five traditions.* Sage.

Crichton, J., & Paige, R. M. (2004). *Integrated resources for intercultural teaching and learning in the context of internationalisation in higher education.* Research Centre for Languages and Cultures Education, University of South Australia.

Criswell, J. R. I., & Zhu, H. (2015). Faculty Internationalization Priorities. *FIRE: Forum for International Research in Education, 2*(2), 22–39.

Crowther, P., M. Joris, M. Otten, B. Nilsson, H. Teekens, and B. W. (2000). *Internationalisation at home: A position paper.* Amsterdam.

Custer, L., & Tuominen, A. (2017). Bringing "internationalization at home" opportunities to community colleges: Design and assessment of an online exchange activity between U.S. and Japanese students. *Teaching Sociology, 45*(4), 347–357. http://doi.org/10.1177/0092055X16679488
Deardorff, D. (2004). Internationalization: In search of intercultural competence. *International Educator, 13*(2), 13–15.
Deardorff, D. (2006). Identification and Assessment of Intercultural Competence as a Student Outcome of Internationalization. *Journal of Studies in International Education, 10*(3), 241–266. http://doi.org/10.1177/1028315306287002
Deardorff, D. (2012). Looking to the future: Leadership perspectives on internationalization—A synthesis. *AUDEM: The International Journal of Higher Education and Democracy, 3*(1), 71–80. http://muse.jhu.edu/journals/audem/v003/3.deardorff.html
De Vita, G., & Case, P. (2003). Rethinking the internationalisation agenda in UK higher education. *Journal of Further and Higher Education, 27*(4), 383–398. http://doi.org/10.1080/0309877032000128082
de Wit, H. (2002). *Internationalization of higher education in the United States of America and Europe: A historical, comparative, and conceptual analysis.* Greenwood Press.
de Wit, H. (2011a). *Trends, issues, and challenges in internationalisation of higher education.* Amsterdam.
de Wit, H. (2011b, October 23). Naming internationalisation will not revive it. *University World News.* http://www.universityworldnews.com/article.php?story= 20111021215849411
de Wit, H. (2015). Internationalisation of higher education. Study requested by the European Parliament. http://www.europarl.europa.eu/RegData/etudes/ STUD/2015/540370/IPOL_STU(2015)540370_EN.pdf .
de Wit, H., & Hunter, F. (2015). The future of internationalization of higher education in Europe. *International Higher Education, 83*, 2–3. http://doi.org/10.6017/ihe.2015.83.9073
de Wit, H., & Leask, B. (2017). Global: Internationalization, the curriculum, and the disciplines. *Understanding Higher Education Internationalization, 83*(2015), 345–347. http://doi.org/10.1007/978-94-6351-161-2_74
de Wit, H. (2019). Internationalization in higher education, a critical review. *SFU Educational Review, 12*(3), 9-17.
de Wit, H., & Altbach, P. G. (2020). Internationalization in higher education: global trends and recommendations for its future. *Policy Reviews in Higher Education*, 1-19.
Dewey, P., & Duff, S. (2009). Reason before passion: Faculty views on internationalization in higher education. *Higher Education, 58*(4), 491–504. http://doi.org/10.1007/s10734-009-9207-z
Durrenberger, P. E., & Pálsson, G. (Eds.). (2015). *Gambling debt: Iceland's rise and fall in the global economy*. University Press of Colorado.
Dweck, C. (2006). *Mindset: The new psychology of success.* Random House.

Egron-Polak, E., & Hudson, R. (2010). *Internationalization of higher education: Global trends, regional perspectives.* IAU.
Ellingboe, B. (1998). Divisional strategies to internationalize a campus portrait: Results, resistance, and recommendations from a case study at a U.S. university. In J. A. Mestenhauser & B. Ellingboe (Eds.), *Evidence, evaluation and outcomes of internationalization* (pp. 198–228). The American Council on Education and The Oryx Press.
Emmanuel, J. (2010). *Motivational factors and worldview dimensions associated with perceptions of global education initiatives by U.S .college professors.* (Doctoral Dissertation). University of South Florida. Scholar Commons Theses and Dissertations. (Paper 1668).
Fields, D. M. (2010). *Faculty internationalization: Experiences, attitudes, and perceptions of full-time academics across Vermont.* (Doctoral Dissertation). ProQuest Dissertations and Theses. (Order No. 3428232).
Finkelstein, M. J., Walker, E., & Chen, R. (2009). The internationalization of the American faculty: where are we, what drives or deters us? The Changing Academic Profession over 1992-2007: *International, Comparative, and Quantitative Perspectives., 13,* 113–142.
Finkelstein, M. J., Walker, E., & Chen, R. (2013). The American faculty in an age of globalization: predictors of internationalization of research content and professional networks. *Higher Education, 66*(3), 325–340. http://doi.org/10.1007/s10734-012-9607-3
Freeman, M., Treleaven, L., Ramburuth, P., Leask, B., Caulfield, N., Simpson, L., … Ave, N. (2009). Embedding the development of intercultural competence in business education. Australian Learning & Teaching Council. http://www.olt.gov.au/resource-library?text=embedding the
Freire, P. (1993). The "banking " concept of education. In *Pedagogy of the Oppressed.* Continuum Books.
Friesen, R. (2011). *Canadian university internationalization: Selective perceptions of five faculty memers.* University of Manitoba.
Friesen, R. (2012). Faculty member engagement in Canadian university internationalization: A consideration of understanding, motivations and rationales. *Journal of Studies in International Education, 17*(3), 209–227. http://doi.org/10.1177/1028315312451132
Gay, G. (2013). Teaching to and through cultural diversity. *Curriculum Inquiry, 43*(1), 48–70. http://doi.org/10.1111/curi.12002
Gee, J. P. (2000). Identity as an analytic lens for research in education. *Review of Research in Education, 25*(1), 99–125. http://doi.org/10.3102/0091732X025001099
George, S. (2014). The politics of the imagination in our globalized world. In *Re-imagined universities and global citizen professionals* (pp. 229–257). Palgrave Macmillan.
Gil-Alana, L. A., & Huijbens, E. H. (2018). Tourism in Iceland: Persistence and seasonality. *Annals of Tourism Research, 68,* 20–29. http://doi.org/10.1016/j.annals.2017.11.002
Gomm, R., Hammersly, M., & Foster, P. (2000). *Case study methodology: Key issues, key texts.* (R. Gomm, M. Hammersley, & P. Foster, Eds.). Sage.

Goode, M. L. (2005). The role of faculty study abroad directors: A case study. *Frontiers: The Interdisciplinary Journal of Study Abroad, 15*, 149–172.
Green, M., & Olson, C. (2003). *Internationalizing the campus: A user's guide. Internationalizing the Campus: A user's guide*. American Council on Education.
Green, M., & Shoenberg, R. (2006). *Where faculty live: Internationalizing the disciplines*. (Vol. 2) American Council on Education.
Green, W., & Mertova, P. (2016). Transformalists and transactionists: Towards a more comprehensive understanding of academics' engagement with "internationalisation of the curriculum." *Research in Comparative and International Education, 11*(3), 229–246. http://doi.org/10.1177/1745499916662372
Gu, Q., & Schweisfurth, M. (2011). Rethinking university internationalisation: Towards transformative change. *Teachers and Teaching, 17*(6), 611–617. http://doi.org/10.1080/13540602.2011.625110
Guba, E. G. (1981). Criteria for assessing the trustworthiness of naturalistic inquiries. *Educational Communication & Technology, 29*(2), 75–91. http://doi.org/10.1007/BF02766777
Guba, E. G., & Lincoln, Y. S. (1994). Competing paradigms in qualitative research. *Handbook of Qualitative Research, 2*, 163–194.
Guo, S., & Alfred, M. (2013). Intensification of faculty engagement in the internationalization of adult education. *Critical Perspectives on International Education, 15*, 135–148.
Gvetadze, S. (2014). Financing the mobility of students in European higher education. European Investment Fund, (January).
Hall, D. E. (2002). *The academic self: An owner's manual*. Ohio State University Press.
Halldórsdóttir Gudjonsson, B. E., & Gollifer, S. E. (2018). A view towards internationalisation at the University of Iceland: Lessons learned from the International studies in Education Programme.
Hanson, C., & McNeil, B. (2012). Faculty understanding and implementation of internationalization and global citizenship. *Collected Essays on Learning and Teaching, 5*, 33–38. http://hrgpapers.uwindsor.ca/ojs/leddy/index.php/ CELT/article/view/3410
Harrison, N. (2015). Practice, problems, and power in "internationalisation at home": critical reflections on recent research evidence. *Teaching in Higher Education, 20*(4), 412–430. http://doi.org/10.1080/13562517.2015.1022147
Hill, C. E. (2012). *Consensual qualitative research: A practical resource for investigating social science phenomena*. American Psychological Association.
Hoffman, D. M. (2003). Internationalisation at home from the inside: Non-native faculty and transformation. *Journal of Studies in International Education, 7*(1), 77–93. http://doi.org/10.1177/1028315302250190

Holm, G. (2014). Photography as a research method. In the Oxford Handbook of Qualitative Research (pp. 380–402). http://doi.org/10.1080/08949468.1991.9966560

Horn, A. S., Hendel, D. D., & Fry, G. W. (2007). Ranking the international dimension of top research universities in the United States. *Journal of Studies in International Education, 11*(3–4), 330–358. http://doi.org/10.1177/1028315306294630

Horn, A. S., Hendel, D. D., & Fry, G. W. (2011). The empirical basis for adopting a civic rationale for internationalization. *Higher Education, 64*(2), 161–175. http://doi.org/10.1007/s10734-011-9485-0

Hudson, R. (2016). Dominated by economics evidence of changing drivers of internationalization and its funding within higher education institutions in Europe. *Higher Education Policy, 29*(1), 1–19. http://doi.org/10.1057/hep.2015.4

Hudzik, J. (2010). *Comprehensive internationalization: From concept to action.* NAFSA.

Hustvedt, G., & Dickson, M. (2011). The challenge of internationalizing FCS. *Journal of Family and Consumer Sciences, 103*(4), 22–30.

Icelandic Quality Board for Higher Education. (2015). *Institution-wide review: University of Iceland.* Reykjavík.

Icelandic Tourist Board (2021). Tourism in Iceland in Figures. August 14, 2022. https://www.ferdamalastofa.is/en/recearch-and-statistics/numbers-of-foreign-visitors

Intercultural Cities Secretariat, Council of Europe (2020). *Intercultural Cities Index Analysis Reykjavik.* Strasbourg Cedex.

Intercultural Cities Secretariat, Council of Europe. (2014). *Intercultural Cities Index Analysis Reykjavik.* Strasbourg Cedex.

International Association of Universities (IAU). (2012, April 19). Affirming academic values in internationalization of higher education: A call for action. GlobalHigherEd.

Jiang, N., & Carpenter, V. (2013). Faculty-specific factors of degree of HE internationalization: An evaluation of four faculties of a post-1992 university in the United Kingdom. *International Journal of Educational Management, 27*(3), 242–259. http://doi.org/10.1108/09513541311306468

Jóhannesson, G. T., & Huijbens, E. H. (2010). Tourism in times of crisis: exploring the discourse of tourism development in Iceland. *Current Issues in Tourism, 13*(5), 419–434. http://doi.org/10.1080/13683500.2010.491897

Jón Hákon Halldórsson. (2017). Íslenska fyrir útlendinga orðin ein vinsælasta greinin innan HÍ - Visir. http://www.visir.is/g/2017170639994/islenska-fyrir-utlendinga-ordin-ein-vinsaelasta-greinin-innan-hi

Jones, E. (2013). The Internationalization of Higher Education. In R. Sugden, M. Valania, & J. R. Wilson (Eds.), *Leadership and cooperation in academia: Reflecting on the roles and responsibilities of university faculty and management* (pp. 161–181). Edward Elgar Publishing.

Jones, E. (2017). Problematising and reimagining the notion of "international student experience." *Studies in Higher Education, 42*(5), 933–943. http://doi.org/10.1080/03075079.2017.1293880

Jones, E., & de Wit, H. (2012). Globalization of internationalization: Thematic and regional reflections on a traditional concept. *AUDEM: The International Journal of Higher Education and Democracy, 3*(1), 35–54. http://muse.jhu.edu/journals/audem/v003/3.jones.html

Jones, E., & Killick, D. (2007). Internationalisation of the curriculum. In E. Jones & S. Brown (Eds.), *Internationalising Higher Education* (pp. 109–119). Routledge.

Jones, E., & Killick, D. (2013). Graduate attributes and the internationalized curriculum: Embedding a global outlook in disciplinary learning outcomes. *Journal of Studies in International Education, 17*(2), 165–182. http://doi.org/10.1177/1028315312473655

Kahn, W. A. (1990). Psychological conditions of personal engagement and disengagement at work. *Academy of Management Journal, 33*(4), 692–724. http://doi.org/10.2307/256287

Kahn, W. A. (1992). To be fully there: Psychological presence at work. *Human Relations, 45*(4), 321. http://doi.org/10.1177/001872679204500402

Kahn, W. A., & Heaphy, E. D. (2014). Relational contexts of personal engagement at work. *Employee Engagement in Theory and Practice, 82*–96.

Kezar, A., Gallant, T., & Lester, J. (2011). Everyday people making a difference on college campuses: The tempered grassroots leadership tactics of faculty and staff. *Studies in Higher Education, 36*(2), 129–151. http://doi.org/10.1080/03075070903532304

Kezar, A., & Lester, J. (2009). Supporting faculty grassroots leadership. *Research in Higher Education, 50*(7), 715–740. http://doi.org/10.1007/s11162-009-9139-6

Klyberg, S. G. F. (2012). *The faculty experience of internationalization: Motivations for, practices of, and means for engagement.* ProQuest Dissertations and Theses. (Order No. 3534672).

Knight, J. (1994). Internationalization: Elements and checkpoints. *Canadian Bureau for International Education, 7*, 1–15. http://quic.queensu.ca/resources/training/files/ CBIE_Internationalization_Elements_and_Checkpoints.pdf

Knight, J. (2004). Internationalization remodeled: Definition, approaches, and rationales. *Journal of Studies in International Education, 8*(1), 5–31. http://doi.org/10.1177/1028315303260832

Knight, J. (2008). Definitions and driving forces for internationalisation. In M. Gaebel, L. Purser, B. Wachter, & L. Wilsons (Eds.), *Internationalisation of European higher education: An EUA/ACA handbook* (pp. 1–22). Raabe Academic Publishers.

Knight, J. (2011, August). Is internationalisation having an identity crisis? Programme on Institutional Management in Higher Education. OECD.

Knight, J. (2015a). Internationalization brings important benefits as well as risks. *International Higher Education, 46*, 8–10. http://doi.org/10.6017/ihe.2007.46.7939

Knight, J. (2015b). Updating the definition of internationalization. *International Higher Education, 33*, 2–3. http://doi.org/10.1177/1028315315602927

Koester, J. (2010). Intercultural matters: The internationalization of higher education. https://global.umn.edu/icc/documents/2010_mestenhauser_lecture _koester.pdf

Kreber, C. (2007). What's it really all about? The scholarship of teaching and learning as an authentic practice. *International Journal for the Scholarship of Teaching and Learning, 1*(1), 1–6. http://eaglescholar.georgiasouthern.edu:8080/jspui/ bitstream/10518/2712/1/IJ_Kreber.pdf

Kreber, C., & Klampfleitner, M. (2013). Lecturers' and students' conceptions of authenticity in teaching and actual teacher actions and attributes students perceive as helpful. *Higher Education, 66*(4), 463–487. http://doi.org/10.1007/s10734-013-9616-x

Kreber, C., Klampfleitner, M., McCune, V., Bayne, S., & Knottenbelt, M. (2007). What do you mean by "authentic"? A comparative review of the literature on conceptions of authenticity in teaching. *Adult Education Quarterly, 58*(1), 22–43. http://doi.org/10.1177/0741713607305939

Leask, B. (2006). Campus diversity, student participation and Internationalization – a case study from Australia. In H. Teekens (Ed.), *Internationalization at home: A global perspective* (pp. 119–130). Nuffic.

Leask, B. (2009). Using formal and informal curricula to improve interactions between home and international students. *Journal of Studies in International Education, 13*(2), 205–221. http://doi.org/10.1177/1028315308329786

Leask, B., & Bridge, C. (2013). Comparing internationalisation of the curriculum in action across disciplines: theoretical and practical perspectives. *Compare: A Journal of Comparative and International Education, 43*(1), 79–101. http://doi.org/10.1080/03057925.2013.746566

Leask, B., Whitsed, C., de Wit, H., & Beelen, J. (2020). Faculty engagement. In A. Ogden, B. Streitwieser, C. Van Mol (Eds.) *Education abroad: Bridging scholarship and practice*. Routledge.

Li, B., & Tu, Y. (2016). Motivations of faculty engagement in internationalization: A survey in China. *Higher Education, 71*(1), 81–96. http://doi.org/10.1007/s10734-015-9890-x

Li, H., Khattak, S. I., & Jiang, Q. (2021). A qualitative assessment of the determinants of faculty engagement in internationalization: A Chinese perspective. *SAGE Open, 11*(3), 21582440211046935.

Livingston, J. (2011*). Defining and measuring faculty engagement: Validation of the faculty engagement survey*. ProQuest Dissertations and Theses (Order No. 3467979)

Loftsdóttir, K. (2017). Being "the damned foreigner": Affective national sentiments and racialization of Lithuanians in Iceland. *Nordic Journal of Migration Research, 7*(2), 70–78. http://doi.org/10.1515/njmr-2017-0012

Lundy Dobbert, M. (1998). The impossibility of internationalizing students by adding materials to courses. In J. A. Mestenhauser & B. Ellingboe (Eds.), *Reforming higher education curriculum: Internationalizing the campus* (pp. 53–68). American Council on Education and Oryx Press.

Macey, W. H., & Schneider, B. (2008). The meaning of employee engagement. *Industrial and Organizational Psychology, 1*(1), 3–30. http://doi.org/10.1111/j.1754-9434.2007.0002.x

Mak, A. S., Grealish, L., Daly, A., Neill, J., Barker, M., Henderson, S., … Buys. (2013). Internationalisation at home: Enhancing intercultural capabilities of business and health teachers, students, and curricula. http://pandora.nla.gov.au/pan/133238/ 201405051402/www.olt.gov.au/system/files/resources/PP10_1810_Mak_Report_2013.pdf

Mangels, J., Butterfield, B., Lamb, J., Good, C., & Dweck, C. (2006). Why do beliefs about intelligence influence learning success? A social cognitive neuroscience model. *Social Cognitive and Affective Neuroscience, 1*(2), 75–86. http://doi.org/10.1093/scan/nsl013

Martin, J., & Nakayama, T. (2014). Thinking dialectically about culture and communication. In M. Asante, Y. Miike, & J. Yin (Eds.), *The global intercultural communication reader* (2nd ed., pp. 190–207). Routledge.

McBurnie, G., & Ziguras, C. (2009). *Higher Education to 2030: Globalisation.* OECD. http://doi.org/9264023984

Merriam, S. B. (1998). *Qualitative research and case study applications in education*. Jossey-Bass.

Merriam, S. B., & Tisdell, E. J. (2016). *Qualitative research: a guide to design and Implementation* (4th ed.). Jossey-Bass.

Merrill, M. (2012). This rethinking exercise is about reinserting the values: An interview with Eva Egron-Polak. *AUDEM: The International Journal of Higher Education and Democracy, 3*, 164–177. http://muse.jhu.edu/journals/audem/v003/3.merrill.html

Mertova, P., & Green, W. (2010). Internationalising teaching and learning: Perspectives and issues voiced by senior academics at one Australian university. Conference Proceedings of the 21st …, 2–3. http://www.proceedings.com.au/isana/docs/2010/paper_mertova.pdf

Mestenhauser, J. A. (1998). Portraits of an international curriculum: An uncommon multidimensional perspective. *Reforming the Higher Education Curriculum: Internationalizing the Campus,* 3–39.

Mestenhauser, J. A. (2002). In search of a comprehensive approach to international education: A systems perspective. In W. Grunzeig & N. Rinehart (Eds.), *Rockin'in Red Square: Critical approaches to international education in the age of cyberculture*, (pp. 165–202). Lit.

Mestenhauser, J. A. (2003). Building bridges. *International Educator,* (Summer), 6–11.

Mestenhauser, J. A. (2006). Internationalization at home: Systems challenge to a fragmented field. In H. Teekens (Ed.), *Internationalization at home: A global perspective* (pp. 61–77). Nuffic.

Mestenhauser, J. A. (2011). *Reflections on the past, present, and future of internationalizing higher education: Discovering opportunities to meet the challenges*. University of Minnesota.

Mezirow, J. (1990). How critical reflection triggers transformative learning. *Fostering Critical Reflection in Adulthood, 20*(1). https://www.ln.edu.hk/osl/conference2011/

Mezirow, J. (1997). Transformative learning: Theory to practice. *New Directions for Adult and Continuing Education,* (74), 5–12. http://doi.org/10.1002/ace.7401

Mezirow, J. (2000). Learning to think like an adult: Core concept of transformation theory. In J. Mezirow (Ed.), *Learning as transformation: Critical perspectives on a theory in progress* (pp. 3–33). Jossey-Bass.

Miller-Idriss, C., & Hanauer, E. (2011). Transnational higher education: Offshore campuses in the Middle East. *Comparative Education, 47*(2), 181–207. http://doi.org/10.1080/03050068.2011.553935

Ministry of Education Science and Culture (2010). *Policy on public universities.* Iceland.

Mitchell, D., & Nielsen, S. (2012). Internationalization and globalization in higher education. In H. Cuadra-Montiel (Ed.), *Globalization - Eduation and management agendas* (pp. 3–22). http://doi.org/10.5772/48702

Mullen, W. (2011). *Factors influencing campus internationalization: A case study of a liberal arts college in the Upper Midwest.* University of Minnesota. ProQuest Dissertations and Theses. (Order No. 3488255).

Ng, S. W. (2012). Rethinking the mission of internationalization of higher education in the Asia-Pacific region. *Compare, 42*(3), 439–459. http://doi.org/10.1080/03057925.2011.652815

Niehaus, E., & Williams, L. (2012). The role of faculty development in curricular transformation for internationalization (Presented at the annual meeting of the American Educaitonal Researach Association.). Vancouver, British Columbia.

Niehaus, E., & Williams, L. (2016). Faculty transformation in curriculum transformation: The role of faculty development in campus internationalization. *Innovative Higher Education, 41*(1), 59–74. http://doi.org/10.1007/s10755-015-9334-7

Nilsson, B. (2000). Internationalising the curriculum. In P. Crowther (Ed.), *Internationalisation at home* (pp. 21–28). European Association for International Education.

Nilsson, B. (2003). Internationalisation at home from a Swedish perspective: The case of Malmö. *Journal of Studies in International Education.* http://doi.org/10.1177/1028315302250178

Northouse, P. G. (2010). *Leadership: Theory and practice* (5th ed.). Sage.

Novelli, M. (2006). Imagining research as solidarity and grassroots globalisation: A response to Appadurai (2001). *Globalisation, Societies and Education, 4*(2), 275–286. http://doi.org/10.1080/14767720600752700

Nyangau, J.Z. (2020). Faculty engagement in internationalization: The role of personal agency beliefs. International Journal of Research in Education and Science, 6(1), 74-85.

Odgers, T., & Giroux, I. (2006). Internationalizing faculty: A phased approach to transforming curriculum design and instruction. York University Annual International Conference on Internationalizing Canada's Universities.

Óladóttir, Á. D. (2009). Internationalization from a small domestic base: An empirical analysis of foreign direct investments of Icelandic firms.

Management International Review, 49(1), 61–80. http://doi.org/10.1007/s11575-008-0125-6

Otten, M. (2000). Impacts of cultural diversity at home. In P. Crowther (Ed.), *Internationalisation at Home* (pp. 15–20). European Association for International Education.

Otten, M. (2009). Academicus interculturalis? Negotiating interculturality in academic communities of practice. *Intercultural Education, 20*(5), 407–417. http://doi.org/10.1080/14675980903371266

Page, S. E. (2007). Making the difference: Applying a logic of diversity. *Academy of Management Perspectives, 21*(4), 6–20. http://doi.org/10.5465/AMP.2007.27895335

Paige, R. M. (1993). *Education for the intercultural experience.* Intercultural Press.

Paige, R. M. (2003). The American case: The University of Minnesota. *Journal of Studies in International Education, 7*(1), 52–63. http://doi.org/10.1177/1028315302250180

Paige, R. M. (2005). Internationalization of higher education: Performance assessment and indicators. *Nagoya Journal of Higher Education*, 99–122.

Paige, R. M., & Goode, M. L. (2009). Intercultural competence in international education administration. In D. K. Deardorff (Ed.), *The SAGE handbook of intercultural competence.* Sage.

Paige, R. M., & Mestenhauser, J. A. (1999). Internationalizing educational administration. *Educational Administration Quarterly, 35*(4), 500–517. http://doi.org/10.1177/0013161X99354005

Patton, M. Q. (2015). *Qualitative research & evaluation methods: Integrating theory and practice.* (4th ed.). Sage.

Phan, L.-H. (2016). *Transnational education crossing "Asia"and "the West": Adjusted desire, transformative mediocrity and neo-colonial disguise.* Routledge.

Prieto-Flores, O., Feu, J., & Casademont, X. (2016). Assessing intercultural competence as a result of Internationalization at Home efforts: A case study from the Nightingale Mentoring Program. *Journal of Studies in International Education, 20*(5). http://doi.org/10.1177/1028315316662977

Raina, K., & Khatri, P. (2015). Faculty engagement in higher education: Prospects and areas of research. *On the Horizon, 23*(4), 285–308. http://doi.org/10.1108/OTH-03-2015-0011

Rannís - The Icelandic Centre for Research. (2017). Quality Enhancement Framework for higher education in Iceland. https://en.rannis.is/activities/quality-enhancement-framework/

Reykjavik University. (2017). University - Reykjavik University. https://en.ru.is/the-university/

Robson, S. (2011). Internationalization: A transformative agenda for higher education? *Teachers and Teaching, 17*(6), 619–630. http://doi.org/10.1080/13540602.2011.625116

Robson, S., Almeida, J., & Schartner, A. (2017). Internationalization at home: Time for review and development? *European Journal of Higher Education*, 8235, 1–17. http://doi.org/10.1080/21568235.2017.1376697

Rumbley, L. E. (2015). "Intelligent Internationalization": A 21st century imperative. *International Higher Education, 80*, 16–17.

Rumbley, L. E., Altbach, P. G., & Reisberg, L. (2012). Internationalization within the higher education context. In *The SAGE Handbook of International Higher Education*. Sage.

Saks, A. M., & Gruman, J. A. (2014). What do we really know about employee engagement? *Human Resource Development Quarterly, 25*(2), 155–182. http://doi.org/10.1002/hrdq.21187

Sanderson, G. B. (2004). Existentialism, globalisation and the cultural other. *International Education Journal, 4*(4), 1–20. Retrieved from http://doi.wiley.com/10.1111/j.1365-2648.2004.03086.x

Sanderson, G. B. (2008). A foundation for the internationalization of the academic self. *Journal of Studies in International Education, 12*(3), 276–307. http://doi.org/10.1177/1028315307299420

Sanderson, G. B. (2011). Internationalisation and teaching in higher education. *Higher Education Research & Development, 30*(5), 661–676. http://doi.org/10.1080/07294360.2011.598455Savishinsky, M. (2012). Overcoming barriers to faculty engagement in study abroad. (Doctoral dissertation). Retrieved from ProQuest Dissertations and Theses. (Order No. 3542383).

Schuerholz-Lehr, S., Caws, C., Van Gyn, G., & Preece, A. (2007). Internationalizing the higher education curriculum: An emerging model for transforming faculty perspectives. *Canadian Journal of Higher Education, 37*, 67–95. Retrieved from http://www.eric.ed.gov/ERICWebPortal/recordDetail?accno=EJ771047

Schwietz, M. (2006). *Internationalization of the academic profession: An exploratory study of faculty attitudes, beliefs, and involvement at the University of Pennsylvania.* (Unpublished doctoral dissertation). University of Pittsburgh, Pennsylvania. Retrieved from http://d-scholarship.pitt.edu/7216/

Scott, P. (2008). The internationalisation of higher education and research: Purposes and drivers. In & L. W. M. Gaebel, L. Purser, B. Wachter (Ed.), *Internationalisation of european higher education: An EUA/ACA handbook* (pp. 1–18). Berlin.

Scriven, M., & Paul, R. (1996). Defining critical thinking: A draft statement for the National Council for Excellence in Critical Thinking. Retrieved from http://www.criticalthinking.org/University/univlibrary/library.nclk

Seeber, M., Cattaneo, M., Huisman, J., & Paleari, S. (2016). Why do higher education institutions internationalize? An investigation of the multilevel determinants of internationalization rationales. *Higher Education, 72*(5), 685–702. http://doi.org/10.1007/s10734-015-9971-x

Seidman, I. (2013). *Interviewing as qualitative research: A guide for researchers in education and the social sciences.* Teachers college press.

Shapiro, J., & Goldberg, B. Z. (2003). Promises. USA: Cowboy Pictures. Retrieved from http://www.promisesproject.org/film.html

Shenton, A. k. (2004). Strategies for ensuring trustworthiness in qualitative research projects. *Education for Information, 22*(2), 63–75. http://doi.org/10.1111/j.1744-618X.2000.tb00391.x

Skaptadóttir, U. D. (2010). Integration and transnational practices of Filipinos in Iceland. E-Migrinter, 5, 36–45. Retrieved from http://www.mshs.univ-poitiers.fr/migrinter/e-migrinter/201005/e-migrinter2010_05_tout.pdf#page=38

Skaptadóttir, U. D. (2014). What happened to the migrant workers? In G. Durrenberger, E. P., & Pálsson (Ed.), *Gambling debt: Iceland's rise and fall in the global economy*. (pp. 175–186). University Press of Colorado. http://doi.org/10.5876/9781607323358.c014

Soria, K. M., & Troisi, J. (2014). Internationalization at Home alternatives to study abroad: Implications for students' development of global, international, and intercultural competencies. Journal of Studies in International Education, 18(3), 261–280. http://doi.org/10.1177/1028315313496572

Stake, R. E. (1995). *The art of case study research*. Sage.

Statistics Iceland. (2009). Immigrants and persons with foreign backgroundin 1996-2008. http://statice.is/publications/news-archive/population/immigrants-and-persons-with-foreign-bakground-in-1996-2008/

Statistics Iceland. (2020a). Immigrants by sex, citizenship, country of birth and year of arrival 1996-2017. March 30, 2020. http://px.hagstofa.is/pxen/pxweb/en/ Ibuar/Ibuar__mannfjoldi__3_bakgrunnur__Uppruni/MAN43001.px

Statistics Iceland. (2020b). Population by country of birth, sex and age 1 January 1998-2020. http://px.hagstofa.is/pxen/pxweb/en/Ibuar/ Ibuar__mannfjoldi__3_bakgrunnur__Uppruni/MAN43001.px/?rxid=201b6495-981b-4d75-9723-c44a4f052807

Stier, J. (2006). Internationalisation, intercultural communication and intercultural competence academia: A global play-ground. *Journal of Intercultural Communication, 11,* 1–12.

Stohl, M. (2007). We have met the enemy and he is ss: The role of the faculty in the internationalization of higher education in the coming decade. *Journal of Studies in International Education, 11*(3–4), 359–372. http://doi.org/10.1177/1028315307303923

Strauss, A., Corbin, J., Denzin, N. K., & Lincoln, Y. S. (1994). *Handbook of qualitative research*. Sage.

Stromquist, N. P. (2007). Internationalization as a response to globalization: Radical shifts in university environments. *Higher Education, 53*(1), 81–105. http://doi.org/10.1007/s10734-005-1975-5

Stromquist, N. P., California, S., Gil-antón, M., Autonoma, U., Colatrella, C., & Mabokela, R. O. (2007). Professoriate: Towards a diversified or segmented profession? *Higher Education Quarterly, 61*(2), 114–135.

Sullivan, J. (2011). *Global leadership in higher education administration: Perspectives on internationalization by university presidents, vice-presidents and deans*. Vasa. Graduate School Theses and Dissertations. http://medcontent.metapress.com/index/A65RM03P4874243N.pdf

Sullivan, J. R. (2012). Skype: An appropriate method of data collection for qualitative interviews? *Hill Top Review, 6*(1), 54–60. Retrieved from http://scholarworks.wmich.edu/hilltopreview/vol6/iss1/10

Tagg, J. (2012, January 4). Why does the faculty resist change? *Change: The Magazine of Higher Learning, 44*(1), 6–15. http://doi.org/10.1080/00091383.2012.635987

Teferra, D. (2020). The Irrelevance of the Re-Configured Definition of Internationalisation to the Global South. *International Journal of African Higher Education, 7*(2).

Teichler, U. (2017). Internationalisation trends in higher education and the changing

role of international student mobility. *Journal of International Mobility, 1*(1), 177-216. https://doi.org/10.3917/jim.005.0179

Thomas, K. (2012). *How international are we? A study of the internal barriers to internationalisation of UK higher education.* (Doctoral Dissertation). University of Northumbria at Newcastle: Newcastle. Retrieved from http://nrl.northumbria.ac.uk/11365/1/thomas.kevin_prof.doct.pdf

Thomas, M. A. M. (2018). Research capacity and dissemination among academics in Tanzania: examining knowledge production and the perceived binary of "local" and "international" journals. *Compare: A Journal of Comparative and International Education, 48*(2), 281–298. http://doi.org/10.1080/03057925.2017.1318046

Trahar, S. (2010). Internationalizing the university. *Compare: A Journal of Comparative and International Education, 40*(5), 679–681. http://doi.org/10.1080/03057925.2010.503371

Turner, Y., & Robson, S. (2007). Competitive and cooperative impulses to internationalization: Reflecting on the interplay between manangement intentions and the experience of academics in a British university. *Education, Knowledge and Economy, 1*(1), 65–82. http://doi.org/10.1080/17496890601128241

Turner, Y., & Robson, S. (2008). *Internationalizing the University.* Continuum.

University of Iceland. (2011). Strategic plan of the University of Iceland rector's forward. http://www.hi.is/files/afmaeliforsida/policy_2011-2016.pdf

University of Iceland. (2014). Equal rights policy 2013-2017. http://english.hi.is/university/equal_rights_policy#primary_objectives

University of Iceland. (2016a). Development of Iceland as a multicultural community. http://english.hi.is/frettir/development_iceland_multicultural_community

University of Iceland. (2020). Facts and figures. Retrieved June 1, 2021 https://english.hi.is/sites/default/files/bryndjo/pdf/lykiltolurfacts2020.pdf

University of Iceland. (2016c). Increased satisfaction among International Students. Retrieved June 18, 2017, from http://english.hi.is/frettir/increased _satisfaction_among_international_students

University of Iceland. (2016d). Strategy of the University of Iceland 2016-2021. https://english.hi.is/sites/default/files/atlityr/pdf/hi21_brochure_ens-01-web.pdf

University of Iceland. (2017). Graduate studies programs always taught in English. http://english.hi.is/

University of Iceland. (2018). University of Iceland - Course catalogue 2018-2019: INT261 international studies in education BA. https://ugla.hi.is/kennsluskra/ index.php?tab=nam&chapter =namsleid&id =730000_20186&kennsluar =2018
University of Iceland (2020). University of Iceland Equality Action Plan 2021-2023. https://english.hi.is/sites/default/files/sveinng/university_of_iceland_ equality_action_plan.pdf
Van der Wende, M. (2009). *European responses to global competitiveness in higher education* . Center for Studies in Higher Education. http://escholarship.org/uc/item/718832p2
Wächter, B. (2000). Internationalisation at home - the context. In P. Crowther (Ed.), *Internationalisation at home: A position paper* (pp. 5–13). EAIE.. http://cdigital.uv.mx/handle/123456789/31163
Wächter, B. (2003). An introduction: Internationalisation at home in context. *Journal of Studies in International Education, 7*(1), 5–11. http://doi.org/10.1177/1028315302250176
Welch, M. (2011). The evolution of the employee engagement concept: Communication implications. *Corporate Communications: An International Journal, 16*, 328–346. http://doi.org/10.1108/13563281111186968
Wenger, E., & Snyder, W. (2000). Communities of practice: The organizational frontier. *Harvard Business Review, 78*(1), 139–146.
Whitsed, C., & Green, W. (2013). What's in a name? A theoretical exploration of the proliferation of labels for international education across the higher education sector. *Journal of Studies in International Education,* 17(2), 1–15. http://doi.org/10.1177/1028315313491117
Wojtynska, A., & Zielinska, M. (2010). Polish migrants in Iceland facing the financial crisis. In *Rannsóknir í félagsvísindum* xi (pp. 1–12). Félagsvísindastofnun Háskóla Íslands.
Yin, R. K. (2018). *Case study research and applications* (6th ed.). Sage.
Yorke, M., & Knight, P. (2004). Self-theories: Some implications for teaching and learning in higher education. *Studies in Higher Education, 29*(1), 25–37. http://doi.org/10.1080/1234567032000164859
Zha, Q. (2003). Internationalization of higher education: Towards a conceptual framework. *Policy Futures in Education, 1*(2), 248–270.
Zimmerman, B. (2002). Becoming a self-regulated learner: An overview. *Theory Into Practice, 41*(2), 64–70.

Made in the USA
Monee, IL
04 November 2026

67376103R00125